CULTURE AND CUSTOMS OF INDONESIA

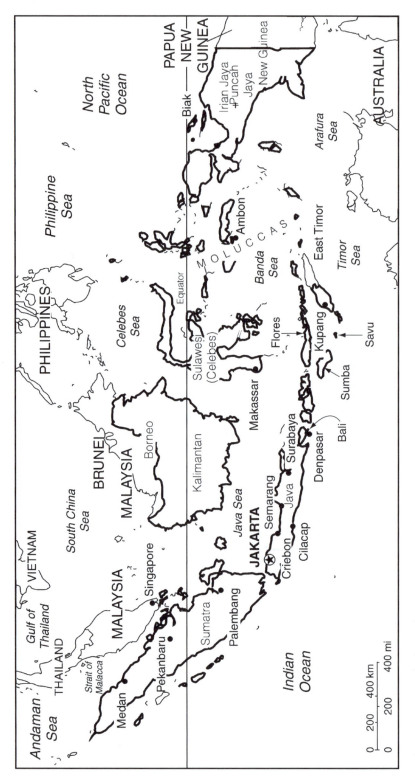

Indonesia. Cartography by Bookcomp, Inc.

Culture and Customs of Indonesia

∽⚬∾

JILL FORSHEE

Culture and Customs of Asia
Hanchao Lu, Series Editor

GREENWOOD PRESS
Westport, Connecticut • London

To the memory of my mother, Erma McMurter Forshee

Library of Congress Cataloging-in-Publication Data

Forshee, Jill.
    Culture and customs of Indonesia / Jill Forshee.
        p. cm.—(Culture and customs of Asia, ISSN 1097–0738)
    Includes bibliographical references and index.
    ISBN 0–313–33339–4 (alk. paper)
    1. Indonesia—Civilization. 2. Indonesia—Social life and customs. I. Title.
    DS625.F64 2006
    959.8—dc22   2006022942

British Library Cataloguing in Publication Data is available.

Library of Congress Catalog Card Number: 2006022942
ISBN: 0–313–33339–4
ISSN: 1097–0738

First published in 2006

Greenwood Press, 88 Post Road West, Westport, CT 06881
An imprint of Greenwood Publishing Group, Inc.
www.greenwood.com

Printed in the United States of America

The paper used in this book complies with the
Permanent Paper Standard issued by the National
Information Standards Organization (Z39.48–1984).

10   9   8   7   6   5   4   3   2   1

Every reasonable effort has been made to trace the owners of copyright materials in this book, but in
some instances this has proven impossible. The author(s) [editor(s)] and publisher will be glad to receive
information leading to a more complete acknowledgments in subsequent printings of the book and in the
meantime extend their apologies for any omissions.

Contents

Series Foreword

Geographically, Asia encompasses the vast area from Suez, the Bosporus, and the Ural Mountains eastward to the Bering Sea and from this line southward to the Indonesian archipelago, an expanse that covers about 30 percent of our earth. Conventionally, and especially insofar as culture and customs are concerned, Asia refers primarily to the region east of Iran and south of Russia. This area can be divided in turn into subregions commonly known as South, Southeast, and East Asia, which are the main focus of this series.

The United States has vast interests in this region. In the twentieth century the United States fought three major wars in Asia (namely the Pacific War of 1941–45, the Korean War of 1950–53, and the Vietnam War of 1965–75), and each had profound impact on life and politics in America. Today, America's major trading partners are in Asia, and in the foreseeable future the weight of Asia in American life will inevitably increase, for in Asia lie our great allies as well as our toughest competitors in virtually all arenas of global interest. Domestically, the role of Asian immigrants is more visible than at any other time in our history. In spite of these connections with Asia, however, our knowledge about this crucial region is far from adequate. For various reasons, Asia remains for most of us a relatively unfamiliar, if not stereotypical or even mysterious, "Oriental" land.

There are compelling reasons for Americans to obtain some level of concrete knowledge about Asia. It is one of the world's richest reservoirs of culture and an ever-evolving museum of human heritage. Rhoads Murphey, a prominent Asianist, once pointed out that in the part of Asia east of Afghanistan and south of Russia alone lies half the world, "half of its people and far more that half of its historical experience, for these are the oldest living civilized traditions." Prior to the modern era, with limited interaction and mutual influence between the East and the West, Asian civilizations developed largely independent from the West. In modern times, however, Asia and the West have come not only into close contact but also into frequent conflict: The result has been one of the most solemn and stirring dramas in world history. Today, integration and compromise are the trend in coping with cultural differences. The West—with some notable exceptions—has started to see Asian traditions not as something to fear but as something to be understood, appreciated, and even cherished. After all, Asian traditions are an indispensable part of the human legacy, a matter of global "common wealth" that few of us can afford to ignore.

As a result of Asia's enormous economic development since World War II, we can no longer neglect the study of this vibrant region. Japan's "economic miracle" of postwar development is no longer unique, but in various degrees has been matched by the booming economy of many other Asian countries and regions. The rise of the four "mini dragons" (South Korea, Taiwan, Hong Kong, and Singapore) suggests that there may be a common Asian pattern of development. At the same time, each economy in Asia has followed its own particular trajectory. Clearly, China is the next giant on the scene. Sweeping changes in China in the last two decades have already dramatically altered the world's economic map. Furthermore, growth has also been dramatic in much of Southeast Asia. Today, war-devastated Vietnam shows great enthusiasm for joining the "club" of nations engaged in the world economy. And in South Asia, India, the world's largest democracy, is rediscovering its role as a champion of market capitalism. The economic development of Asia presents a challenge to Americans but also provides them with unprecedented opportunities. It is largely against this background that more and more people in the United States, in particular among the younger generation, have started to pursue careers dealing with Asia.

This series is designed to meet the need for knowledge of Asia among students and the general public. Each book is written in an accessible and lively style by an expert (or experts) in the field of Asian studies. Each book focuses on the culture and customs of a country or region. However, readers should be aware that culture is fluid, not always respecting national boundaries. While every nation seeks its own path to success and struggles to maintain its own identity, in the cultural domain mutual influence and integration among Asian nations are ubiquitous.

Each volume starts with an introduction to the land and the people of a nation or region and includes a brief history and an overview of the economy. This is followed by chapters dealing with a variety of topics that piece together a cultural panorama, such as thought, religion, ethics, literature and art, architecture and housing, cuisine, traditional dress, gender, courtship and marriage, festivals and leisure activities, music and dance, and social customs and lifestyle. In this series, we have chosen not to elaborate on elite life, ideology, or detailed questions of political structure and struggle, but instead to explore the world of common people, their sorrow and joy, their pattern of thinking, and their way of life. It is the culture and the customs of the majority of the people (rather than just the rich and powerful elite) that we seek to understand. Without such understanding, it will be difficult for all of us to live peacefully and fruitfully with each other in this increasingly interdependent world.

As the world shrinks, modern technologies have made all nations on earth "virtual" neighbors. The expression "global village" not only reveals the nature and the scope of the world in which we live but also, more importantly, highlights the serious need for mutual understanding of all peoples on our planet. If this series serves to help the reader obtain a better understanding of the "half of the world" that is Asia, the authors and I will be well rewarded.

Hanchao Lu
Georgia Institute of Technology

Preface

Indonesian cultures include those of forest-dwelling hunters and foragers, rice growers, fisher folk, village artisans, urban office and factory workers, intellectuals, artists, wealthy industrialists, street vendors, and homeless people. They involve villagers in customary societies, sophisticated and cosmopolitan urbanites, as well as people who struggle to survive on city streets: beggars, peddlers, prostitutes, and pedicab drivers. Moreover, waters engulfing all Indonesian islands support seafaring peoples in contrast to societies of the lands.

An extraordinary range of belief systems, material culture, and arts enliven these thousands of islands—composing one of the most ethnographically rich and diverse countries in the world. Majestic temples, complex poetry and literature, lavish theatrical performances, rich mythologies, sophisticated thinking, and splendid visual arts have distinguished Indonesia for centuries and continue into the present. By the seventh century, people were creating exquisite gold jewelry, elaborately detailed stone carving, and intricately beautiful textiles that rival anything in the world today. Indonesians carry on an artistic genius, constantly reinterpreting and refining their cultures in the modern world. Yet, aside from Bali's exotic reputation as an "island paradise," many Westerners (and most Americans) are almost unaware of this country of 242 million people, the fourth most populous nation in the world.

Indonesia has suffered a tumultuous past in stages: under the oppression of local rulers, European colonists, Japanese invaders, corrupt military dictatorships, and currently multinational corporations. This history produced a permanent underclass of people, but also instilled strength of spirit and skill at survival in most ordinary Indonesians. In this new century, the future of

Indonesia, as of much of the world, remains problematic and uncertain. This book attempts to give glimpses of some of the marvels, ingenuities, dilemmas, social realities, diverse cultures and customs, and complex pasts and presents of the Indonesian people.

Europeans have produced most of the modern written histories of this region, although Indonesians have contributed much. Most general literature about Indonesia focuses upon the central islands of Bali and Java. This book will expand the scope to other islands of the world's largest archipelago, revealing something of the rich diversity of this nation.

Acknowledgments

I would first like to thank Hanchao Lu for the opportunity to write this book and for his supportive input while doing so. I appreciate the help and patience of my editor, Wendi Schnaufer, at Greenwood Press and the enthusiasm and assistance of Kaitlin Ciarmiello. For critical comments while writing, I am grateful to Wendi Schnaufer, Herbert Phillips, and Pierre Horn. I thank Elizabeth Oley, David Weitzman, Astri Wright, and Joe and Clare Fischer for helping me sort out matters concerning photographs. Several people contributed photographs of places and events that otherwise would not be illustrated in this book. I appreciate the generosity of Marie Jeanne Adams, Ian Fischer-Laycock, Joseph Fischer, David Weitzman, Andrew Causey, Kathleen Adams, and Elizabeth Oley for sharing their fine pictures. Over the years, I received funding from generous institutions such as the Fulbright Foundation, the Wenner-Gren Foundation for Anthropological Research, and the Australian Research Council, which permitted me to carry on prolonged research in Indonesia. I also thank the Indonesian Academy of Sciences (LIPI) for facilitating my research periods. The number of Indonesians who assisted and befriended me through the years is too great to list. Their kindness has been immeasurable. I owe my truly meaningful knowledge of Indonesia to the people who allowed me into their lives. I hope that this book will do them justice and I apologize for any omissions or inaccuracies, which are solely my own. *Terima kasih banyak.*

Because of the immense scope of this book and the limitations on space within it, I have had to selectively include information, while leaving much out. I regret that I could not include more topics and pictures from a number of places. Thus, this book is a necessarily partial portrayal of Indonesia, but one that I hope will inspire the reader to further exploration of the culture and customs of this marvelous country.

Chronology

1.3 to 1.8 million years from present	*Homo erectus* ("Java Man") fossils discovered in East Java in 1891. Whether the fossil represents an ancestor of *Homo sapiens* in Java remains uncertain.
40,000 years from present	First traces of *Homo sapiens* in Indonesia, as people were able to migrate back and forth from the Asian mainland. The islands of western Indonesia formed a peninsula with mainland Southeast Asia, some call Sundaland. Papua New Guinea and neighboring islands formed an extension of Australia.
17,000 years from present	The Ice Age began to subside and sea levels gradually rose to cover landmasses and form islands of the Indonesian archipelago.
5,000–3,000 B.C.	Austronesian migrations from Southern China began to move through Indonesia.
100 A.D.	Rulers of the archipelago opened trade routes between China and India, creating great wealth in some local regions and permitting foreign influences. Indians arrived in Sumatra, Java, and Bali.
Third century	The area of southern Sumatra near Jambi and probably western Java became main entrepots linking the Java sea region with China.
Fourth century	First known inscriptions of South Indian *Pallawa* script used in announcements by King Mulavarman in East Kalimantan.
Fifth century	Based on Chinese chronicles, Indonesian ships controlled most trade in the archipelago and were sailing as far as China.

Eighth century	Srivijaya emerged in Sumatra as the first great power in the region. Inscriptions reveal teaching of Tantric Mahayana Buddhism. Srivijaya controlled trade in the Melaka Straits through providing a safe upriver port base at Palembang. Sailendra dynasty developed a great rice plane polity in Central Java. They ruled for 200 years, constructing the giant Buddhist monument Borobudur.
Tenth century	Most Javanese rulers, for reasons unclear (but perhaps through wars with Srivijaya of Sumatra) lost power. Airlangga became the founder of Java's first great empire, bringing central and eastern Java and Bali under some semblance of a united kingdom.
Thirteenth century	Kertanegara began a reign of rapid development in Javanese culture and expansion beyond Java. After his death, his son-in-law founded the most powerful kingdom ever to arise in Java: Majapahit.
1292	Italian explorer Marco Polo wrote of Islamic sultanate in Aceh, northern Sumatra.
Fourteenth century	Majapahit's fleets sailed to outer islands, in an expansive plan by its prime minister Gajah Mada. A chronicle written at this time, *The Nagarakertagama,* claimed that the empire held sovereignty from Sumatra to Papua New Guinea. Srivijaya had declined after losing control of maritime commerce to Chinese shipping.
Fifteenth century	Majapahit went into decline after losing control of island shipping trade and the opposition of the expanding Muslim kingdom of Demak.
Sixteenth century	The Islamic Mataram kingdom rose to power, subjugating most of Java and invading the formerly Hindu–Buddhist interior.
1511	Portuguese conquered the city of Melaka, thus controlling the Straits. Months later they sailed to eastern Indonesia seeking spices.
Seventeenth century	The seafaring Makasar from South Sulawesi reached northern Australia, on coastal Arnhem Land, in search of *trepang* (sea cucumbers) to sell to Chinese. They interacted with Aboriginal people, leaving Makasar descendants and terminology.
1641	The Dutch took Melaka from the Portuguese and began to establish factories and plantations in Sumatra and Java. Jan Pieterszoon Coen, Governor General of the Dutch East Indies, took control of the spice trade in the Banda Islands and other parts of eastern Maluku.

1664	Atrocities in the Indies and ongoing trade battles with the Dutch led to an unexpected invasion of Manhattan (then a Dutch colony) by a British armada. This resulted in Holland's forced swap of Manhattan Island to the English in exchange for the small Banda island of Run—a major turn in American history.
1799	The Dutch East India Company began to lose money. The Netherlands government took over its enterprise in the future Indonesia.
1811	Java fell under control of the British East India Company. Thomas Stamford Raffles, as lieutenant governor, rediscovered Borobudur, buried under centuries of volcanic soil. He arranged for excavation.
1815	Mt. Tambora erupted on Sumbawa Island, obliterating an entire language group.
1825–1830	A period called the "Java Wars" raged against the Dutch. The Netherlands also faced resistance in western Sumatra from Islamic leaders of the Minangkabau.
1830	A great commercial expansion of Dutch colonialism under "The Cultivation System" demanded a percentage of crops from all farmers. This period secured position and wealth for the elite *priyayi* Javanese in complicity with Dutch colonists.
1860	Publication of the novel *Max Havelaar,* written by a former Dutch official, Douwes Dekker (under the pen name Multatuli) describing the abuses of combined Dutch and Javanese elite rule toward peasants.
1883	The volcano Krakatoa erupted in the sea west of Java.
1901	The Dutch created a more liberal Ethical Policy, in response to criticism within Holland and other European nations. At this point, the Netherlands controlled most of Indonesia.
1906	On September 20 the Dutch advanced upon Denpasar, Bali. The entire royal family and entourage marched toward them, carrying only daggers. All were shot or committed suicide. This day is remembered as *Puputan* (Ending).
1907–1911	Borobudur excavation and restoration was completed under Dutch administration.
1911	Publication of Raden Kartini's letters as a book in Holland. In 1920, it was published in English as *Letters of a Javanese Princess,* telling of a young Javanese woman's struggles with traditional values and European modern ideas.

1900–1930	Indonesian nationalism began to spread among a variety of organized groups, from Muslims to Communists. Many became organized under the Indonesian Nationalist Party, formed by future President Sukarno.
1941–1942	World War II broke out and the Japanese conquered Indonesia.
1945	After news of Japanese surrender, Sukarno proclaimed Indonesia an Independent nation on August 17, 1945.
1949	Holland had attempted to regain control of Indonesia, but ceded it under international pressure, retaining only West Papua. Indonesia gained full sovereignty in 1949. Sukarno and Muhammad Hatta became the first president and vice-president, respectively, and developed a policy called Guided Democracy.
1963	Mt. Gunung Agung erupted in Bali killing more than 1,000 people.
1965	An attempted coup occurred on September 30, leaving six military generals and one child murdered. General Suharto, senior surviving officer, seized command, becoming the new leader of Indonesia. The full reality behind this coup remains a mystery.
1965–1967	Rumors circulated widely after the failed coups that a communist women's group had also mutilated the murdered generals. A violent frenzy swept Indonesia as the army and citizens killed communists and others. In Bali up to 80,000 were murdered. Tens of thousands died in North Sumatra and Java. The total number of deaths over these years is estimated at more than a half million people.
1966	In March Sukarno officially handed the Presidency over to Suharto, and then went into exile. Suharto rapidly centralized power in a tight system of military control. Under his absolute authority, New Order Indonesia began.
1967	Indonesia joined the United Nations. A new Indonesian foreign investment law began a wave of international capital in the country. Oil exports brought much revenue into Indonesia, and a program of economic development began. Achievements were phenomenal, involving infrastructure, industry, healthcare, and schools.
1969	The Dutch ceded its last outpost, West Papua New Guinea to Indonesia. The region was then renamed Irian Jaya (Victorious Papua).
1975	Indonesian forces invaded East Timor, recently independent from Portugal, with acquiescence (if not prompting) of the United States and Australia. A battle ensued lasting almost 25 years, as people resisted occupation and Indonesian forces killed many thousands of East Timorese.

1980	A book of political dissident, Pramoedya Ananta Toer, *This Earth of Mankind,* was published in Indonesian in Jakarta. Three more novels followed, written while Toer was in a prison camp on the island of Buru, called the *Buru Quartet.* Suharto banned the books in Indonesia.
1980s–1997	The New Order under Suharto retained power and political repression and corruption progressed. Simultaneously, economic growth continued, producing a growing Indonesian middle class.
1997	The Asian financial crisis hit after the dramatic fall of the Thai baht. Currencies of Southeast Asia plummeted. The Indonesian rupiah lost 80 percent of its former value. Suharto failed to comply with reforms demanded by International Monetary fund and continued "crony capitalism." This caused further economic woes and massive public disgust with Suharto.
1998	Suharto was re-elected unopposed to his seventh presidential term. Security forces shot four protesting university students in Jakarta, and the "May Riots" swept the city. Rioters attacked mostly government and commercial buildings as the city ignited in flames. Thugs targeted the Chinese community, looting, raping, killing, and burning their homes and businesses. Three thousand buildings were razed. On May 21, having lost support of the military, Suharto passed the Presidency to his Vice-President, B. J. Habibie.
1998–1999	Violence raged across Indonesia: Kalimantan Dayaks murdered transmigrants from Madura; religious war between Christians and Muslims created death and devastation in Ambon; gangs controlled streets of provincial cities; and a war between clans left many dead in Sumba. Much of Indonesia was in anarchy.
1999	In January President Habibie announced publicly that East Timor could vote for autonomy or independence. This fueled a wave of separatist movements across Indonesia and upset the military. Losing a vote of confidence in parliament, Habibie resigned from upcoming elections. In national elections, after much delay, debate, and confusion, on October 19 Abdurrachman Wahid became fourth Indonesian President and Sukarno's daughter, Megawati Sukarnoputri became Vice-President. Under the auspices of the occupying United Nations, East Timor voted overwhelmingly for national independence on August 30. Upon exiting the new nation, the Indonesian army and pro-Indonesian Timorese incinerated much of the region and forcibly evacuated thousands across the border to Indonesian West Timor.

2001	Following his liberal policies, openness to autonomy of various regional groups, and his poor health, President Wahid was impeached through military efforts in July. Megawati Sukarnoputri became President of Indonesia.
2002	On October 12 a terrorist car bomb exploded at a Bali nightclub, killing over 200 and destroying a city block. The group responsible claimed that they meant to kill Americans in retaliation for George W. Bush's Middle Eastern policies. Other attacks would follow in Jakarta and then again in Bali. Islamic Fundamentalism was growing in Indonesia through groups like *Jemaah Islamiyah* (Islamic Congress).
	Megawati ruled as a detached elite, and Indonesia deteriorated. Conflicts and anarchy raged across the archipelago. The military became involved in organized crime rackets, and people became ever more disillusioned.
2003	Discovery of small human-like fossils on the island of Flores, named *Homo floresiensis.*
2004	Indonesians elected a new President, Susilo Bambang Yudhoyono ("S.B.Y") a retired general offering hope of strength, reform, and much needed order. His Vice-President was Jusuf Kalla. S.B.Y. won the first direct election in Indonesian history, as people voted for individuals and not parties.
	On December 26, a massive tsunami devastated the region of Aceh on the north coast of Sumatra, killing thousands.
2005	Indonesian military forces withdrew from Aceh, after 31 years. Acehnese agreed to surrender weapons and drop demands for independence. The national government ceded to Aceh much of its natural gas and oil resources and agreed to limited self-government for the region. A staunchly Islamic region, Aceh voted *sharia* (conservative Islamic) law into its government.
	A free press continued and some government reforms were slowly progressing. The Constitutional Court and Judicial Commission began to flex some power independent of politics and cronyism.
2006	On March 8 women's groups took to the streets in Jakarta to protest *sharia* (conservative Islamic) law, as a "porn bill" before the House of Representatives would apply strict Muslim dress codes and conduct to them, but not to men. They demanded that the government focus on more valid issues, like domestic violence and human trafficking.

On April 12, 5,000 trade union workers swarmed Jakarta and Surabaya, Java, protesting the government's support of business interests over their own.

On April 30, writer Pramoedya Ananta Toer died in Jakarta at the age of 82.

2006   From April through July, Mt. Merapi in Central Java issued signs of an imminent eruption, spewing lava and clouds of gas.

On May 27, a 6.2 earthquake struck near the city of Yogyakarta, Java, killing more than 6,200 and leaving much of the region in ruins.

On July 17, a major tsunami devastated the southwest coast of Java, following a 6.8 earthquake. More than 50,000 people became homeless and as many as 1,000 perished.

1

Land, People, and History

LAND AND CLIMATE

On December 26, 2004, a massive earthquake jolted the shores of northwest Sumatra, Indonesia. Within hours immense tsunami waves virtually obliterated the area of Banda Aceh, killing thousands. The quake's ripple effect sent tsunamis as far as Africa, Sri Lanka, and Thailand, wreaking devastation in the southeastern hemisphere—particularly ravaging coastal populations in nine countries of Southeast and South Asia. Resulting tremors followed in places as distant as Alaska. The tectonic shift centered in the sea near the Sumatran coast and the destruction in Banda Aceh and well beyond dominated the global media. Many in the western hemisphere viewed the first televised images they had ever seen of Indonesian people, from a region they knew little about.

The region of Banda Aceh, Sumatra, long had been a landing point for less catastrophic but nonetheless profound influences—such as the spread of trade from India and Arabia and probably the introduction of Islam to the Indonesian and Malay archipelagos. Marco Polo traveled to Aceh in 1292 and reported the first Islamic sultanate in Southeast Asia.[1] In more recent times, Aceh has experienced intense political strife and violence in a struggle for independence from Indonesia. But this is one region of many this book will explore, and there is much to cover.

A Volcanic Archipelago

Imagine a country made up of more than 17,000 islands—over 6,000 inhabited, roughly over 300 languages, and hundreds of ethnic groups stretching on either side of the equator for nearly 3,200 miles. Traveling by air across the length of the world's largest archipelago, scores of volcanoes appear through the clouds, some with colorful crater lakes. Intricate ecologies of uniquely formed islands and waterways have shaped the vibrant cultures inhabiting them.

This vast stretch of wildly diverse islands formed through tumultuous geological events over thousands of years. A slow, perpetual movement of continental plates from the Indian and Pacific Oceans shaped the archipelago, causing some land masses to rise and others to sink into surrounding seas. Indeed, the earthquake and tsunamis of December of 2004 followed an abrupt tectonic shift deep in the ocean bed west of Sumatra.

An enormous series of arcs creates the southern Indonesian islands; a concentric sweep beginning northwest of Sumatra and stretching thousands of miles eastward through the Maluku islands (formerly called the Moluccas) to West Papua (Irian Jaya), continuing far beyond Indonesia across the Pacific Ocean.

Before the end of the last Ice Age (about 17,000 years ago), shallow straits connected much of the archipelago. As late as 10,000 B.C., people and animals migrated from mainland Southeast Asia on foot to the Indonesian islands. Known by geographers as the Sunda Shelf, approximately 15,000 years ago Sumatra, Java, Bali, and Borneo (Kalimantan) were one land mass connected to the Asian mainland, with shallow waters from the Gulf of Siam to the Java Sea.

Mountains, forests, rivers, and savannahs dramatically contour these ever-changing lands, altered by volcanic eruptions, earthquakes, erosion, and sedimentation. Explosive volcanoes produced or annihilated islands in the past and continue to transform them. Among hundreds of volcanoes across Indonesia, sixty-one remain active. Krakatoa, the most historically famous, exploded in 1883 in the seas west of Java, killing more than 35,000 people and changing climate patterns around the world for a year.[2] A yet greater eruption (the second largest ever recorded in the world) took place on the island of Sumbawa on Tambora mountain in 1815, killing approximately 50,000 people, obliterating the Tambora language group, and causing a worldwide "year without summer."[3] Lake Toba in North Sumatra appeared after an ancient volcano literally blew its top about 74,000 years ago—the largest known eruption ever.

Other explosions, such as of Mount Gunung Agung in Bali in 1963, destroyed villages and terrain, simultaneously strengthening people's beliefs in the supernatural. Indeed, to many Indonesians volcanic eruptions, earthquakes, droughts, wildfires, famines, and floods signal immanent changes in human and metaphysical powers that be. Natural disasters often portent the fall of a national or local regime. Such catastrophes preceded the fall of ancient kings in Sumatra, Java, and Bali as well as the more recent demises of President Sukarno in 1965 and President Suharto in 1998. Thus, geology (and all of nature) reinforces belief systems of Indonesian societies.

Volcanoes also provide the rich soils nourishing communities clustered at their feet. Volcanic ash reinforces a fertility that would otherwise wash away in the nearly two hundred inches of rainfall drenching Indonesia each year. Most islands remain verdant from frequent rainfall, supporting rain forests or intensive agriculture. Southeast islands such as Flores, Sumba, Savu, Rote, Alor, and Timor lay dry and relatively barren of vegetation for half the year or more, sitting within climate zones of Australia.

The Wallace Line, Upland and Lowland, Coastal and Aquatic

In the mid-nineteenth century British explorer and naturalist Alfred Russel Wallace perceived a distinction between two zones of the Indonesian archipelago.[4] He then proposed a bio-regional border, now accepted internationally as the Wallace Line. Wallace observed sharp contrasts in flora and fauna across an aquatic border running north to south between Bali and Lombok and separating Kalimantan and Sulawesi. To the west of this line, animals and plants compared to those of Asia, including monkeys and tigers living amid jungle trees. To the east, natural species resembled those of Australia, including Eucalyptus trees, marsupials, and emus. Climate east of the border was notably drier than islands to the west.

A largely monsoonal and volcanic region, Indonesia contains about 10 percent of the world's (ever-shrinking) rain forests. Historically based upon agricultural production, groups in Indonesia have practiced wet-rice cultivation in fertile lowland floodplains and swidden (slash-and-burn) agriculture, hunting, and foraging in the less fertile upland regions. Populations and political centers tended to cluster in lowland or coastal areas for rich soils and commerce. People maximized many different ecological conditions, creating complementary needs and interests between groups. Thus, necessities of reciprocal trade and services between highland peoples with those of coastal regions, and between swidden and wet-rice agriculturalists, established interdependant economies. For example, inland peoples might trade wood products, crafts, or garden produce for fish, salt, and imported goods from port communities.

Indonesia is a hot, equatorial land, becoming chilly at high altitudes. Snow falls only in West Papua around the mountain *Puncak Jaya* (16,503 ft.), which contains permanent glaciers. Two seasons envelop the remaining islands, the relatively cool rainy season between November and April, when monsoons ride the winds from the South China Sea. For the rest of the year, a hotter, drier season engulfs the archipelago. Annual temperatures typically range from 61 to 91 degrees Fahrenheit with humidity from 50 to 90 percent. Dense atmospheric moisture saturates days with sultry heat. Indonesians customarily take a mid-day break from activities, much like the Spanish *siesta*. At the hottest time of day (between 11 A.M. and 2 P.M.), people return from the fields, businesses close, and many sleep.

Water defines Indonesia as much as does land—to the extent that Indonesians refer to their nation as *tanah air,* meaning "land and water." In a vast region of long maritime commerce and sustenance, oceans define the archipelago as essentially as land in terms of human environments and resources. The ubiquitous Indonesian seas abound in life supporting fishing communities. In fact, some fisherfolk, such as those from the Sulu Islands between the Philippines and Sulawesi, live on boats all year. Floating communities of people animate the waters of some regions, regarding the sea as home and the land as a place for trade, not settlement.

People Utilizing Land

Human impacts upon the land, such as wet-rice and swidden (slash-and-burn) agriculture, reconfigured regions of Indonesia drastically. Wet-rice agriculture versus swidden methods form a classic distinction between geographical regions for scholars—contrasting the "Inner Indonesia" of Bali and Java and the "Outer Indonesia" of all other islands.

People in heavily forested regions such as Kalimantan or West Irian practice a slash-and-burn type of agriculture called *ladang.* These clearings cut from forests support crops for two to three years, until exhausting soil nutrients. Then people clear a new *ladang.* When farmed on a small scale, slash-and-burn regions recover their original growth to a good degree. This type of cultivation does not permit the population density of wet-rice agricultural communities. Swidden settlements require about ten times the land that they actually cultivate in a year. As people must walk long distances to their fields, villages normally number a few hundred people, often living at some distance from each other. Historically, these were fairly egalitarian societies, with no place for kings. Swidden agriculturalists practiced animism, centering on their plants, water, and ancestors.[5] They based beliefs in complex perceptions of natural and supernatural realms.

Bali presents a marvel of cultivation through an intricate environment of rice terraces, as water systems intrinsically sculpt much of the island.[6] Moreover, the elaborate irrigation systems required for wet-rice agriculture (called *sawah*) are only possible through organized communities built upon social cooperation. In Bali, *subaks* form such communal systems involving people in associations for all aspects of maintaining extensively irrigated rice paddies.

People adhere to the *subak* system not only for reasons of survival and social cooperation, but also following religious beliefs defining the correct and moral way of doing things in life. The religion of Bali is Hinduism, but like belief systems throughout Indonesia, it incorporates many ancient animist elements. Thus, geography, survival, activities, and beliefs mix in cultural and metaphysical ideas throughout Indonesia.

PEOPLE

Societies in Indonesia reflect the natural diversity and splendor of the routes, moorings, and interiors among thousands of sea-bounded land masses forming this archipelago. Although interconnected historically through politics, trade, wars, colonialism, and the formation of the Republic of Indonesia, each island remains distinctive. Moreover, remarkable social, religious, or geographical differences emerge within islands as large as Sumatra or as small as Savu.

With such variety, Indonesia defies simple categorizations. For example, eastern Indonesian islands could as logically fall under categories of Western Polynesia as of those of Southeast Asia, in terms of location, land, climate, and headhunting and chieftain cultures. Western Indonesia experienced more historical connections with mainland Southeast Asia, shares similar climate and geographical features, and developed refined court cultures incorporating Indian influences.

Cultures of Indonesia vividly reflect adaptations to land, climate, and seas; the variety of languages and societies across the archipelago developed through an insularity of islands (some far more than others) as well as the many influxes of peoples and influences upon them. Communities in some regions lived in relative isolation while others were part of great trading or seafaring networks. Outside influences constantly arrived throughout the past and while most evident in multi-ethnic port communities, they eventually made their ways to the hinterlands through trade. Aside from some inland mountain tribes, such as the Dani in West Papua (Irian Jaya), few people in Indonesia have lived in complete isolation for long periods of time.

The oldest known human histories in Indonesia surfaced through archaeological discoveries in Java. Human fossils termed *Homo erectus* ("Java Man") from Java date back to approximately 1.3 to 1.7 million years.[7] Recent findings in 2004 in a cave on the island of Flores revealed fossil remains of a small statured being (less than four feet tall). This newly-found human was named *Homo floresiensis,* dated as living 18,000 years ago (other similar remains were then found dating to 13,000 years). Discoverers of this fossil nicknamed it "The Hobbit" because of its small size. Myths in Flores carry on to this day about a separate race of "little people," which makes this human fossil all the more compelling for anthropologists.[8] At this writing, *Homo flore-siensis* holds the status of an individual species amid continuing controversy.

One scholar considers that the first Indonesian humans were of the broad ethnic group we now call Australo-Melanesians and that they were the ancestors of the Melanesians of New Guinea, the Australian Aborigines, and the small Negrito communities of the Malay Peninsula and the Philippines.[9]

Archaeological speculation suggests that due to the ancient exposure of the Sunda Shelf (between the Malay peninsula and the western Indonesian archipelago), many different peoples migrated and intermixed in prehistoric times.[10] This explanation also traces the Indonesian islands and beyond linguistically, with the beginning of the migration of peoples of the Austonesian language group from Taiwan about 5,000 years ago—expanding as numerous divisions migrated to various island regions. Some words derived from the Austronesian language remain similar from Indonesia to Hawaii. The Austronesians ventured as far as Madagascar, off the east coast of Africa and to Easter Island in the eastern Pacific. They dramatically distinguished a huge sweep of islands between Africa and the eastern Pacific as a megalithic arch. Places Austronesians settled typically display large stone monuments. The immense heads of Easter Island are the most famous examples.

Because ancient people across the Indonesian islands largely used tools and built structures made from decomposable materials like bamboo, rattan, wood, palm leaves, coconut shells, and grasses, little remains of their daily lives for archaeological finding. In this wet, hot climate, organic matter rots quickly, leaving few traces. Generally stone constructions like temples and graves, and tools and artifacts of metal or stone remain of the past.

People living in the western region of Indonesia—including the islands of Sumatra, Java and Bali—generally resemble those of the Malay peninsula (now part of the nation of Malaysia), with straight black hair, round eyes, and dark complexions. Toward the eastern areas of the Lesser Sunda Islands (Nusa Tenggara Timur) and the Maluku archipelago, Papuan or Melanesian features characterize populations. Tightly curled hair and darker skin tones distinguish people of islands such as Flores, Timor, Ambon, or Papua. Before the last Ice Age, the island now politically divided into Papua New Guinea and Irian Jaya (West Papua) was connected by land to Australia. Indigenous peoples of the Papuan island physically resemble Aboriginal peoples of Australia.

Throughout a vast region, however, all sorts of people have mixed over many centuries; and on almost any sizeable island, might descend from ancestry including Chinese, Indians, Arabs, Persians, Europeans, Africans, or islanders across Southeast Asia and beyond. Portuguese brought Africans into their colonies in Flores and East Timor. In East Timor today, some claim descent from Mozambique and Angola. Intermixing between all groups occurred to the extent that there certainly is no one Indonesia physical "type," and likely there never was.

Languages

Linguists have distinguished two major language groups in Indonesia: Papuan and Austronesian. In modern Indonesia it is possible to identify more than 200 Austronesian and more than 150 Papuan (Melanesian) languages.[11] Papuan languages persist in eastern regions of the archipelago, including one group in East Timor, and stretch through some islands in Maluku and much of inland West Papua. Austronesian also weaves through these regions and delineating borders for language groups is difficult. Austronesian language bases predominate through the archipelago west of Timor Island.

Since the seventeenth century, languages in many areas have become extinct. This followed situations such as the Dutch capture of the Banda Islands in 1621, their extermination of most of the indigenous people, and thus the extinction of their language.[12] The massive eruption of Mt. Tambora, Sumbawa in 1815 obliterated people of the Tambora language group. Other languages disappeared as people migrated or mixed with others coming to their regions. Since Indonesian independence in 1949, many formerly remote communities have attended school, learned the national language of Bahasa Indonesia, and have absorbed wider influences. Now, only thirteen Indonesian languages have a million or more native speakers; linguists generally believe that languages with fewer than this number are vulnerable to extinction.[13]

The Malay language originated in Sumatra and spread through mercantile centers of the Straits of Melaka, becoming the main trade vernacular of coastal regions beyond. Javanese was a complex language, steeped in social class distinctions and too difficult for traders to learn and use. Thus, Malay spread through Java's ports. In the colonial era, the Dutch insisted upon using Malay as their language of law and administration. A publishing industry beginning in the 1920s further established Malay as a language of legitimacy. In 1928, the nationalist movement adopted Malay as the language of the future independent state of Indonesia, calling it *Bahasa Indonesia* (Indonesian Language).[14]

Ways of Life

The Chinese traded with Indonesia long before Europeans knew it existed and some settled early on. Chinese became established traders and middlemen in port towns, growing in numbers after Europeans arrived in the sixteenth century. A solid merchant class thus evolved adept at business management and the accumulation of wealth. Many Chinese became some of the most well-to-do business people in modern Indonesia, supported by the national regime in return for political patronage. This caused resentment among common Indonesians, who typically did not practice the Chinese business acumen and work ethic. Chinese came to dominate commerce and set up shops and enterprises on the outermost islands.

Today roughly 50 percent of Indonesians occupy the densely populated island of Java. The capital city of Jakarta contains about 10 million people and Surabaya (the second largest) numbers almost 6 million. Less than half of the nation's population now lives in rural areas. Rural people support themselves through wet-rice cultivation in Bali and Java. Through a program called *transmigrasi* (transmigration), the Indonesian government (during the 1970s and 1980s) transposed this agricultural system along with Javanese farmers to other islands. This policy aimed to relieve population pressures in Java and to "Indonesianize" other island peoples by converting them to wet-rice farming. Javanese rulers have long equated wet-rice agriculture with being civilized. Transmigration was not without problems, as Javanese tried to adapt to extremely different environments and cultures. Further, they often faced resentment (for the land the government allotted them) from indigenous peoples of the islands where they resettled.

Enclaves of wet rice paddies grow in Sumatra, coastal areas of Kalimantan, the Makasar and Manado regions of Sulawesi, and lowlands of the Lesser Sunda and Maluku islands. In places with low rainfall such as Sumba and Timor, people grow rice and produce along rivers and invest much of their energy into livestock. The small, dry island of Savu cultivates the *lontar* palm for most of its needs, providing sugar, paper, oil, building materials, and trade goods. As mentioned, people in deeply forested regions such as Kalimantan and West Irian carry on slash-and-burn agriculture. Multi-national corporations leasing large regions from the Indonesian government, however, have displaced many such people from forests to allow massive logging and mining operations. These businesses have pushed indigenous peoples off of their lands and devastated environments.

HISTORY

The Archipelago before European Contact

Indonesia's aquatic passages carried traders from India, Arabia, Persia, China, and mainland Southeast Asia in prehistoric time, later followed by Europeans. The generally warm waters and rarity of storms in Indonesian seas provided an hospitable, inviting meeting place in comparison to seas such as

the Mediterranean,[15] offering a favorable maritime environment. Boat building and navigation reached sophisticated levels on islands such as Sulawesi,
Bali, Java, and Sumatra, permitting people to travel widely, trade between
islands and mainland Asia, and migrate to other regions. The first European
boats arrived following a demand for Indonesian spices, especially nutmeg and
cloves—stimulating trade relations with the eastern islands of Maluku (the
famed "Spice Islands") beginning in the sixteenth century. The seas became
avenues for widespread penetration of European ships with advanced naval
technology. This enabled conquest of people throughout the archipelago, followed by colonialism.

By way of ocean routes, India had established trade with Java from about
the first century A.D. and the outermost Indonesian islands received goods from
China and India many centuries ago. Because of the rhythms of the monsoons
in island Southeast Asia, traders moving between India and China generally
needed to spend a season in port somewhere near the Straits of Melaka to
wait for the winds favorable for an onward journey.[16] Effects from these countries were manifold through the islands, principally from India. Yet the waters
allowing Chinese and Indian trade also hindered the massive invasions these
powers carried out on mainland Southeast Asia. Thus, many islands absorbed
influences of world civilizations—trade goods, ideas, new foods, technology,
religion, material culture, agricultural innovations, and domestic animals—
gradually over centuries. People adapted such elements to their societies and
purposes.

An historical account of Indonesia characterizes indigenous ways of accounting
history, in describing early Sumatran kingdoms:

Affirming a particular version of the past was never an urgent priority in a culture with
relatively diffuse awareness of authority, where the sea offered countless options for
people who were at home in boats and where agriculturalists were dispersed in many
small riverine enclaves.[17]

In fact, there are few written early accounts of history from the Indonesian
region, although some do exist, especially from Bali, Java, and Sulawesi.
Chinese court visitors to the islands and eventually Europeans such as Marco
Polo provided descriptive writings of life in the archipelago many centuries
ago. Particularly in Sumatra and Java, much international trade and political activity took place in thriving societies, drawing in foreigners with their
developed Hindu–Buddhist centers.

Through the Indonesian islands and Southeast Asia, political power has
functioned through what scholars call a center and periphery model.[18] That
is, rulers exerted influence from the center of an area surrounded by followers
extending out to a periphery. Imagine a circle with a powerful light at the

center. The intensity of this light gradually becomes diffused toward the edges of the circle. Beyond the circle would be the dimmed outer boundaries of another region of people allied to a ruler at the center of their political area. This model typified large kingdoms and small village regions.

An important ancient mark of political power throughout Southeast Asia rests in the ability of leaders to attract large followings of people. One analysis concludes, "What Euro-Americans commonly regard as 'real' power (influence over other persons) would only be possible to one already favored by invisible forces. The real question was how long those forces would continue to confer their favor."[19] Such views toward power or its deterioration profoundly affected recent elections in Indonesia and changing political conditions. To comprehend modern Indonesian politics, one must acknowledge deeply historical ideas of the meanings and workings of power through the potency of leaders.

Throughout history, controlling populations was far more important than owning land. Subjects would serve a ruler in exchange for protection, gifts, prestige, or simply peace. If he ruled too harshly or failed to care for his surrounding population, many would simply move to a more favorable region. Thus followings were flexible and populations could suddenly shift.

The Rise of the Great Hindu-Buddhist Kingdoms

During the last half of the seventh century, the region around the city of Palembang in southeastern Sumatra became the center of the Srivijaya Empire. Palembang at that time controlled trade and shipping through the Straits of Melaka—a vital commercial route for many Asian powers and later Europeans. This maritime control produced immense wealth for the Srivijaya Empire, who sent ships to China and Sri Lanka. Although information of Srivijayan history is scant, it dominated the Malay Peninsula, Sumatra, and western Java for much of five hundred years. After centuries of power, Srivijaya went into decline following the expansion of Chinese shipping through the archipelago, involving Malay, Thai, and Javanese ports and dispersing control of the Palembang kingdom.[20]

During an architecturally flamboyant period (eighth and ninth centuries) in central Java, the immense Buddhist temple Borobudur arose under the Sailendra dynasty. The region grew clustered with numerous temples, including Hindu structures in the mountain-bordered Dieng Plateau and a large Hindu complex at Prambanan. These monuments represented rice plain societies, with different political dynamics than those of the cosmopolitan ports. These inland societies involved specific types of eco-regions, with leaders controlling the water associations essential to maintain wet-rice agriculture. One historian wrote that "the behavior of the gods, like the behavior of the farmers, was shaped by the human planting cycles, for they came down to inhabit their shrines only on special days, usually related to the planting schedule."[21] This remains the case throughout Indonesia, whether involving rice paddies in Java or Bali or cornfields in Timor. People appeal to supernatural forces to provide land with water and ensure fertility of their crops. In this way, ongoing relations between people, gods and goddesses, ancestors, spirits, and agriculture are vital to Indonesian societies.

The great Javanese empire of Majapahit rose as a rice plain polity. Coming to power in the late thirteenth century, Majapahit gained political authority over central Java and the island of Madura. This empire sent emissaries afar between 1294 and 1478 and considered itself sovereign over what centuries later became islands of the Republic of Indonesia. Kertanegara, who ruled in the late thirteenth century, had visions of a large archipelago domain ruled by the Javanese, which he expressed in the term *nusantara* (archipelago). Today, Indonesians refer to their nation by this term. An epic poem, the *Nagarakertagama* (1365), tells of the grandeur of the Majapahit Empire and is a rare indigenous record of this period of Javanese history.

Majapahit reached its peak of power under Rajasanagara in the fourteenth century through the brilliant vision and diplomatic skill of its minister, Gajah Mada. Representatives from this empire reached most of the major Indonesian islands and beyond during his time, and Gajah Mada ventured out himself to distant lands. To this day, some people in the eastern Indonesian islands claim that they descend from the Majapahit or particularly from its dynamic minister. Legends from Bali tell of many cultural origins from Majapahit, including the founding of Bali's most sacred temple to this day, Besakih. Majapahit later became an exemplary model for twentieth century nationalist leaders in Java. Conditions, however, eventually changed drastically in the archipelago, leading to the decline of this great empire.

One summarizes that the "hemisphere-wide access of Majapahit's spice trade was its undoing. And the spices, like the islands themselves, had developed a siren quality that was irresistible."[22] The spice trade in the eastern islands grew so enormous and international that the Majapahit could no longer control it—particularly after ships sailed in from Europe, upsetting the balance of power in the archipelago. Atlantic shipping through the Indonesian islands solidified powers of the port communities, subsequently beginning a process of European colonization.

Coastal communities in Java eventually defeated the Majapahit and established a new empire of Mataram in the sixteenth century. Its leaders were Javanese Muslims, likely converted through exposure to Islamic influences in port cities. After this, Islam diffused through Java. While some of the regal families converted, Islam nonetheless represented a rejection of the special religious connections formerly available only to royals. This compelling new faith was open to all people, who could pray directly to a central God. Hinduism and Buddhism had developed as court cultures not accessible to common people. Indeed, many commoners had been severely exploited in constant, unpaid laboring to construct the Hindu–Buddhist megastructures of their kings. The centuries-long construction of Borobudur probably bankrupted the region of central Java, exhausting its population.

Ironically, many ports in Indonesia today with sizeable Muslim populations once allied with the Majapahit Empire. On the eastern Indonesian island of Sumba, a number of Muslims adamantly claim descent from the Majapahit minister, Gajah Mada. In 1994, a high-school English teacher declared fervently, "I was born to say that Gajah Mada died in Sumba!"[23]

Buddhism and Hinduism, however, never took hold in eastern islands such as Sumba, Timor, and Flores. Islam came through traders in port towns (where it tended to remain as a religious enclave), but these islands had developed strong animistic cultures apart from the mainstream of world faiths and felt little need to change. In fact, outside religions posed a serious threat to their locally based power structures. House societies characterized the eastern islands, with ancestral homes as cosmological centers of people's notions of the universe. Such systems continue to an extent in this region, which differs significantly from western Indonesia. Eastern islands long had developed headhunting societies, with domains in frequent warfare with one another. Headhunting formed part of a cosmological belief system related to power and fertility and also a rite of passage to manhood.

The Spread of Islam and the Arrival of Europeans

In the early fifteenth century, A Srivijaya prince founded the city of Melaka on the Malay Peninsula. This port city grew to be the most important trade center in Southeast Asia, controlling regional commerce from the east, west, north, and south, and drawing in peoples from around the world. Melaka gained power early on through Chinese protection and trade. Yet the Portuguese seized Melaka in 1511. The former leaders and many residents moved upriver and formed a new settlement to avoid their control. Still, this situated the Portuguese in a profitable location from which to control an immense amount of commerce. The fall of Melaka to Catholic Portugal prompted a rippling religious fervor through Indonesia and a rise in power of Islamic sultanates, such as Aceh and Minangkabau in Sumatra, Banjarmasin in Kalimantan, Makasar and Bugis in Sulawesi, Ternate and Tidore in Maluku, and kingdoms throughout Java. The Aceh people of northern Sumatra waged continuous war against the Portuguese in Melaka until finally they assisted the Dutch in conquering the port in 1640. Yet Aceh gained nothing as the Dutch seized command. After this, Aceh went into relative decline.

By the fifteenth century, Islam had spread through Indonesia and a number of sultanates were established across the islands, notably in port towns. As in Java, this new religion likely attracted many because it professed egalitarianism in regions dominated by oppressive class systems. However, at least early on, Islam was not a liberating force for the general population, which long had been suppressed by the kings and aristocracy.[24] Aristocratic Javanese Muslims became known as the *priyayi* (upper class) and Islamic kings ruled from palaces through the same feudal system that had gripped the island for centuries. Islam mixed with Javanese mysticism and its practice became determined by former realities of the Indonesian situation,[25] as had other new religions in the past.

In southern Sulawesi, the Muslim empire of Makasar of Gowa grew extremely powerful between 1550–1660 because of its dominant port and strong leadership.[26] Bugis (also Muslims) were sea-faring rivals of the Makasar. Like much of Indonesia, Sulawesi practiced slavery. People either captured in warfare or born into hereditary servitude were traded between islands. South Sulawesians were brilliant boat builders and navigators (and remain so to the present). Both Makasar and Bugis seamen sailed to the west coast of West Papua seeking slaves. Many migrated to other islands and some actually reached the northern coast of Australia by the seventeenth century in search of sea cucumbers (called *trepang*) to trade with China. Today, Aboriginal communities in a coastal region of the Northern Territory, Australia, use certain south Sulawesi terms and include some descendants of the Indonesian seamen, who also took some Australians back to Sulawesi.

Thus, Indonesian ships spread Islam and trade goods through the archipelago and brought diverse groups into contact with one another. They also spread the Malay language, the *lingua franca* of trade in many ports, learned by foreigners to trade or rule. Eventually, Malay became the official language of the Republic of Indonesia, taking on its own character as *Bahasa Indonesia,* spoken now by most people across the nation in addition to their local languages.

The Imposition of Colonialism

European colonialism largely operated through co-opting Indonesian leaders. Colonial ventures are best understood in terms of how they "fit" into local regimes of political power—whether as cooperative or adversarial forces. An important historical insight relates how "both European and Indonesian histories put the Dutch at the center of the narrative. … This mode of writing history answers and satisfies the demands of imperialism and nationalism, but obliterates the histories of Indonesian societies."[27] The nationalist versions of histories across the archipelago typically cast Indonesians as victims of outsiders (mainly Dutch) rather than revealing how Indonesian elite classes were also in league with foreigners. Moreover, European colonists moved among many other trading peoples throughout the archipelago. In most of Indonesia, the Dutch did not take hold until the late nineteenth and early twentieth centuries. Nonetheless, colonialism was an imposition causing major changes in some regions, while creating fateful repercussions in the Western world.

By the early sixteenth century, the Portuguese had ventured into Indonesian waters in search of spices—such as cloves, nutmeg, mace, and pepper. Nutmeg and cloves had attained an almost magical quality in Europe, where people carried pomanders made from these spices as protection against the plague. The Banda Islands of Maluku drew the spice-seeking Europeans to follow. Shortly thereafter this escalated into a spice race, a furiously competitive marathon for control of one of the world's smallest island groups drawing ships from Portugal, Spain, England, Denmark, and Holland.

As the western islands of Java and Sumatra were predominantly Islamic by the sixteenth century and Bali had developed a strong Hindu culture, Portuguese settlements and missionaries faced less resistance in infiltrating animist regions of eastern Indonesia, such as Flores, Timor, and Maluku. European ships entering the archipelago were mostly war galleons. The foreigners thus conquered and maintained control of ports through superior firepower, experience in naval warfare, and sheer aggressiveness.

The Portuguese established Catholic missions in North Sulawesi, in Ternate and Ambon in Maluku, and in Flores and Timor. In the early 1600s, however, they were supplanted by the Dutch and thereafter remained only in parts of Flores and Timor. Portuguese years in Maluku were violent, echoing a European medieval spirit of invasive Catholic Crusaders. Moreover, the colonists were more bent on looting and gaining personal wealth than with any sort of trade. Thus, their demise in Maluku came about through the hatred of the people they were trying to colonize.

The Dutch East India Company (Vereenigte Oost-Indische Compagnie—generally called the VOC) began trading in Indonesia in the seventeenth century, eventually developing into a colonial power across the archipelago and ousting the Portuguese (who retained two colonies in Timor until 1974). Initially, Dutch interests were limited to the Maluku Spice Islands.

One Dutch Governor General during the time of the VOC merits special mention, so extreme was his ruthless imperialism. Jan Pieterszoon Coen established a post in the Banda Islands of Maluku in 1621 to exploit the flourishing nutmeg crops. Coen sold off most of the population into slavery and set up medieval torture chambers to deal with enemies. He hired Japanese mercenaries to behead, burn, and dismember people, including English attempting to trade in the islands. Afraid the English might gain control and despising the local people, Coen ordered the uprooting of many of Banda's nutmeg trees for transport to other islands. Later, the English did the same, robbing the islands' trees and taking tons of its unique soil to places as far as Sri Lanka. Under Coen's vicious rule, Dutch chopped down the nutmeg trees on the small island of Run, part of the Banda archipelago. The ecology of the Banda Islands, on which nutmeg had thrived, never fully recovered from this period.

Extremely hostile relations continued to grow in the seventeenth century between England and Holland over worldwide colonial rights, battles, and atrocities in Indonesia. Eventually, the English mounted an armada and invaded Manhattan Island, then administered by the Dutch under Pieter Stuyvesant as New Amsterdam. What eventually transpired from this invasion was that on September 8, 1664 Stuyvesant signed off the rights to Manhattan Island in exchange for the tiny British-controlled Banda island of Run (a rather bitter irony after Coen's earlier destruction of its nutmeg trees) and Surinam, South America. This remains one of the least known and most bizarre real estate deals ever and a major turn in American history.

The Netherlands government took over the bankrupt Dutch East India Company in the eighteenth century and proceeded to create an efficiently organized colonial administration across Indonesia. The colonists developed a small port of northwestern Java into their central post, which they named Batavia. Much later, this became the city of Jakarta. Holland constructed a colonial empire over three hundred years and the Indonesian islands became world-famous as the Dutch East Indies. Many islands, however, did not experience a Dutch presence until the late-nineteenth and early-twentieth centuries.

Dutch missionaries converted people to the Protestant Dutch Reformed Church in largely non-Muslim areas of Indonesia: the Batak of Sumatra, the Dayak of Kalimantan, peoples of the Lesser Sunda Islands of eastern Indonesia, the Toraja and Manado peoples of Sulawesi, and peoples of West Papua. These were all animistic regions where the Dutch categorized inhabitants as "heathens." Europe funded Christian missionaries, Catholic and Protestant. To this day many receive financial support from churches in the Western world.

The colonists exploited Indonesians in numerous ways, through land seizure, unpaid plantation labor, forcing new crops upon them (such as coffee and rubber) for Dutch benefit, exacting taxes, and inflicting severe punishments. As did European colonists the world over, Holland controlled the types, production, and prices of products in Indonesia and exported them to their own profit. They also stimulated a serious population boom in Java, however, not necessarily out of avarice. Colonists provided medicines that enabled more children to survive. Also, people began to have larger families to earn more from their children's labor. Today, Java is one of the most densely over-populated places in the world and this began through Dutch colonial policies. At the same time, the colonists introduced new technologies and materials (such as rubber) to Indonesians, facilitated world exposure to Indonesian dyes, textile trades, and other arts, and provided many elite Indonesians with Dutch educations and political ideas.

Holland also strengthened and perpetuated the power of the elite *priyayi* class in Java. The novel *Max Havelaar* describes *priyayi* corruption and complicity with the Dutch, written by the colonial official Douwes Dekker living in Java, using the pen name Multatuli. Greatly disturbed by the abuses he witnessed, Dekker's book describes life for the unfortunate common folk under joint Dutch and Javanese elite control. First published in 1860, the novel profoundly affected Dutch progressives and Indonesian nationalist leaders planning for independence.

For a brief time the British took command of Indonesian ports during the early nineteenth century, but Holland regained control and remained the dominant power in Indonesia until World War II. By the 1920s, students across Indonesia were organizing youth groups against the Dutch. In 1926, they merged as the Youth Congress, voting to unite Indonesia as one nation, with Malay as its language. Their symbol became a red-and-white flag, eventually becoming the banner of the Indonesian nation.

The Republic of Indonesia

Japan invaded Indonesia in 1942. Initially, many Indonesians looked to the Japanese as Asian liberators, but their optimism was short-lived. While the Dutch had often been harsh in their colonial rule, Japanese occupation was far worse and Indonesians were relieved when this period ended in 1945. Many recall the Japanese era as a time of extreme hardship and starvation. Much of the rice that Indonesians were forced to produce was exported to Japan. After Japanese departure, Indonesian nationalists led by president-to-be Sukarno[28] and vice-president-to-be Muhammad Hatta declared the archipelago an independent nation—the Republic of Indonesia. Ironically, knowledge of European political ideas learned from the Dutch galvanized the nationalists to oust the former colonists. As summarized below:

The first generation to benefit from the expansion of Dutch schooling under the so-called "ethical policy" (developmentalism in today's terminology) then began to absorb ideas of progress, education, science, freedom, and democracy to form organizations to promote them.[29]

During their occupation, the Japanese actually put Sukarno and Hatta in power and oversaw the writing of their constitution. These Nationalist leaders

Indonesia's first president, Sukarno, Jakarta, September, 1950. © Bettmann/CORBIS.

initially worked within the framework of Japan's World War II propaganda against the Europeans and American Allies. This period permitted the growth of Nationalist aspirations throughout the Indonesian population, especially among young people.[30] After Japan's wartime defeat, Indonesians moved rapidly for independence. Sukarno became President and Hatta became Vice-President. The first country to recognize the new republic was Egypt.

For three years following the end of World War II, the Netherlands strove to re-establish control in Indonesia. Following fierce resistance from Indonesians and facing international pressure to concede independence to the nation, in 1949 Holland transferred sovereignty to the entire archipelago except West Papua. In 1950, a new Indonesian constitution went into effect, creating on paper a united nation-state.

The Sukarno years to follow, however, became a bizarre and disappointing era for the new country, characterized by the president's grandiose schemes that never materialized. Much political chaos resulted through widespread disorganization. Sukarno was far more adept at revolutionary rhetoric than good governance. Under his presidency, Indonesia relapsed into a kind of neo-feudal system, although Sukarno's stated policy was "Guided Democracy."

Colonial-era laws restricting freedom of expression and the right to assemble remained in effect and dissidence was treason.[31] While building exorbitantly expensive, self-aggrandizing monuments (as had ancient Javanese kings), he ignored worsening economic conditions in Indonesia. He gained a tawdry reputation as a womanizer, marrying six times. His extramarital affairs made him a legend.

Still, Sukarno had skillfully motivated Indonesians to nationhood, was loved by common folk, and many remember him with gratitude. One historian considers that Sukarno genuinely loved the heterogeneous nation that he had helped to build. He had spread national consciousness and ideals of freedom to even the poorest of the poor. Moreover, he was without racial prejudice and attempted to protect minorities and different religions, including animism.[32] While a highly charismatic leader able to rally immense support, as president, Sukarno, nonetheless, was unable to plan for his people with any practicality. His stalwart ideology closed him to dealing pragmatically with much of the world, in a time when Indonesia needed international support.

Sukarno turned his back on Western aid while catering to Soviet Russia and Communist China. He pulled Indonesia out of the United Nations in protest of its recognition of Malaysia. Politically and economically for his nation, such moves were unrealistic, self-defeating, and cost him international assistance in a country that desperately needed it. By 1965, inflation in Indonesia had reached 650 percent. Economic conditions severely worsened as aid stopped from Western nations along with a vital shipping trade. Extremist Islamic groups gained strength in parts of the archipelago. Corruption grew as government officials began pocketing funds; many had no other dependable income. An Indonesian writer regards the Sukarno years as "almost 10 years of the darkest and most irrational period in the Republic's history."[33] Sukarno's health began to fail by 1965, and he appeared to be losing his capabilities to those around him in Jakarta. Some regarded the volcanic eruption of Gunung Agung in 1963 on the island of Bali as confirming the deterioration in the president's leadership powers.

On September 30, 1965, an unsuccessful attempt at an alleged communist coup took place in Jakarta. Details of this event remain a partial mystery, but Sukarno's presidential guard was attempting a power grab. Several army generals were murdered and their bodies thrown into a dry well. A gunshot also killed the small daughter of a surviving general. Newspapers and radio stations reported that the men had been tortured and sexually mutilated, blaming the atrocity on a communist women's group. Later, autopsies ordered by Suharto himself showed no evidence of torture or mutilation, but the news already had swept Indonesia and spread around the world. A counter coup took place, where the Indonesian military took control. When lurid stories of the torture-murders multiplied, a mass reaction of rage and violence ignited Indonesia.

A mad ferocity erupted, resulting in the slaying of hundreds of thousands of people, communists and non-communists. Frenzy particularly raged through communities in Java and Bali, as people slaughtered known communists, but also settled countless personal animosities and grudges through murders under the guise of national patriotism. Bali, famed in the Western world as an exotic and tranquil tropical paradise, became rife with executions during this horrific period in Indonesian history, as neighbor turned against neighbor. The killings became the largest domestic slaughter in Indonesian history, with uncounted numbers of people dead, but certainly more than half a million. The army went unchecked, as did civilians carrying out "anti-communist" purges.

While some Indonesians expressed pride in extinguishing the Indonesian Communist Party, others still feel ashamed of the barbarous mayhem of these times,[34] and few can make sense of it. An historian argues that such an extreme wave of killing gripped Indonesia at this time as "an intensification of modern state violence, the foundations for which were laid during the colonial period."[35] That is, Indonesian civilians carried out what they had witnessed European colonists and later the Indonesian army doing, but motivated by their own frustrations and grievances. Yet the extent of the violence during 1965–1966 remains a largely inexplicable tragedy in Indonesian history.

New Order Indonesia

Sukarno lost all support at this time and resigned in March of 1966, handing the presidency over to General Suharto. Exiled to the city of Bogor, near Jakarta, the ex-president bitterly lived out his years largely under house arrest. The new regime was called New Order Indonesia (*Orde Baru*). President Suharto immediately set into motion a process of centralizing power involving a tight system of military control. Suharto's authority was absolute and his party, Golkar, became the only one legal—forbidding freedom of expression or criticism of its policies. Newspapers were shut down and dissidents jailed, as Indonesia became a yet further resolved military dictatorship.

Human rights aside (and the abuses were countless), the New Order Years did accomplish much. Suharto had promised to improve the welfare of Indonesian commoners and to an appreciable extent this happened. His party's achievements in agriculture, education, and other welfare areas were impressive, especially when compared to the record of the Dutch regime.[36] Medical clinics, roads, bridges, and schools were built in remote parts of Indonesia, and a new generation across the archipelago became literate and learned to speak the national language. These achievements were all the more remarkable, as they happened over a relatively short period of time in a geographically vast and ethnically diverse new nation.

However, all those absorbed into the Republic of Indonesia did not necessarily want to be. Aceh in northern Sumatra and some of the eastern islands were disinclined to accept Javanese rule. Many regions preferred to function as they were while achieving autonomy. In Ambon and surrounding Maluku Islands, Christians fought to attain their own republic at the time of national independence, even asking help against Java from the Netherlands. Controversially, the United Nations ceded the formerly Dutch-controlled, western portion of Papua New Guinea to the Republic of Indonesia in 1969 and it was renamed Irian Jaya. Since that time, local independence movements have persisted. After Portugal withdrew from East Timor in 1974, Indonesia, under Suharto (encouraged and funded by the United States, which feared the spread of communism in Southeast Asia after the Vietnam War), invaded one year later and set up command. Many in East Timor fought for decades for independence, which they finally gained through a popular vote in 1999 (after Suharto was no longer Indonesia's president). This independence came with much devastation and bloodshed. The Indonesian years in East Timor had been harshly oppressive and violent against local resistance movements. Nonetheless, Indonesia provided East Timor with an infrastructure and public schools that the Portuguese had not. As the Indonesian army left the newly independent nation, they vengefully incinerated much of what stood, leaving the region in scorched ruins.

The New Order had constantly felt threatened by both the left (communists) and the right (Islamic militants). It fervently promoted the founding principles of Indonesian statehood—the *Pancasila*—(meaning "Five Principles," originally devised by Sukarno) to instill an ideology of harmony and order among the people. These principles are: belief in one God, nationalism, humanitarianism, social justice, and democracy. The regime also adopted and spread the slogan of "Unity in Diversity" to demonstrate an inclusive policy to the many religious and ethnic groups in Indonesia and thus gain their support.

Suharto's own fear and mistrust of the Indonesian people, however, characterized his thinking about politics.[37] Anyone in opposition to him faced prison or execution. Indonesians grew weary of the military's unbridled power over them. Moreover, the army controlled tremendous resources in Indonesia, such as management of forests, which they were selling out to multi-national corporations. This not only displaced communities, but destroyed eco-systems. People became fed up with the blatant corruption and greed of the Suharto family. Suharto's wife and children controlled fortunes, television stations, and businesses for which they were never held accountable. The family also directed much of the propaganda of the Suharto regime.

Natural disasters, such as a tsunami hitting Maumere, Flores in 1992 (killing about 2,500 people and leaving many homeless) exposed to many the rottenness of the Indonesian political system. Virtually nothing of the foreign aid money in response to this tragedy actually reached the victims, but was pocketed by corrupt New Order officials.

In 1997, an economic crisis swept Southeast Asia, beginning with the devaluation of the Thai baht. As a never stable economy internationally, Indonesia suffered tremendously as its rupiah plunged, at one point losing 80 percent of its former value. This brought hardship upon many common people, further increasing resentment of the wealth and corruption of those in power. This period became known as the *Krismon* (monetary crisis), progressively escalating into the *Kristal* (total crisis). During this time, the global ecological calamity of El Niño caused a long drought and failed harvests across Indonesia. These natural and economic disasters signaled to many a need for political change.

The aging Suharto was losing leadership potency after more than thirty years in office, as violence broke out across the islands: riots and firestorms raged in Jakarta, pro-Indonesian militias were destroying East Timor, and Aceh was in a vicious battle for independence. Indonesia fell into catastrophic disorder. Foreign investment and tourism—an important industry in Indonesia that had supported many people—dropped dramatically, leaving numerous destitute. Still, Suharto continued his "crony capitalism" and did not make necessary economic reforms. Thus, he took the brunt of blame from Indonesians for their dire conditions.

As Suharto prepared to be elected to his seventh five-year term as president, student protests began to grow. Four students were shot and killed in Jakarta on May 12, 1998. Their deaths and funerals unleashed rage throughout the city. Rioting people, largely the poor, incinerated large sections of Jakarta. This turning point became known as the "May Riots." Chinese businesses were targets of much of the violence, as they represented wealthy affiliates in the New Order regime. Simultaneously, gangs of thugs in league with the New Order raped Chinese women. After this, the army deserted Suharto, leaving him powerless. The German-educated B. J. Habibie became president under the Golkar party for a transitional period.

Sometimes history takes a surprising turn, regardless of political affiliations. Influenced by Western notions of democracy, Habibie began to create policies to curb the tremendous power of the Indonesian military and to allow the media and people more freedoms, including expression of discontent. He also made public that he was willing to consider autonomy for regions like East Timor. This new liberalism, however, ultimately led to his undoing. In 1999, Habibie lost a vote of confidence in parliament and withdrew from the upcoming presidential election.

Despite his reformist policies, most Indonesians regarded Habibie as a weak leader, especially as violence across the nation continued to rage. Conditions had become too dire during the late Suharto years, producing a spirit of anarchy, and reform became irrelevant in a country torn apart by intense regional conflicts. War between clan groups such as had not erupted for a century broke out in areas like western Sumba. In November of 1998, scores of villages burned and many decapitated bodies filled a river—echoing head-hunting times of the past. This battle arose from resentments of the political abuses of a local New Order official.[38]

A new subversive fervor escalated through Indonesia near the end of the New Order regime, after years of repression. Growing access to international media and a new freedom of expression under Habibie unleashed a wave of anti-government sentiments, even on Indonesian television. This never before had happened and grew into a popular cultural rage. But perhaps the most revolutionary influence during this time was an uncontrollable and increasing access to the Internet. Not only could Indonesians now enjoy unrestricted exposure to international information, but they also could freely communicate between themselves. This gave them a powerful tool for subversion, as well as for organizing political factions.[39]

The End of the New Order

In the national election of 1999, Sukarno's daughter, Megawati Sukarnoputri of the Democratic Party of Indonesia, actually won the popular vote. Parliament largely resisted her inauguration, however, partly due to Muslim disapproval of a female public leader. Golkar, the losing party, in control since 1965, also played a central role in blocking her assent. When news of this reached the people, riots ensued in Jakarta. Finally a compromise took place: Abdurrahmin Wahid (popularly called Gus Dur) of the National Awakening Party became President and Megawati, Vice-President. The new president's party was Muslim but favored accommodating all kinds of Indonesians. Wahid proceeded to fire a top general, Wiranto, accused of supervising genocide in East Timor. This did not endear him to the military.

Civilian-military clashes swept Indonesia during this time, and violence escalated between Muslims and Christians. "Ethnic cleansing" became a reality in Kalimantan as local Dayaks murdered residents transmigrated from the island of Madura. A full-scale religious war and devastating fires broke out on the island of Ambon, incited by a fight between a Christian bus driver and a Muslim passenger. Local gangs were taking control in provincial cities like Kupang, West Timor, and much of the island of Lombok. Many thought that the Golkar party and hard-line military men were behind much of the disorder to destabilize the new presidency. People in a number of port cities reported that boatloads of young men arrived and began inciting violence while traveling in gangs. Many suspected that the Suhartos and Golkar were funding them.

President Wahid was the first Indonesian president to try to find peaceful solutions to regional conflicts and favored autonomy for areas such as West Papua and Aceh so that they might still remain in the fold of the Republic.[40] This infuriated the military and the formerly ruling Golkar party, who then subverted Wahid, feeling his policies supported separatism. Wahid had suffered strokes, was blind, and in poor health. Through military efforts he was impeached in July 2001, and Megawati became President. She filled her cabinet with elite supporters who would keep her in power.

Her presidency, while an important symbolic gain for the aspirations of Indonesian women, was nonetheless dishearteningly ineffectual for her supporters and most others. In basic ways, she ruled as an aloof, elite *priyayi*, out of touch and inactive in dealing with problems of common people. As described by one political scientist: "The entire government, not just the presidency, appeared to be on auto-pilot."[41] Political parties broke into many factions as anarchy and violence further flared across Indonesia. Infrastructures crumbled through mismanagement of funds and lack of maintenance, and Megawati's promise of Reformation became irrelevant. Conflicts in Aceh, Maluku, West Papua, and parts of Sulawesi worsened; crime increased everywhere; and people throughout Indonesia took justice into their own hands. Disarray and decay pervaded the nation, to a degree that even the rain gutters of Jakarta's streets were left uncleaned and floods then devastated parts of the city. Only the military retained some cohesion.

Disaster struck Indonesia on October 12, 2002, when a terrorist car bomb exploded in front of a Bali nightclub, killing more than two hundred people and destroying much of a city block. A radical Islamic group claimed responsibility, stating that their target had been Americans, in retaliation for George W. Bush's Middle Eastern policies. Most of those in the nightclub, however, were Australians and Indonesians. A total of 88 Australians and 38 Indonesians died, as well as 6 Britons, 6 Germans, and 4 Dutch people.[42] While international investigative agents flew in from the United States and Australia, the Balinese police succeeded in capturing some of the perpetrators, tracing them through reports of local residents. Tourism all but ceased to Bali. Indonesians everywhere were in shock.

With Megawati as president, the military grew fractured and their budgets plummeted. Some became involved in organized crime such as prostitution and drug trafficking. Common people across Indonesia grew ever more disillusioned. Megawati had, ironically, run for office as the "people's candidate," yet the price of rice continued to rise, medical clinics closed in rural regions for lack of funds, and regional conflicts were rampant. One eastern Indonesian woman expressed with dismay during the Megawati period: "Maybe under Suharto things were not good, but they were better than this. Now we have chaos and decay all around us."[43]

A Shift in Power

In September, 2004, Indonesia elected a new president, Susilo Bambang Yudhoyono (called "S.B.Y." by Indonesians). A retired general who conveyed hope of strength, reform, and much-needed order through the Republic, many Indonesians viewed S.B.Y. as a man who could get things done after the desultory Megawati years. With his Vice-President, Jusuf Kalla, S.B.Y. won the first direct election for president in Indonesian history, where citizens could vote for an individual and not a party.

Since Yudhoyono's presidency, efforts at reforming the Indonesian system have made some progress, and many have worked earnestly for this. Indonesia enjoys a relatively free press and much-needed reforms in the judicial system have begun to take hold. Anti-corruption commissions have succeeded in indicting politicians, to a degree formerly not possible. Yet S.B.Y. inherited an immense international debt and a nation in turmoil. Apart from regional separatist movements, he now faces the spread and violence of radical terrorist groups across Indonesia. Importantly, he must appear strong to Indonesians, who expect a leader to deal harshly with opponents or law-breakers. Yet the cronies of Suharto still hold considerable sway, as they dominate large businesses and capital ventures. The task of bringing together government, business, and society to create a more equitable and balanced Indonesia will take an immense amount of dedication and work from those committed to this goal. As ever, they may ask help from the supernatural to help them succeed through this period.

NOTES

1. James Siegel, *The Rope of God* (Berkeley: University of California Press, 1969), 4.

2. The atmospheric debris from Krakatoa dramatically affected sunsets in Europe in the 1880s. Many believe that this influenced artists of the time, such as the British painter, Turner, famed for his vivid skyscapes. See Simon Winchester, *Krakatoa—The Day the World Exploded: August 27, 1883* (New York: Perennial, 2003), 280n.

3. Winchester, *Krakatoa*, 292.

4. See Alfred Russel Wallace, *The Malay Archipelago* (New York: Dover, 1962).

5. David Joel Steinberg, ed., *In Search of Southeast Asia: A Modern History*, rev. ed. (Honolulu: University of Hawaii Press, 1987), 22–23, paraphrased.

6. See Clifford Geertz on Balinese irrigation organizations in *Negara: The Theatre State in Nineteenth- Century Bali* (Princeton, NJ: Princeton University Press, 1980).

7. See Peter S. Bellwood, *Prehistory of the Indo-Malaysian Archipelago* (Honolulu: University of Hawaii Press, 1997).

8. See Gregory Forth, "Hominids, Hairy Hominids, and the Science of Humanity." *Anthropology Today* 21, no. 3 (June 2005): 13–17.

9. Robert Cribb, *Historical Atlas of Indonesia* (Honolulu: University of Hawaii Press, 2000), 31.

10. See Bellwood, *Prehistory of the Indo-Malaysian Archipelago.*

11. Cribb, *Historical Atlas of Indonesia,* 29.

12. Paraphrased from Cribb, *Historical Atlas of Indonesia,* 37.

13. Cribb, *Historical Atlas of Indonesia,* 37.

14. Cribb, *Historical Atlas of Indonesia,* 36.

15. Anthony Reid, *Southeast Asia in the Age of Commerce 1450–1680—Volume One: The Lands below the Winds* (New Haven, CT: Yale University Press, 1988), 2.

16. Cribb, *Historical Atlas of Indonesia,* 76.

17. Keith W. Taylor, "The Early Kingdoms," in *The Cambridge History of Southeast Asia: Volume One, Part One, From Early Times to C. 1500,* ed. Nicholas Tarling (Cambridge: Cambridge University Press, 1999), 136–182.

18. Benedict Anderson refined this model, as described in his essay "The Idea of Power in Javanese Culture," in *Culture and Politics in Indonesia,* ed. Claire Holt (Ithaca, NY: Cornell University Press, 1972), 1–69.

19. Wiener, Margaret J. *Visible and Invisible Realms: Power, Magic, and Colonial Conquest in Bali* (Chicago: University of Chicago Press, 1995), 74.

20. See Taylor, "The Early Kingdoms," 173–176 for a succinct history of Srivijaya.

21. Kenneth R. Hall, "Economic History of Early Southeast Asia," in Nicholas Tarling, ed., *The Cambridge History of Southeast Asia: Volume One, Part One, Early Times to C. 1500* (Cambridge: Cambridge University Press, 1999), 205.

22. Taylor, "The Early Kingdoms," 227–228.

23. Personal communication to Jill Forshee, February 5, 1994.

24. Mochtar Lubis, *Indonesia: Land under the Rainbow* (Singapore: Oxford University Press, 1990), 60.

25. Lubis, *Indonesia,* 59.

26. Anthony Reid, "Merdeka: The Concept of Freedom in Indonesia," in *Asian Freedoms: The Idea of Freedom in East and Southeast Asia,* ed. David Kelly and Anthony Reid (New York: Cambridge University Press, 1999), 147.

27. Jean Gelman Taylor, *Indonesia: Peoples and Histories* (New Haven: Yale University Press, 2003), 144. Taylor's book provides numerous insights into specific and diverse histories across the Indonesian archipelago, taking account of a rich variety of people, communities, and interactions.

28. Many people in Java customarily use one name. Sukarno was the official name of this leader, as Suharto was the name of the president to follow him.

29. Reid, "Merdeka," 152.

30. Lubis, *Indonesia,* 173.

31. See Taylor, *Indonesia,* 343.

32. See Benedict Anderson, paraphrased here from "Bung Karno and the Fossilization of Soekarno's Thought," *Indonesia* 74 (October 2002): 1–19.

33. Lubis, *Indonesia,* 183.

34. See M. C. Ricklefs, *A History of Modern Indonesia since C. 1300,* 2nd ed. (Stanford, CA: Stanford University Press, 1993), 284–303.

35. Henk Schulte Nordholt, "A Genealogy of Violence," in *Roots of Violence in Indonesia,* ed. Freek Colombijn and J. Thomas Lindblad (Leiden: KITLV Press, 2002), 44.

36. Ricklefs, *A History of Modern Indonesia,* 304. Even Suharto's staunchest critics often concede his accomplishments.

37. R. E. Elson, "In Fear of the People: Suharto and the Justification of State-Sponsored Violence under the New Order," in *Roots of Violence in Indonesia,* ed. Freek Colombijn and J. Thomas Lindblad (Leiden: KITLV Press, 2002), 171–195.

38. See David Mitchell, "Tragedy in Sumba: Why Neighbors Hacked Each Other to Death In a Remote Part of Indonesia," *Inside Indonesia,* April–June 1999, 18–20.

39. See Lorraine V. Aragon's in-depth analysis of how new media freedoms and access to the Internet in the post-Suharto period played out concerning belligerence and violence between Christians and Muslims in the region of Poso, Sulawesi in "Mass Media Fragmentation and Narratives of Violent Action in Sulawesi's Poso Conflict," *Indonesia* 79 (April 2005): 1–55. Also see David T. Hill, "East Timor and the Internet: Global Political Leverage in/on Indonesia," *Indonesia* 73 (April 2002): 25–51.

40. Liem Soei Liong, "It's the Military, Stupid!" in *Roots of Violence in Indonesia,* ed. Freek Colombijn and J. Thomas Lindblad (Leiden: KITLV Press, 2002), 197–225.

41. Dan Slater, "Indonesia's Accountability Trap: Party Cartels and Presidential Power after Democratic Transition," *Indonesia* 78 (October 2004): 61–92.

42. "Bali Death Toll Set at 202," *BBC News.* Accessed February 19, 2003 from http://news.bbc.co.uk/go/em/fr/-/2/hi/asia-pacific/2778923.stm.

43. Personal communication to Jill Forshee, December 1, 2002, from a businesswoman on the island of Sumba.

SUGGESTED READING

Bellwood, Peter. *Prehistory of the Indo-Malaysian Archipelago,* rev. ed. Honolulu: University of Hawaii Press, 1997.

Cribb, Robert. *Historical Atlas of Indonesia.* Honolulu: University of Hawaii Press, 2000.

Ellen, Roy. *On the Edge of the Banda Zone: Past and Present in the Social Organization of a Moluccan Trading Network.* Honolulu: University of Hawaii Press, 2003.

Forth, Gregory. *Beneath the Volcano: Religion, Cosmology and Spirit Classification among the Nage of Eastern Indonesia.* Leiden: KITLV Press, 1998.

Lev, Dan S., and Ruth McVey. *Making Indonesia.* Ithaca: Cornell University Southeast Asian Studies Publications, 1999.

Lubis, Mochtar. *Indonesia: Land under the Rainbow.* Singapore: Oxford University Press, 1990.

Milton, Giles. *Nathaniel's Nutmeg: How One Man's Courage Changed the Course of History.* London: Hodder and Stroughton, 1999.

Owen, Norman G. *The Emergence of Modern Indonesia.* Ithaca: Cornell University Southeast Asian Studies Publications, 2005.

Ricklefs, M. C. *A History of Modern Indonesia Since c. 1300.* 2nd ed. Stanford: Stanford University Press, 1993.

Taylor, Jean Gelman. *Indonesia: Peoples and Histories.* New Haven: Yale University Press, 2003.

Vickers, Adrian. *A History of Modern Indonesia*. New York: Cambridge University Press, 2005.

Wallace, Alfred Russel. *The Malay Archipelago*. New York: Dover, [1869] 1962.

Winchester, Simon. *Krakatoa, The Day the World Exploded: August 27, 1883*. New York: Perennial (HarperCollins), 2004.

2

Thought and Religion

Indonesians have adopted world faiths in myriad manners, blending them with their pre-existing cosmological systems and reconfiguring them to adapt to unique societies. This merging has produced extremely complicated ways of thought and religious practices that have intrigued scholars throughout the years. Indonesian religions are multi-layered. For instance, Islam reveals many mystical elements of animism in Java and beyond, as does Hinduism in Bali, and Christianity throughout the islands. The intricacies of Indonesian thought and religion emerge through other aspects of life, such as arts, cuisine, social relations, and architecture.

While nearly 90 percent of Indonesians are Muslims, most practice their faith with a synthesis of former beliefs, including Hindu–Buddhism and native animism. A mystical quality imbues Indonesian Islam, and leaders still visit pre-Islamic spiritual sites for strength. Christians also have fused their newer religion with older belief systems. Most Indonesians thus maintain a hybridism in religious creeds and practices.

ANIMISM

Talking about thought and religion throughout Indonesia is a complicated matter, as in any part of the world. To begin to understand various Indonesian ways of thinking and religious convictions, one needs to first consider animism, which long preceded imported world religions in the archipelago and currently weaves through most of them. Animism is a type of belief system (indeed, a kind of religion) that regards all of nature to contain spiritual power. In Europe or North America, this is called "paganism." In Indonesia beliefs in spirits of the earth, air, and waters combine with concerns about the ongoing supernatural powers of ancestors; visible and invisible realms both hold sway in everyday life.[1] Nature includes guardian spirits as well as evil ones, residing in houses, trees, rocks, mountaintops, or any number of places. To stay in the good graces of these spirits, people make offerings or acknowledge them through ceremonies, chants, songs, or simple respectful phrases. Departed relatives become ancestors requiring ceremonial offerings and prayers to avoid offending them and creating anger toward the living.

People often consider natural and supernatural spirits as the primary causes of misfortunes as well as successes. As Indonesia is so diverse in cultures and geography, specific beliefs about spirits vary greatly from place to place. If, as in Bali and Java, world religions such as Hinduism and Islam have been in place for centuries, local people have blended and even elaborated their previous beliefs with these newer faiths in ways that seem to fit. This is also true of many Indonesian Christians. Unconverted animist societies persist in Indonesia, especially in the eastern islands.

Many animists express that they feel no need to convert to another religion, explaining that their own still works for them. Often events reinforce their beliefs. Elaborate rituals after a long, dry season on eastern islands like Sumba or Timor do appear to bring on the rains. Certain bends in roads or rivers are sites of numerous deaths—so people consider them haunted by dangerous spirits. Jealousy or hatred produces curses, from which people fall ill or die, from all appearances. All such phenomena may seem like superstition, but animists view them as cause and effect logical events to explain their worlds and lives.

All contemporary world faiths include elements of animism (or paganism), based upon what people believed and did in ancient times, before newer religions took hold. These elements include miracles, divine interventions, invisible spiritual realms, taboos, mythic beings, and the need to make offerings and pray to unseen powers. Considered comparatively, such religious views are no less plausible than doctrines of world faiths. In fact, most major world religions retain something of former animist or pagan rituals, symbols, and ideas—like the Christmas tree of Christianity, tales of the magical parting of waters (like the Red Sea) of Judaism, or dietary prohibitions of Muslims, Hindus, Jews, and others.

Animism usually differs from world religions in that its tenets and practices relate to specifically indigenous spirits, places, and ancestors. Also, animists generally seem less concerned with being a "good person" in the greater world than with adhering to local ways and moral codes. This might involve one village or even one household. An animist from Sumba expressed: "Following custom, outside of the clan home and village there is no right and wrong."[2] This is not to say that animists necessarily abandon morality when away from their home regions, but it does emphasize the centrality of clans, villages, ancestors, and local nature spirits in their thought and behavior. In much of eastern Indonesia, people live in what anthropologists have called "house societies"[3] where clan houses and their ancestral spirits are central cosmological forces in people's lives—establishing their senses of place in the world and a shared moral universe.[4]

In its most intense form, the locality of animist allegiances emerged in headhunting societies, where people of a warrior's home region considered themselves fully human, while those outside were not. In basic ways, this is little different from current groups and nations at war. Throughout history the world over, people have dehumanized others to justify carrying out violent acts against them.

As noted of headhunting in Southeast Asia, "Manliness and bloodshed are linked in the sexual politics of many societies" (including modern, industrialized ones).[5] In Indonesian regions, headhunting proved a young man's bravery, travel prowess, ferocity, and duty to his village or clan. It also competitively demonstrated masculinity to women, who often goaded men off to warfare and sang upon their return carrying the heads of enemies. These human "trophies" proved a local victory and reinforced potency and fertility beliefs and rituals. In warfare, headhunting accomplished the complete separation of an enemy from his being through an ultimate destruction of selfhood. Many saw this as a way to keep the dead from ever reaching their ancestral realm, because they could never be recognized without their faces—the worst imaginable fate.

While now outlawed for many decades and currently practiced on symbolic forms, such as coconuts, heads have been at the center of recent violence. Crimes occasionally involve villagers taking the law into their own hands— killing and then cutting off the head of a thief or murderer. This follows old systems of punishment for violating customary law, or *adat*. In West Sumba in 1998, a full-scale war erupted between two clans (during a period of anarchy throughout Indonesia after the resignation of Suharto), leaving many people decapitated.[6] Indonesian soldiers and East Timorese fighting on their side displayed severed heads of local rebels fighting for independence on the end of rifle bayonets in East Timor, in the late 1990s. Thus, this violent practice retains symbolic (and terrorizing) power in current times. Not all animists have carried out headhunting and certain groups across Indonesia converted to world faiths have continued to use decapitation against wrongdoers and enemies.

Indonesians are no more prone to violence than other people around the world. In fact, in daily life, they generally may be less so following a social emphasis on composure and balance. Still, as do other beliefs and customs, ancient means of bloodshed sometimes resurface in current conflicts.

RELATIVE SOCIAL STATUS

Throughout most of Indonesia relative social status forms the base of people's ideas about society and correct behavior. Some languages contain "high" and "low" levels of speech and people customarily behave deferentially to seniors and those of higher social level. When an elder approaches a porch to visit, younger people will shift their positions to a lower level to show respect. This especially holds true in Bali, but also occurs on many other islands. The Indonesian national language (Bahasa Indonesia) does not contain the extent of class-marking (i.e., "high" and "low") ways of speech, as do some local languages—especially Javanese. However, more polite, formal terms are always used to superiors and people address adults by the terms *Bapak* or *Pak* (for men) and *Ibu* or *Bu* (for women). These translate literally as "father" and "mother," but in Indonesia also mean "Mr." or "Mrs." Indonesians become uncomfortable when asked by well-meaning Westerners to drop these formal titles when talking to them, as they then feel disrespectful and unsure of their relationship to those with whom they are speaking. Such formality confuses Americans and Europeans, especially in casual situations.

Societies of the Indonesian Islands have never followed wholly democratic systems but, rather, make decisions based in consensus or follow regional leaders in matters of politics and voting. As democracy has never fully permeated most people's thinking or aspirations, so with religions brought from other lands. In modern political life, old class systems and ideas persist and the same is true regarding the practice of world religions in the archipelago. Relative status plays out in all social situations in Indonesia, in good part determining etiquette, speech, and attitude.

WORLD RELIGIONS

People gradually adopted new religions (Buddhism, Islam, Hinduism, Christianity) after the conversion of a regional head. Old belief systems persisted, however, and today even the most "modern" of Indonesian Christians, Hindus, or Muslims incorporate ancient animist ideas and ritual elements into their newer world faiths. Indonesians absorbed influences from India and made them their own. Ancient Indian epics, such as the *Ramayana* and the *Mahabharata* became localized and spread through Indonesian culture through storytellers, dances, puppet shows, and visual artistry. These themes elaborated through centuries and today the epics still inspire theatrics and arts of all sorts, including films and soap operas. Indonesians love these ancient Indian epics with a devotational quality, adapting them to become tales within Indonesia. Characters of these mystical stories are moral examples and their struggles exemplify those of humanity.

Most people of the nation follow Islam (roughly 90 percent), although Christians are growing in number. Buddhism, which once dominated much of Java and parts of Sumatra, now is a minor religion in Indonesia. Judaism is largely unfamiliar to Indonesians in their own country. Hinduism is mostly limited to Bali and western Lombok.

Hinduism

Hinduism evolved from early Indian philosophy, incorporating an immensely complex body of literature, oral traditions, visual arts, sciences, rituals, metaphysics, and social systems. The holy Mount Meru, a cosmological abode of gods and goddesses, centers Hindu religious focus. Hindus seek to overcome desire and maintain harmony in their lives by following *dharma*, or religious duty, which balances forces of order and disorder. *Dharma* applies to diet, sex, thinking, desires, occupations, and social life. Following Hindu thought, souls incarnate repeatedly as animals and humans (a chain of lifetimes called *samsara*) until they achieve a state of enlightenment, balance, bliss, and purity called *moksa*. Conditions of each lifetime echo the deeds of a soul in a previous one. People create *karma* through their right or wrong actions and desires, according to Hindu *dharma*. Thus punishment or reward becomes the basis of each incarnation. Hindus strive to maintain purity by avoiding pollution, which can take form in thoughts, actions, foods, and association with those of lower character or caste. This is but a basic definition of an ancient, sophisticated, and dynamic system of belief. Hinduism includes a vast range of principles, deities, rituals, and religious practitioners too intricate to name here.

Hinduism spread to Indonesia from India around 100 A.D. As mentioned, as local rulers adopted new religions, these diffused to surrounding populations. On the islands of Java and Sumatra, large empires developed with Indian philosophies adapted to and mixed with local beliefs. Hinduism also took hold in Bali through long, close links with Java, including intermarriage between royal families. Bali kingdoms in ancient times, however, primarily functioned independently from Java. Hinduism arrived on Bali's shores from

India around the same time that it did on Java, as suggested in old Balinese inscriptions dating from the late ninth century.

Today, Bali remains the only predominantly Hindu island in Indonesia. Hinduism becomes especially complex in Bali, producing a riotously elaborate religion, combining the enormous Indian Hindu pantheon of Gods and Goddesses with countless Balinese deities and spirits of earthly and supernatural realms. Balinese follow a three-tiered caste system, but with far less severity than do Indians. Firm believers in the laws of *karma,* Balinese hold that their deeds will come back to haunt them or even cause them to reincarnate as an animal in the next lifetime. Bali–Hindu is rife with ceremonies and rituals and the religion is tenacious through modern times.

Hindu–Buddhism

Buddhism grew out of Hinduism, following the teachings of Gautama Buddha in India in the sixth century B.C. Emphasizing the importance of knowledge, moral thought, and controlling desire, Buddhists also aspire to a state of perfect enlightenment and an end to reincarnations in this world. Buddhism does not follow notions of social caste, but recognizes that some people are more advanced than others on the path to spiritual enlightenment. Many Hindu principles such as *karma* and *dharma* carry on through Buddhism. In Indonesia, people long combined ideas and deities of Hinduism and Buddhism. Early Indonesian adaptations of these faiths are generally referred to as Hindu–Buddhism. To the present, Balinese combine elements of both religions.

Chinese records from the seventh century report a flourishing, international community of Buddhists in the Sumatran kingdom of Srivijaya, including Indians and Chinese, studying Buddhism with teachers from India. Of course, the ruler of Srivijaya was a patron of Buddhism, influencing its spread to surrounding areas. The type of Buddhism adopted in Indonesia was Mahayana (in contrast to Theravada Buddhism of Thailand). It teaches that the way to heaven (*Nirvana*) is through practicing compassion in life and following spiritual practices like meditation. Many kings adopted Hinduism or Buddhism to claim relations to divine powers and strengthen their earthly authority. The Sailendra dynasty of central Java began the world's largest Buddhist temple, Borobudur, in the ninth century. In early Indonesian kingdoms, Buddhism and Hinduism were practiced alongside each other, with no evidence of conflict. In Javanese courts of the fourteenth century Majapahit, Buddhist and Hindu senior ministers held equal status.[7]

Through the Srivijaya period in Java and Sumatra, the demonstration of Hindu–Buddhist devotion stimulated many arts, which developed great refinement. Poetry, theatrical performances, dance, the indigenous artistry of *batik* textiles and other complex sorts of weaving, metalworking, and wood and stone carving all reached extremely sophisticated levels that continue to this day. These profoundly reflect Indonesians sensibilities and thought, revealing how the past lives in the present. Many Indonesians today consider their arts and cultures among the most refined in the world. The term *halus,* meaning refined or polite, reflects a central value in Indonesian societies, as opposed to *kasar,* meaning crude or vulgar. These terms apply to aesthetics as well as social behavior, and echo ancient Hindu–Buddhist teachings and ideals. After the fall of the Srivijaya empire, Buddhism went into decline, although perhaps as many as 2 million people still practice it in Indonesia.

Islam

Islam (meaning "surrender" in Arabic) holds that God's final revelation was told in the seventh century to the Prophet Muhammad in Arabia, becoming the sacred *Qur'an* (Koran). Muslims follow five religious duties (called pillars): acknowledging that there is one God (Allah) and that Muhammad is his prophet; ritual prayer facing the Muslim holy city of Mecca at five specific times each day; fasting during daylight hours for the month of Ramadan to honor Muhammad receiving God's revelations; making a pilgrimage to the holy Arabian sites of Mecca and Medina during one's lifetime; and paying taxes or alms to support religious leaders, travelers, and the poor. Islam incorporates a vast system of religious doctrine, law, government, spiritual leadership, pilgrimages, mosques, schools, dress, and other customs.

Although Indonesia is the largest predominantly Islamic nation in the world, through its islands Islam surfaces in distinctly adapted forms with particular historical backgrounds. When compared to Muslim ideology and practice in parts of the Middle East, Indonesian Islam is moderate and tolerant. This religion arrived through traders and missionaries from Arabia, China, and India, beginning in Sumatra and Java and spreading through the archipelago by largely peaceful means. Islam formed a connection between Arabia and China of a vast and developed Muslim sea network.[8] It attracted commoners early as it preached equality in the eyes of God—a compelling alternative to the elitism and exclusiveness of the Hindu and Buddhist kingdoms, where rulers and priests enjoyed relationships with the divine and others did not. Some Hindu and Buddhist kingdoms exploited commoners wholly to construct lavish monuments demanded by rulers. The most dramatic of these was Borobudur.

As Islam took hold in Java, it divided to suit three levels of society. Commoners practiced *abangan,* an Islam blended with previous folk ideas of healing, sorcery, and magic. The more affluent merchant class adopted the *santri* version of Islam, concerned with carrying out the basic rituals of the faith, but also forming a complex of social, political, and charitable Islamic societies. The third type of Islam practiced by the aristocratic class, the *priyayi,* incorporated Hindu elements into the newer faith and carried on a love of refinement and mysticism.[9] Islam became entrenched in Javanese society through boarding schools for boys, called *pesantren,* headed by religious scholars and supported by Muslim taxes.

However, these distinctions apply to Java and Islam takes multiple forms across Indonesia. As regions became Islamic, local systems of power and patronage largely continued across the islands. Yet the vastness of Muslim trade networks brought many regions into a wider world of goods, ideas, and people.

Christianity

Christianity came to Indonesia largely through the Dutch, although the earlier Portuguese had set up monasteries and convents in Timor and Flores and converted many to Catholicism. Today, Flores and East Timor remain largely Catholic. The Dutch set up a number of mission schools throughout the archipelago during the colonial era, although these were mostly limited to local elites. One scholar considers that certain elites converted to Dutch Protestantism because it offered them an avenue to literacy—a skill they perceived as the source of the inexplicable technological and supernatural powers for the invading Dutch.[10] Thus, some of the nobility "converted," following an old inclination to form alliances with outside powers to maintain and increase its own control. In this way, status and power provided impetus for becoming Christian in some regions.

Most Indonesian Christians are Protestants, largely adapting the Dutch Reformed Church to their societies. Indonesian Christians are often devout, and many hold vigils during holy times of year like Easter. Most of the eastern Indonesian islands are Christianized, as well as parts of northern Sumatra (mainly Batak areas) and Sulawesi (the Manado region and Torajaland). Catholic missions exist on most sizeable islands. Indonesian Chinese tend to follow Christianity, practicing all denominations.

In recent decades, Protestant evangelical churches have taken hold in Indonesia, following missionaries from the United States. Unlike other world faiths that permitted a synthesis of old and new ideas and practices, this recent fundamentalist creed often denounces traditional ways. For instance, in some congregations people are discouraged from wearing local dress and carrying out rituals that are non-Christian, including dancing. Yet services in these churches involve charismatic preachers, lively singing, and emotion; thus, they appeal to some people more than the staid Dutch Protestant services. It remains to be seen how this type of Christianity will evolve within Indonesian cultures.

ADAT

Imported religions take on distinctive combinations with customary laws—called *adat* throughout Indonesia. To most Indonesians, *adat* maintains the appropriate way of doing things, from religious ceremonies, to daily social interactions, to marriage agreements, to law enforcement regarding crimes such as theft or murder. It also signifies indisputably correct ways of thought and living established for centuries. *Adat* long has preceded influences such as colonialism, world religions, Indonesian state laws, and new ideas and mores of modern life. Through recent times of international media, tourism, and increased education and mobility of Indonesians, *adat* provides cohesion to life after centuries of impositions and disruptive changes. Veneration of ancestors forms a basis of Indonesian belief and *adat* represents the proper ways set down by those that came before. In this way, in village or urban neighborhoods across the archipelago, people view *adat* as a time-tested, civilized system that works. Religion and moral virtue throughout Indonesia involve social obligations, etiquette, and rituals which then create and perpetuate harmony and order—living conditions valued above all else. *Adat* provides a clear foundation for such conditions.

For example, the *slametan* ceremony given by many Muslims in Java sustains community harmony while celebrating a family event. This is a communal feast in response to any change in a family's life: birth, death, circumcision, illness, starting a new business, and so on:

The *slametan* is the Javanese version of what is perhaps the world's most common religious ritual, the communal feast, and, as almost everywhere, it symbolizes the mystic and social unity of those participating in it. Friends, neighbors, fellow workers, relatives, local spirits, dead ancestors, and near-forgotten gods all get bound … into a defined social group pledged to mutual support and cooperation.[11]

Although the *slametan* appears to be an Islamic event, with appropriate speakers reading from the Koran and people sitting in prayerful postures with upturned hands, it echoes ancient pre-Islamic rituals held to sustain group solidarity and protection against animistic evil spirits. Malign forces might exist in animals, in parts of a yard, under rocks, near toilets, in rivers

Neighborhood *slametan*, Yogyakarta, Java, 1990. A
woman, seven months pregnant, ceremoniously eats
a hard-boiled egg to symbolize and assure the viabil-
ity of her unborn child. Courtesy of Jill Forshee.

or the sea, or just about anywhere. Often they carry a vivid historical basis:
Following a drowning, people might believe that an evil spirit plagues them
from a river, or a series of traffic accidents could indicate a malevolent force
near a section of a road. Violation of *adat* principles or unruly behavior—such
as disrespect of parents—might attract spiritual retribution to the wrongdoer,
causing calamities such as physical accidents, loss of a job, illness, or mental
disorders. Ceremonies such as the *slametan* and the resulting offering of food,
however, appease such spirits. The *slametan* is an *adat* practice based in Java,
combining animistic and Islamic elements into a unique ritual event.

Ancestors and the Powers of the Dead

Belief in spiritual interventions manifests across Indonesia in many ways.
Scholars note that almost all Indonesians have a respect for deceased ancestors

and role models that to outsiders borders on the supernatural.[12] Indeed, people more often than not explain misfortune as supernaturally caused, in response to human misdeeds, bad faith, or community failures to carry out proper ceremonies—all provoking an upsetting of social and cosmological balance. Such explanations especially follow illness or death of children, whom people believe the ancestors especially affect.

On the island of Sumba in 2000, villagers interpreted the sudden, inexplicable death of a healthy ten-year-old boy (while sleeping) as supernatural retribution for a ritually inadequate funeral for his grandmother held weeks before. People commented that the quality of the textiles wrapping the deceased were not up to standard and too few in number, and that this "skimping" had angered her spirit.[13] Spirits of the dead, when offended, will then take a descendant among the living for retribution. Similarly, one notes the importance of death rites in Bali:

There is a pervasive belief that no expense must be spared in this final sendoff of the soul, as any skimping would constitute disrespect. And since the soul will shortly become a deified ancestor, with great power to help or hurt, a cheap funeral is a very bad way to start off this relationship.[14]

Throughout Indonesia funeral rites and graves are extremely important. Bali is generally the only island where people carry out cremations, following Hindu tradition. Cremation ceremonies are as extravagant as a family can afford and might include a decorated tower built over the deceased. In 2004 in Ubud, Bali, a cremation event involved a tower that was 60 feet high. Festooned with colorful cloth, gold ornaments, and paper, this supported a sarcophagus in the form of a bull (constructed of wood, paper, and cloth). Many men bore planks on their shoulders as they moved the tower to the cremation site.

Typically when transporting cremation towers, men swerve and take indirect routes during processions to confuse any evil spirits that may be lurking nearby. Large groups of people—dressed in their finest—join the colorful march, adding to the display of family status. Men eventually bring the funeral tower to a cremation site, where someone lights it on fire. After a fantastic display of sparks and flames, the fire engulfs and cremates the corpse beneath. Ideally, the family will throw the ashes of the corpse into the sea, after a high priest (called a *pedanda*) chants the last *mantra*s (words used to concentrate in meditation). After this there might be merriment throughout the crowd, as the final rites are ultimately happy events, freeing up the soul of the deceased. Throughout much of the process of Balinese death rites, people converse, laugh, eat, and behave as if at a kind of party. Dressed in their best finery, many wear silken fabrics woven with gold or display golden ornaments in their hair. These spectacular rituals have attracted many foreign tourists, who often have been welcomed to join processions, provided they comply with minimum standards of proper dress—which always includes a sash around the waist. An observer summarizes:

A Balinese cremation is a dramatic event, but one that leaves many casual onlookers puzzled. Where is the dead body? Why is everyone so happy? Why all the horseplay? What kind of death rite is this after all? The cremation, as witnessed by most visitors, is just one afternoon of weeks, sometimes months, of ceremonies and preparations. A Balinese cremation is a big event, and almost none of it has to do with the dead body.[15]

This emphasizes how Balinese consider the human body as a temporary and impure shell that houses the soul while on earth. Balinese concentrate their thoughts on the spirit and not the actual corpse at a death rite, and they consider the body as something that needs to be disposed, as quickly as possible. Families, however, will sometimes bury a corpse until they have the means for an elaborate funeral, and then dig it up later for the cremation ceremony. Years may pass during this waiting period. The most crucial concern is that the death ceremony be as splendid and ritually correct as possible. Poor families frequently ask permission to include their dead (with modest decoration)

Burning bull sarcophagi at a multiple cremation scene, Ubud, Bali, 2004. Courtesy of Ian Fischer-Laycock. Used by permission.

along with a wealthy family's ritual and procession, to save on costs. This often happens. These are not sorrowful occasions, but times of great celebration believed to assist the departed soul in reaching heaven (*suarga*) or, in the case of a highly developed soul, to a state of oneness with God (*moksa*).

Offerings are central to Balinese religious practice. At death rites, temporary structures fill up with brightly colored, small sculptures of rice paste, shaped as people, animals, boats, and so forth. Cakes, fruits, flowers, eggs, and meats of pig and duck add to the array. Perhaps 25 to 40 women will work daily for several weeks making decorative offerings for an average-sized cremation. These colorful and elegantly displayed creations function to honor and please the ancestors and the spirit that will make its departure after cremation. Offerings also appease the hungry evil spirits of Bali, called *bhutas* and *kalas*. If ignored, these spirits will cause trouble for the living or interfere with the ceremony.

On other islands, burials involve extravagant ceremonies and sometimes stone megaliths. The southern region of Indonesia, including Nias, Sumba, and Timor, are part of a chain of islands regarded as a "megalithic arch." That is, people of these islands create large, stone grave markers (megaliths) to honor their dead and assert prestige for living relatives.[16] Chiseling stones weighing many tons from a quarry and then dragging them some distance to a burial site persists today in some areas.

In 1993, a megalith weighing 40 tons was dragged over mountainous terrain in western Sumba for 3 miles, involving up to three thousand people pulling in unison with ropes and rolling the stone over logs. This mammoth community undertaking took place over 6 weeks sponsored by a high-ranking family. Most of the money to finance the event came to the family from sons working at professional jobs in Jakarta, more than 1,000 miles to the west of Sumba. Beliefs and status associated with these megaliths remain strong in parts of Indonesia, despite many outside influences and including educated people who otherwise carry on modern lifestyles.

In Sumba, although many have converted to Christianity, perhaps half of the population still carries out rituals of the indigenous *Marapu* (meaning "our roots") religion. This includes many converts who seem to combine the faiths without difficulties. Sumbanese take funeral rituals most seriously and villages on the island contain central yards with megalithic graves of all shapes and sizes. The term *Marapu* also denotes the ancestors, and people forever carry out ceremonies involving special priests using ritual speech and sacrifice animals to stay in ancestral good graces. Divination—forecasting the future or the auspiciousness of an undertaking—takes many forms in Sumba, from drawing pictures to reading the entrails of pigs or chickens. People still regard *Marapu* ideas and rituals most seriously. As a highly stratified society, with

Dragging a hand-chiseled, 40-ton stone funeral megalith in West Sumba over 3 miles of terrain. 1994. Courtesy of Jill Forshee.

castes of nobility, commoners, and slaves, Sumbanese are extremely conscious of social position.

Nowhere in Indonesia do people carry out grander pageantry to honor the dead than the Torajans of highland southern Sulawesi. People of the Tana Toraja Regency occupy a mountainous area, geographically and culturally distinct from the neighboring Muslim lowlands. As were people in Sumba, Torajans remained isolated from colonialism until the twentieth century, when Dutch missionaries converted some to Christianity. After the founding of the Indonesian nation, they remained cloistered geographically through the 1960s, when their main visitors became tourists. Ironically, more Torajans converted to Christianity after the departure of Dutch colonialism and the following encouragement by Indonesian national policy to convert to a mono-theistic faith.[17] Toraja culture remained largely intact in 1968, at which time half the population adhered to the ancestral religion, *aluk to dolo* (meaning "ways of the ancestors"), while the other half adhered to Christianity.[18]

Torajans hold extravagant funeral rituals at which they slaughter many water buffalo and stage processions and dances. As do funerals through-out Indonesia, these rituals honor the deceased and relations while making public individual or family social status. In 1987, an anthropologist attended a Torajan funeral and wrote: "The more guests a funeral attracts, the more water buffalo are slaughtered and the more prestige accrues to the sponsors. This particular funeral had been widely publicized: thirty thousand guests were to attend, including three cabinet ministers, two governors, a foreign ambassador, and van loads of tourists."[19]

Although by recent estimates, more than 80 percent of the Toraja are Christian converts, they continue to sponsor and partake in elaborate funeral rituals replete with pig and water buffalo sacrifices.[20] These costly events might seem wasteful to outsiders, but to the people involved they are of the highest priority in social life. Like Sumba, Toraja is a stratified society, indeed following what could be called a caste system. People are born into a certain caste level and remain there, regardless of what successes they might have in life. As do people of Sumba, those of Toraja historically belong to noble, commoner, or slave castes. To retain one's higher caste level has become even more crucial in modern times, within a nation that expounds democracy and outlaws slavery. Thus Torajan elites have more at stake than in the past, when they lived in relative isolation. The importance of social status has become intensified throughout Indonesia in recent times, in the face of modern changes. As summarized regarding the importance of cockfighting in Bali (in 1958), "the cockfight talks most forcibly about ... status relationships, and what it says about them is that they are matters of life and death."[21]

WAYS OF LIFE, THOUGHT, AND BEHAVIOR

The village remains the basic home of less than half of the Indonesian people. Yet even within cities such as Jakarta, Yogyakarta, Surabaya, or Denpasar, areas often divide into small alleys (*gangs*) where kin and neighbors live in close quarters, recreating a village sociability and ambience. These types of neighborhoods have suffered in recent decades through massive urban renewal projects, succeeding in displacing many of the urban poor from their modest living quarters. Many Indonesian city-dwellers also claim an outlying village region as their true home, and some return for special ceremonies or to help during harvest time.

Village political life typically centers around a ruling clan group or an elected village head (*kepala desa*). People engage in a system of mutual assistance called *gotong royong* (meaning "mutual cooperation"), in which help or goods received by a family eventually becomes returned in kind. "What goes around comes around" aptly describes Indonesian ways of thinking about sustaining communities. This may involve building a new house, contributing to a funeral, helping with a wedding, or a gift of fresh fish. Often "debts" between villagers are not monetary, but rely upon physical assistance.

Maintaining a communal water system or building a new roof on a home may involve the entire village and relations beyond.

In terms of rules and disputes, Indonesians strive to reach consensus in making decisions. Often meetings, called *musyawarah,* take place among relatives or neighbors for decisions on marriages, funerals, agricultural matters, trade obligations, crimes, or to settle disagreements. A resolution follows (ideally) when all present reach agreement rather than merely sharing a majority opinion.

Indonesians value a peaceful social order and strive for balance in their relationships and activities (when order is lost, mayhem can take over, and the earlier section on history in Chapter 1 demonstrated how this has happened). People rarely openly disagree or argue with each other face-to-face. To Westerners they might seem indecisive or evasive in the ways they do not respond to questions with "yes" or "no" answers but, rather, with "maybe" or "not yet." Indonesian etiquette involves a formal politeness to others that requires deference. Behaving with too much certainty might appear aggressive. Kin and elders enjoy respect and people carry on their lives through complex systems of family obligations. To be blatantly individualistic is considered egotistical (*egois*) and childishly selfish and the extent of honor and consideration Indonesians give to others often surprises foreigners.

To be alone for any length of time is an aberration in Indonesia. Young and old prefer the company of family and friends. Sometimes Indonesians strike Westerners as intrusive, clinging, and knowing no sense of privacy. This is because they often belong to large extended families living in close quarters and are accustomed to the constant company of others. In fact, Indonesians generally relish close contact with family and friends. Many people will express that they feel isolated (*sepi*) when by themselves. When venturing out to market or a late day stroll, Indonesians usually go with one or several companions.

Gendered Behaviors

Western observers of Indonesia noted in the past the relatively high status enjoyed by women, who sell goods at the market place and are visible, active, and vocal in home life and beyond. Although usually men dominate public and ritual events, women largely set the tone for domestic life and handle the finances. Yet, officially sanctioned, traditional roles for women in Indonesia particularly emphasize a role of wife and mother. President Suharto, after his rise to power in the mid-1960s, stated that women's organizations in Indonesia should bring women to their correct role, as the mother of a household and the motor for development.[22] Women's roles and status vary throughout Indonesian societies. They have become educated, outspoken, and have entered all sorts of professions in recent decades.

To many Indonesians of all faiths, everything possesses a soul. Moreover, human souls succumb to evil forces, to physical traumas, or to sudden shocks. One such consequence is called *latah,* which befalls women who have been startled, sometimes by something as simple as an abrupt loud noise. This causes a severe nervous condition where women react to the surprise by behaving irrationally, by using uncharacteristically foul language, or by falling to the ground in a kind of fit. People explain that *latah* results from the soul leaving the body through sudden fright. Local healers or priests will then call back a woman's soul and cure her of the affliction.

Amok is another psychological phenomenon that strikes Indonesians. Most Americans have heard the expression, "running *amok*" (or *amuk*) without knowing its Indonesian origins. This seems to largely affect men and typically occurs in Indonesian societies that encourage emotional restraint, such as in Java or Bali. To run *amok* is to rage violently, striking out at anything nearby. Someone in this state has lost all control and acts out with madness. People will eventually subdue the person, who will usually not bear the blame for his behavior, unless he has caused injury or death. Reasons of job stress, recent loss, pent up anger, a grievous insult, and so forth, often explain the affliction. *Amok* occurs from a serious loss of personal balance and highlights how harmony prevents chaos and frenzy. This might occur on an individual or collective level, as during historical collapses of order in Indonesia.

Living with the Natural and Supernatural

Many Indonesians believe that there are dangers everywhere, visible and invisible. Balinese will eat food quickly and in silence, fearing risks in the prolonged opening of their mouths, inviting the possible entry of evil forces. In Sumba and other parts of Indonesia, people dread nocturnal spirits called *suangi.* Sumba villagers keep lamps lit all night to prevent these spirits of the dark from entering their rooms and preying upon them while they sleep. *Suangi,* they say, will feed upon human organs or, like vampires, suck blood from sleeping people and thus strengthen their own powers. Frequently, people who fall ill or weakened for a length of time will suspect such a spirit has attacked them in their sleep. Sometimes they also regard living individuals as *suangi*s and avoid contact with them. One anthropologist received constant warnings in Sumba to never go out at night and to always keep a lamp lit in her room.[23] Moreover, a person alone attracts such spirits so it is best to live in a household with others. People often fear empty houses and even consider them as haunted. Only the presence of humans and social order makes spaces safe.

Across the island of Timor (including now independent East Timor), sacred sites provide spiritual meaning to the landscape—on mountaintops, among rock outcroppings, in forests, and so forth. These contain *lulik* (meaning "sacred" and also "forbidden") wooden carvings, often posts or figures, which people of the region traditionally have considered protective and beneficial.[24] These are secret places, visited by elders and animist priests. Sometimes the carvings are very old. In recent times, some of these objects have been stolen and sold into the world market of ethnic arts. In one region of East Timor, a *lulik* figure in the form of a wooden angel disappeared from a mountaintop in the 1950s. People of the region report that after this loss, their region was not as prosperous as before.[25] In his autobiography, Xanana Gusmão, the current president of the nation of East Timor, reports that in the days when he was a resistance fighter against the Indonesian army, he went to *lulik* sites in the mountains to renew his strength.[26]

Animism accounts for many helpful earthly and ancestral spirits and even national leaders sometimes appeal to them. These spirits provide life and its blessings or assist in times of crisis. Following beliefs throughout rice-growing areas of Indonesia, spirits abide in the plants. In Bali, the rice goddess, Dewi Sri, commands immense respect. When harvesting rice, women use a small, crescent-shaped blade concealable in the palms of their hands. This is to avoid frightening rice sheafs by the sight of the knives in their harvesting. Similar means of cutting rice at harvest take place across other Indonesian islands.

After the "Green Revolution" in parts of Indonesia, fostered by Western rice hybrids and chemical fertilizers and pesticides, many Balinese (who had been brilliant rice-growers for centuries) became distraught at the environmental consequences. Although harvests were more frequent and abundant, and certain pests were at bay, other creatures of the rice paddy eco-system (and sources of food), such as minnows, shrimp, and frogs, died from the chemicals. Ducks, an important part of fertilization and pest control in paddies to this day, became irrelevant to the rice fields or sick from the new chemicals. Moreover, people said that the rice did not taste as good as the type they had always grown. Some formerly unknown diseases began to attack crops in Bali and Java. Some Indonesians claimed that Dewi Sri and spirits were upset by these modern "developments."

At one point, then-President Suharto outlawed some of the more toxic pesticides, in response to concerns of offense to the rice goddess. Suharto, a Muslim, was also a life long adherent to Javanese mysticism, including its gods, goddesses, and spirits. He was a striking example of how animistic beliefs underlie and persist through Indonesian thought—even that of modern, high-ranking political leaders (President Wahid visited the grave of a long-dead spiritual leader before making political decisions). Now some people have resumed growing rice through traditional, largely organic methods, particularly in Bali where the grain holds a central nutritional, social, and cosmological place in life.

Recent Challenges to Indonesian Thought, Religion, and Order

As mentioned in Chapter 1, the terrorist bombing of the Bali nightclub on October 12, 2002 created upheaval in Indonesia, not only through the lives it took and ruined, but also in the effects it had upon the way many Indonesian people thought about their worlds. In Bali, many Hindus believed that they had grown too commerce oriented in their involvement with tourism and had thus neglected the sacred. Muslims were dismayed and confused as to why the Islamic fundamentalist group *Jemaah Islamiyah* (meaning Islamic Community)[27] claiming responsibility would take the lives of Indonesians (including other Muslims) and all but destroy the livelihoods of many of all faiths in Bali.

The massive tsunami destroying Aceh on December 25, 2004, in the northern region of Sumatra, also signified to many either discontent within their metaphysical worlds and faulty religious practice, or the weakening and even immorality of the national government of Indonesia—another geological disaster heralding the wrongs of the powers that be. The catastrophe provided an earthly and supernatural message that the ethical bases of religion of Indonesian peoples have been violated—whether by ordinary citizens or political leaders. Such times have caused introspection, anger, confusion, further violence, and tremendous sorrows for those affected. Most appeal to higher powers for help. Many Indonesians blamed political corruption (*korupsi*)—a system so entwined with power, especially regarding the national government, that most consider it as the main attribute of those who rule over them and the cause of their woes. The earthquakes and tsunami in Java in May and July 2006 have caused many to again lose confidence in their leaders.

Further terrorist bombings in Jakarta, such as that of August 2003 (killing 12 people) at the Marriot Hotel and that of September 2004, killing 11 people at the Australian Embassy have escalated the terrorism and caused many foreigners to stay away from Indonesia altogether. But the October 2005 bombing, once again in the tourist section of Bali, physically and emotionally devastated people who were just beginning to believe that their lives had returned to normal. Thus far, there have been no reprisals against Muslims and, indeed, the many Muslims doing business in Bali have suffered equally.

Indonesians now must struggle with their religious diversity and a minority of people prone to terrorism and violence (which includes Muslims, Christians, and animists), threatening the stability of their lives, communities, and nation. Terrorism, as throughout the world, will likely continue, as peoples of the archipelago strive for peace and order. Indonesians live with a multiplicity of moral standards and now juggle social and religious systems that shift between a nationally promoted ideal of monotheistic religion (recognized as *agama,* which differs from older beliefs of *adat*) and local, customary ideas of the right ordering of the world. As always, this "right ordering" will take account of natural and human-inflicted disasters, as people try to find ways to balance the many forces—both earthly and metaphysical—affecting their lives.

NOTES

1. See Margaret J. Wiener, *Visible and Invisible Realms: Power, Magic, and Colonial Conquest in Bali* (Chicago: University of Chicago Press, 1995).

2. Told to Jill Forshee by a young man in Sumba in 1998.

3. Claude Levi-Strauss, *The Elementary Structures of Kinship* (Boston: Beacon Press, 1969).

4. See Jill Forshee, *Between the Folds: Stories of Cloth, Lives, and Travels from Sumba* (Honolulu: University of Hawaii Press, 2000), 17–19.

5. Janet Hoskins, "Introduction: Headhunting as Practice and Trope," in *Headhunting and the Social Imagination in Southeast Asia* (Stanford: Stanford University Press, 1996), 20.

6. This warfare has been described at length by David Mitchell, "Tragedy in Sumba: Why Neighbors Hacked Each Other to Death in a Remote Part of Indonesia," *Inside Indonesia* 58 (1998): 8–20. See also Jacqueline Vel, "Tribal Battle in a Remote Island: Crisis and Violence in Sumba (Eastern Indonesia)," *Indonesia* 72 (2001): 141–158.

7. James J. Fox, ed., *Religion and Ritual, Indonesian Heritage Series* (Singapore: Archipelago Press, 1999), 50, paraphrased.

8. See Jean Gelman Taylor, *Indonesia: People and Histories* (New Haven: Yale University Press, 2003), 60–87.

9. Clifford Geertz, *The Religion of Java* (Chicago: The University of Chicago Press, 1960), 5–7.

10. See Janet Hoskins, "Entering the Bitter House: Spirit Worship and Conversion in West Sumba," in *Indonesian Religions in Transition,* Rita Kipp Smith and Susan Rodgers, eds. (Tucson: University of Arizona Press, 1987), 136–160. Also discussed in Forshee, 19–21.

11. Geertz, *The Religion of Java,* 11.

12. See Henri Chambert-Loir and Anthony Reid. "Introduction," in *The Potent Dead Ancestors, Saints, and Heroes in Contemporary Indonesia,* ed. Henri Chambert-Loir and Anthony Reid (Honolulu: University of Hawaii Press in association with Allen and Unwin, Australia, 2002), xv–xxvi.

13. This was Jill Forshee's (2001) personal observation and conclusion through discussions with a number of people in the family and village.

14. Fred B. Eiseman, Jr., *Bali: Sekala and Niskala. Volume I: Essays on Religion, Ritual, and Art* (Hong Kong: Periplus Press, 1990), 116.

15. Eiseman, *Bali,* 115.

16. This arch actually sweeps around half of the globe, from the island of Madagascar off the east coast of Africa, through Indonesia and across the Pacific Ocean to Easter Island—the site of immense and mysterious stone heads. Originally, the Austronesian peoples spread megalithic culture across this vast region.

17. This is mentioned in Chapter 1 as one of the five founding principles of *Pancasila* set out by President Sukarno.

18. Eric Crystal, "Rape of the Ancestors: Discovery, Display, and Destruction of the Ancestral Statuary of Tana Toraja," in *Fragile Traditions: Indonesian Art in Jeopardy* (Honolulu: University of Hawaii Press, 1994), 30.

19. Kathleen Adams, "Taming Traditions: Torajan Ethnicity in the Age of Tourism," in *Converging Interests: Traders, Travelers, and Tourists in Southeast Asia,* ed. Jill Forshee, with Christina Fink and Sandra Cate (Berkeley: Center for Southeast Asia Studies, Monograph No. 36, University of California at Berkeley, 1999), 253.

20. Adams, "Taming Traditions," 252.

21. Geertz, Clifford, "Deep Play: Notes on the Balinese Cockfight," in *The Interpretation of Cultures* (New York: Basic Books, 1973), 447.

22. Sylvia Tiwon discusses Suharto's stand toward the position of women in New Order Indonesia in "Models and Maniacs: Articulating the Female in Indonesia," in *Fantasizing the Feminine in Indonesia,* ed. Laurie J. Sears (Durham: Duke University Press, 1996), 59.

23. Jill Forshee, personal observation.

24. For a fuller ethnographic description of the region and beliefs, see Elizabeth Traube, *Cosmology and Social Life: Ritual Exchange Among the Mambai of East Timor* (Chicago: University of Chicago Press, 1986).

25. See Jill Forshee, "Tracing Troubled Times: Objects of Value and Narratives of Loss from Sumba and Timor Islands," *Indonesia* 74 (2002): 65–77.

26. See Xanana Gusmão, *To Resist Is to Win: The Autobiography of Xanana Gusmão* (Victoria, Australia: Aurora Books, 2000).

27. In the early 1970s, Muslim youths hostile to the religious repression of Suharto's New Order regime started supporting local Muslim groups, and the diverse band of believers became collectively known as Jemaah Islamiyah, which literally means "Islamic Community." These small groups agreed to live by Islamic law and were blamed for arson attacks on churches, nightclubs and cinemas. Quoted from Bill Guernin, "Indonesia's Terror Dilemma," *Online Asia Times,* October 7, 2005, http://www.atimes.com/atimes/Southeast_Asia/GJ07Ae01.html.

SUGGESTED READING

Aragon, Lorraine V. *Fields of the Lord: Animism, Christian Minorities, and State Development in Indonesia.* Honolulu: University of Hawaii Press, 2000.

Chambert-Loir, Henri, and Anthony Reid, eds. *The Potent Dead: Ancestors, Saints, and Heroes in Contemporary Indonesia.* Honolulu: University of Hawaii Press, 2002.

Eiseman, Fred B. *Bali, Sekala & Niskala, Volume 1: Essays on Religion, Ritual and Art.* Hong Kong: Periplus Editions, 1990.

Fox, James J. *Religion and Ritual: Indonesian Heritage Series.* Singapore: Archipelago Press, 1999.

Geertz, Clifford. *The Religion of Java.* Chicago: University of Chicago Press, 1976.

Hooker, M. Barry. *Indonesian Islam: Social Change through Contemporary Fatawa.* Honolulu: University of Hawaii Press, 2003.

Kipp, Rita Smith, and Susan Rodgers, eds. *Indonesian Religions in Transition.* Tucson: University of Arizona Press, 1987.

3

Literature and Art

Indonesian visual arts long have graced international museum exhibitions, stunning onlookers with their beauty, uniqueness, and complexity. These include carving, weaving, drawing, and painting—and encompass puppetry, masks, temple art, and modern, eclectic forms of artistic expression. Currently, as Indonesian artists produce ingenious works with extraordinary standards of excellence, international institutions and collectors avidly seek them out. Today, Indonesians exhibit their arts at galleries in Paris, New York, London, Tokyo, Sydney, and cosmopolitan centers the world over.

The concept of *halus* (refinement) persists through Indonesia's arts and literature, reflecting many centuries of exquisite works evoking a moral rightness. Terms for "beauty" in Indonesian societies (in both the Indonesian national and many local languages) often also mean "goodness," as does *halus* and also the word *bagus* (meaning "beautiful" or "good"). The reverse is also true—the term for "ugliness" in Indonesian is *jelek,* also denoting "bad" or "evil." *Kasar* ("crude") also describes a low moral character. Through its history, visual art and literature in Indonesia represent both the light and dark sides of life and cosmological order. These creative forms embody balance while permitting ambiguities and complexities in expressions and interpretations.

Modern Indonesian art and literature do not necessarily focus upon the beautiful as their subject matters, but frequently paint, carve, or write of life's hardness, inequities, and sorrows. In recent decades, such expressions became powerful media for political criticism. For decades, authors and artists critical of the national government faced imprisonment, most drastically during the Suharto New Order regime.

Art and literature implicate values and social realities beyond the written story or painted picture. Like other aspects of Indonesian life and thought: such as relative social status, spiritual beliefs, balance, etiquette, and gender, expressive culture cannot be separated out as a category by itself. Rather, creative media entwines with all elements of cultures of the archipelago. Adopting a holistic approach eventually reveals patterns toward understanding something of cultures and customs of Indonesia.

VISUAL ARTS

Premodern Indonesian Visual Arts

The classical Indianized art of Java is possibly the greatest art produced by any peoples of Southeast Asia. ... It represents an intimate blending of religious and artistic aims and methods, achieved by the native genius of the peoples of Indonesia.[1]

Before Indian or other foreign influences, indigenous artistry and skill flourished across the Indonesian islands longer than anyone knows. Certain early imported designs, studied by international and Indonesian art scholars and archaeologists, appear to have spread to the Indonesian archipelago at around three to four centuries B.C. from the Dong Son culture of what is now Vietnam. Whether by migrations, diffusions, or trade, ornate metal axes and round, bronze ornamental kettledrums typical of Dong Son made their ways to Indonesian islands. One such drum, called the "Moon of Bali" (between one and two thousand years old) exemplifies an elaborately decorated piece and the largest of its kind ever found. Stylized faces and much ornamentation embellish the drum. Some argue that this drum (and others like it) was produced locally. People of the island of Alor (near Timor) continue to prize and use similar, smaller drums called *moko*.

Scholars now recognize that while Indonesian islands absorbed influences from mainland Southeast Asia, India, China, Arabia, Europe, and beyond— much local skill, inventiveness, and artistry developed independently. Today, anyone observing Indonesians carving, weaving, working with clay, metalworking, drawing, painting—or creating offerings of sculpted rice paste—will note the meticulousness of the artists and their superb senses of design and detail.

Arts of Indonesia generally involve a highly organized horizontal and vertical schematic design, which then contains complex patterns. As an art historian summarized: "Throughout even the most complex pattern, an ordered regularity, a balance, between horizontal and vertical prevails."[2] This visually mirrors cultural emphases upon balance and order prevailing through life.

Indian artistic influences had taken hold in parts of Indonesia by the third century A.D., following centuries of trade and immigrated Indians. The early Sumatran kingdom of Srivijaya and the Javanese kingdom of Majapahit absorbed and reconfigured Indian ideas and aesthetics, which then powerfully influenced the arts of Indonesia. Many reasons explain the historical openness among people and rulers of Indonesia to Indian principles. Buddhism and Hinduism came from India, bringing a highly developed religious and aesthetic heritage. Indian learning offered Indonesians a written script, an administrative system, codes of law, politics, metaphysics, mathematics, astronomy, medicine, and practical magic. Multiple rulers derived inspiration, prestige, and practical assistance from these systems. Their assimilation of Indian ideology and aesthetics became a major factor in the success of dynasties that later erected the great stone monuments of central and eastern Java.[3]

Further, the sinuousness and sensuality of Indian arts clearly appealed to Indonesian aesthetic sensibilities. Early Indian-influenced artistry (and Indonesian arts to the present) was rich in curves, detail, and flourish. The intricacy and elegance of the bas-relief stone panels on Javanese monuments reveal the advanced carving skills and sophisticated design senses of artisans of the times.

A carved stone panel of Borobudur, central Java, illustrating one story of Buddha's many incarnations on earth. Courtesy of Jill Forshee.

Hundreds of these panels and freestanding, three-dimensional stone figures embellish one of the most impressive monuments ever created anywhere in the world—Borobudur in central Java. The carved reliefs along the path to the temple summit illustrate early stories of Buddha's incarnations on earth, called *Jataka* tales. The monument also includes depictions of heaven (*nirvana*) and hell (*neraka*). While these artistic representations come from Buddhist literature brought from India, Borobudur embodies the doctrines of Buddhism as adopted in Java, beautifully rendered pictorially—illustrating rights and wrongs of life and ideals of religion. Now refurbished, Borobudur is a major tourist and pilgrimage site, a largely open-air museum of ancient stone artistry and architectural magnificence.

Puppets

One art form is so popular in parts of Indonesia (especially in Bali and Java) and so magnificently exemplifies indigenous artistry, storytelling, cultural values, and performative skill that it often appears on book covers and travel brochures as a kind of "emblem" for the country. The flat, leather puppets called *wayang kulit* (meaning "leather puppet") represent many characters, animals, and natural forms as both a visual and performing art. Through fantastic imagery and a mystical theatrical ambience, *wayang* performances transport audiences to other worlds—whether of a glorious past or a godly realm. These puppets enact all-night dramas behind a stretched white cloth screen, backlit with a hanging oil lamp. Seated on the other side of the screen, the audience sees only the shadows of the puppets—thus *wayang kulit* is called "the shadow play."

Although people view the *wayang* in performance as shadows, puppets receive colorful and meticulously painted details and often gold highlights. This renders them attractive as they are, but the colors usually do not appear through the screen to an audience. Carvers produce the puppets with special knives and chisels, using master stencils. The leather characters contain rich, lacy detail in the empty spaces carved through them: meanders, curves, eyes, mouths, patterns on clothing and hair, and small holes of various shapes or slits to define sections of each form. This demands great care and skill and each puppet requires highly specific facial features, body type, hairstyle, clothing, jewelry, and so forth, which must be clearly visible in shadow form.

Thus, while often beautifully painted, the exquisite quality of the carving enables the puppets to carry the show. When finished, leather puppets become mounted on bamboo or bone rods running spine-like up their centers for support and serving as handles for the *dalang* to hold from beneath. The same

The *dalang* as a one-man theatre, reenacts ancient epics such
as the *Ramayana* and *Mahabarata,* without pause from dusk
to dawn, manipulating scores of shadow puppet characters and
speaking in many voices and dialects. American Society for
Eastern Arts. Courtesy of David Weitzman.

material forms rods to manipulate moveable parts of the characters, such as
arms, legs, or opening jaws. Puppet making skill in Indonesia often passes
down through families, as do many arts. Typically a master crafter creates
the most intricate sections of a character and younger family members learn
gradually through producing simpler parts of puppets.

The most refined puppets feature black, white, or yellow faces, while those
of coarser manner wear red or pink-faces, with various shades from either
extreme group coloring characters in between. A large stature symbolizes
great physical strength and a violent nature or lack of self-control. This is
in contrast to well-proportioned, medium-sized figures that do possess self-
control and finesse. A slim, small body is indicative of refinement.[4]

Other popular types of puppets include flat, wooden puppets from eastern
Java, called *wayang klitik,* and wooden, doll-like puppets from western Java,
called *wayang golek.* All types include hinged, wooden arms attached to

rods; however, the three-dimensional *wayang golek* puppets do not appear in shadow plays, but as they are—colorfully painted with specially sewn clothing of a variety of fabrics. These enact similar tales as do shadow puppets, with regional variations and modern innovations.

Some puppeteers take their characters to the streets, with mini-theaters pushed on carts. These are not the elite *dalang* puppet masters of renown, but common people trying to make a living through their arts and imaginations. The cover of an issue of the sophisticated Indonesian magazine *Latitudes,* published in Bali in English, features an engaging photograph of a one-toothed, old Javanese man with a small stage on a cart (made from an old bicycle) framing simply painted, three-dimensional puppets. The puppeteer in the picture smiles proudly behind his modest yet colorful mobile theater.[5]

Masks

Perhaps of all Indonesian arts, masks embody the greatest power for transformation of people and dramatic characters. Called *topeng* in the Indonesian language, masks of all sorts animate dance dramas, festivals, and rituals—assisting in offerings and personifying good and evil. In some regions, men have donned masks in battle, and healers have worn them in rituals for the sick. Highly skilled carvers and painters create the best masks used in momentous events. Sacred pieces in some regions (such as Bali and Timor) require special trees for their wood.

As remarked of Balinese arts: "images most important in the political and social organization of Bali in one era did not simply die out, but new images were added to them, so that each generation saw itself as continuing the same culture, while at the same time transforming it."[6] This is true of most Indonesian arts, which all chronicle events and influences of their times and change as time goes on.

While masks of Bali are among the most extravagantly constructed, those of other Indonesian islands are also finely made and ritually important. The Toba Batak people of northern Sumatra have worn large, simply carved wooden masks at funeral rituals and the neighboring Karo people wore large helmet-like masks of wood representing either people or horses. Traveling medicine men of Sumatra wear simple wooden masks to advertise their healing powers as they sit behind their wares at open markets. The wood of the masks emulates the magical powers of the herbs and barks the healers sell and use.

Dramatic and complex, masks of the Dayak people in regions of Kalimantan portray animist spirits and earthly creatures. Some bear elaborate extensions and resemble those of northwest coast indigenous peoples of North America. Dayak masks portray pigs, deer, tigers, dragons, and people. Men wear them at important times of year during rice planting or harvesting, sometimes as they dance within the community longhouses for which Dayak are famous. Some say that gods descend from the mountains and enter the men to help attract rice spirits that will bestow fertility upon the crops and that these earthly masks serve as a sort of disguise against any malevolent forces.[7]

Masks of Timor Island are simply carved of wood, then darkened with soot. People say that warriors or local priests wore them in dances. These masks differ greatly from the finely detailed ones of Bali and Java and express creatures and concepts of animist cultures of eastern Indonesia. Arts of this region sharply contrast with those of the more Indian-influenced areas of central and western Indonesia. Sometimes Timor masks derive their shapes from certain pieces of wood, and the tangled roots of a tree might become the "hair" of a mask. People believe that these objects receive their powers from particular trees and places, in keeping with local spirits of nature.

Temple Painting

Illustrating sacred tales, people historically created paintings on large cloths, and then hung these on walls and eaves of temple pavilions.[8] Figures in these paintings appear in standard three-quarters view, as do shadow puppets. Bali is famed for such paintings, especially near the Klungkung region (an old kingdom). Balinese tend to fill all of the space in a picture with imagery. In temple pieces, otherwise empty spaces teem with birds, vegetation, or water drops to portray an atmosphere full of vibrancy. Moreover, large paintings often contain sequential episodes of a long story, each defined by a highly decorative border. This lends the scenes a comic strip-like appearance. In fact, they similarly tell stories through a succession of pictorial frames, some including written script in ancient Balinese.

As do many arts of Bali and Java, temple paintings frequently portray images from revered Indian epics, the *Mahabharata* and the *Ramayana*.[9] These paintings use little "perspective" to suggest space, instead composing everything at the same distance from the viewer; all forms occupy the same plane. Other paintings depict tales of royal pageantry; some tell of warfare, or even *kasar* (coarse) commoners celebrating together.[10] Elaborate, decorative, and repetitious, these paintings draw viewers into their details and stories.

The Kertha Gosa (Palace of Justice) is filled with paintings, built in the early eighteenth century at Klungkung, Bali (a region also renowned for modern paintings). These lavish pictures decorate the entire sectioned ceiling

Balinese temple painting depicting a scene of hell. Courtesy of Joseph Fischer. Used by permission.

of this pavilion, numbering 267 panels. The paintings vividly reflected an aesthetic penchant for artistic precision, opulence, and excellence throughout Bali during this era.[11]

Modern Indonesian Art

An art scholar from Java considers that "Modern Indonesian visual art was born in a rush and then developed quickly without following any prolonged or traditional natural course. Its birth was a product of strong Western influences and its character for a long time was conditioned by this circumstance."[12]

While true to a great degree regarding initial factors bringing "modern art" to Indonesians, this statement seems too dismissive of indigenous artistry and ideas. In any case, it does not sufficiently credit Indonesian artists of the time, who adopted new forms but continued to develop their own subjects and styles, thus making their marks in various art worlds. As Indonesians took on Western concepts in their art, they did not routinely abandon their intrinsic artistic sensibilities and subject matters, much less their creativity.

The modern art movement in Java and Sumatra largely came out of study clubs in the early twentieth century, in which elite Indonesians grew acquainted with foreign art and literature. Following this, "the future Indonesians became aware of Western art history, and suddenly 'painter' became a new career-option, an option with a certain modern, international aura—a new category which it would be up to the Indonesian artists to interpret according to their own ideas and needs."[13] Through the 1920s and 1930s, Indonesian painters increasingly took part in shaping contemporary culture, mixing the international with their own and the modern with the traditional, "into a series of individual syntheses which could not have happened anywhere else." Indeed, Indonesians contributed much to a "global history of contemporary art" no longer centered in the Western world.[14]

In the early twentieth century, Bali experienced an exhilarating, revolutionary period of artistic transition to Western-style framed and individualized drawings and paintings—and stylized wood carvings of nonreligious themes. In the 1930s, a community of Western artists resided in Bali. Some provided Balinese artists with paper, pencils, paints, canvases, frames, brushes, and other imported art materials. They also instructed them in Western art techniques and themes, such as linear perspective, modern artistic styles, and scenes of everyday life. Accordingly, for some Balinese, visual subject matter moved from the sacred spheres of the gods to the ordinary realm of the living, and artists began to draw, paint, and carve such imagery with fervor. They also began to sign their work, thus individualizing art.

In the 1920s, 1930s, and 1940s, few tourists visited Bali, but enough went (as did visiting friends of resident foreign artists and celebrities, such as Charlie Chaplin) that a growing market developed for Balinese "village

Painting of village life in Bali, 1933, by I. Reneh, Batuan. Courtesy of Joseph Fischer. Used by permission.

life" painting that continues to this day. Anthropologists Margaret Mead and Gregory Bateson researched in Bali during this time and collected paintings of the period, many of which they commissioned.[15] Such patronage, encouraged Bali artists to develop individual styles and themes. Older subjects continued in popularity, however, as the Balinese began to portray just about everything in their real and imaginary worlds in framed pictures.

Artists in Java, influenced by colonialism, Dutch education, European art books, tourism, and so forth, had also begun to create nontraditional art. As noted, "Up to about 1920 this art largely consisted of landscape painting, still life and portraiture...a break from traditional artisanship and a precursor of a new art movement."[16] In the 1920s, led mainly by the artist Soedjojono, artists in Java broke radically with conventions and progressed to address themes of social realism. These included now famous artists such as the painter Affandi.

Following World War II, such artists, along with a new generation, continued to express their sentiments toward colonialism, Japanese wartime occupation of Indonesia, and a national revolution resulting in independence from the Dutch. They did not paint pretty pictures of the idyllic tropics, but depicted horrors and sorrows of recent Indonesian life. During the national independence struggle from the Dutch, many artists were involved in the battlefields, which emerged in their later artwork.[17] Revolutionary themes appeared well before independence in paintings by Affandi, Soedjojono, and others—passionately striving to portray what was truly Indonesian. Simultaneously, in the region of Ubud, Bali, the artist Gusti Nyoman Lempad began drawing and painting scenes dignifying everyday Balinese life, such as women preparing food in kitchens or people working in yards.

The birth of modern painting in Indonesia coincided with the birth of the nationalist movement,[18] and the portrayal of ordinary Indonesians—as typical Indonesian labor and activities became themes with a revolutionary message. Such portrayals continued into the new era, as artists conveyed the poverty and social inequities under the Sukarno and Suharto regimes. However, scenes of lives of commoners or anything suggesting poverty became increasingly associated with Communist affiliations and anti-government intentions. Some, such as the painter Hendra Gunawan, imprisoned during the Suharto reign in the 1960s for his subversive political ideas, suffered particular government censure for the socially controversial subjects of his paintings, which included scenes of street prostitutes.[19] Prison, however, for artists and writers, profoundly strengthened their ideas and political resolve. This enriched modern Indonesian art and literature with a passion and social and historical consciousness that came to define it worldwide.

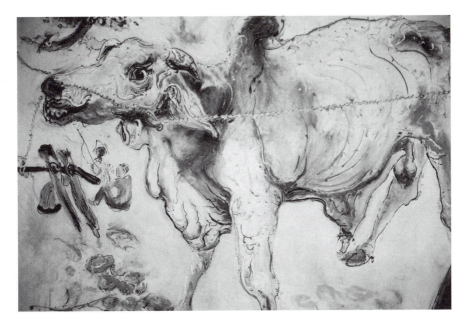

A village scene attributed to Javanese artist Kartika Affandi. Courtesy of Jill Forshee.

In the 1950s, Hendra moved to Yogyakarta, Java, where he joined a newly formed group, Young painters of Indonesia, headed by Soedjojono (the early leader in advocating modern art true to Indonesian realities). Later he joined painters Affandi and others in the group People's Painters and with his wife set up a sort of ashram where artists could stay, and even enabled some to study for free. This drew many painters to the city. Yogyakarta also had created an institution called ASRI, The Yogyakarta Academy of Art. Because of this school and the many artists living in Yogyakarta, there developed a lively arts community in a section of the city near ASRI and the home of Hendra, hosting creative people and events.[20] Affandi's daughter, Kartika, eventually gained acclaim as a contemporary painter with deep Javanese sensibilities.

By the mid-1980s, artistic communities and schools were thriving in Jakarta, Bandung, Bali, and Yogyakarta. The creative neighborhood in Yogyakarta had taken on an international bohemian atmosphere where numerous artists lived humbly and worked, exhibiting their pieces at various places. By the late 1980s, the art scene was increasingly centered upon a small, sophisticated venue called the Cemeti Gallery. Here many young artists had their first showings and some went on to national and international acclaim. Founded and run by artists Mella Jaarsma and Nindityo Adipurnomo, the gallery drew talented people from everywhere. Some stayed on to enjoy the pleasant village-like community and learn from local artists. Painters began experimenting with traditional Javanese arts, such as *batik* cloth, and this ancient form gained in its contemporary expression.

By the late twentieth century, some successful Indonesian artists of Bali and Java had developed a view of their own urban modernism to the extent that they began traveling to remote regions of the archipelago, generally deemed as "primitive" ("*primitif*"), to visit simpler societies. They sought artistic inspiration from less cosmopolitan people and more "authentic" designs of outer island cultures, especially followers of animism. For most Indonesians the term "primitive" does not evoke romantic notions of a "noble savage," close-to-nature spirituality, or exotic handcrafts as it tends to in the West. Rather, middle-class Indonesians largely regard *primitif* peoples as uncivilized, unsanitary, and even as godless heathens.

The artists seeking out such peoples and their arts were among the first relatively elite Indonesians (aside from native anthropologists) to acknowledge outer island cultural validity—even if they were copying and eventually profiting from arts largely unrecognized by central Indonesians and the national government. By the 1990s, artists in Java and Bali included all sorts of Timor, Sumba, West Irian, Toraja (Sulawesi), Batak (Sumatra), and Maluku imagery in their paintings and sculptures. Perhaps also influenced by foreign interest and patronage, a "primitive art" trend developed among urban artists of Indonesia.

Mass tourism produced the most recent and pervasive effect upon modern Indonesian art, on the heels of world collecting of "ethnic arts." Global fashion culture constructed from motifs of non-Western societies created a Euro-American phenomenon of "ethnic *chic*."[21] This reached its economic peak in the mid-1990s, before the Asian monetary crisis, the resignation of Suharto, and the terrorist bombings in Bali curtailed tourism.

For more than thirty years, Indonesia hosted hoards of international visitors. Bali was a thriving hub for surfers, Hollywood film stars, honeymooners, New Age self-improvement groups, budget travelers, wealthy tourists renting idyllic villas, and seekers of a tropical paradise. Bali became the entrepôt for the arts of Indonesia, drawing in countless outer island traders and designers and impressing them within its cosmopolitan, multi-cultural environments. Here Indonesians could see the main showcase for arts of the archipelago, along with contemporary world trends in design. And just had other artists for centuries, they began to adapt and alter their creations to both reflect their knowledge of other worlds and to appeal to a global market.[22]

Textiles

Complex in the making and visually splendid, of all of the Indonesian arts, textiles most readily signal social importance and relationship to the supernatural. The types of cloth and weaving techniques in Indonesia are the most diverse and complex of any in the world and go back for well over a millennium. A ninth century bas-relief carving on Borobudur, Java, shows a woman pulling a yarn from a skein. To this day, hand-woven fabrics are central as status markers, in all rituals, exchange between families, indicators of ethnic identity, appearing stylishly modern, and in needs of everyday life. One anthropologist noted that "history often has a physical, tactile form in Southeast Asia"[23] and this is especially so in Indonesia, where cloth enfolds people and history on numerous levels. Through time, Indonesian textiles have transformed consistently in their designs and uses, responding to many influences—most recently world fashion trends. As a social, economic, and aesthetic medium—an art—cloth is also a channel for passions that underlie people's endeavors. Cloth excites elusive realms of the imagination, playing upon memory while inviting new designs. In current times, designs in fabrics reveal profound shifts in the perspectives of those who create them.[24]

Textiles immediately communicate their value through materials they contain and in the amount of time and expertise involved in their creation. This generally holds true for most Indonesian visual arts—the more detailed and time-consuming, the better. Fine fabrics long were prized regalia for royals and continue to distinguish those able to own them. Limitations on space make description of all textile types impossible here. Chapter 5 provides more discussion of fabrics.

Two major customary fabrics are *ikat* (from the Indonesian word *mengikat,* meaning to tie or bind) and *batik* (perhaps originally from the Indonesian word *betik,* meaning to come into appearance or come to light). These are both "resist-dye" methods, in which patterned sections of fabrics are finely drawn or stamped with wax (for *batik*) to resist dye, or pre-woven yarns are tightly bound in patterns with palm fibers (for *ikat*) so that they will not absorb colors when immersed into dye baths. *Ikat* roughly compares to the "tie-dye" method popular in creating T-shirt patterns in the United States and elsewhere. When the wax or palm fibers are removed, a specific pattern appears, in contrast to the dyed areas of the piece left unbound.

Ikat cloths receive their colors and patterns before the cloth is actually woven. This technique is common to Bali, eastern Indonesia, Sulawesi, and the Kalimantan and Borneo interior. Such fabrics range from delicately patterned pieces from Flores to the vividly pictorial cloths from Sumba. In these regions, people carefully bind sections of the warp threads in distinct patterns. Even before a warp is dipped into the first dye bath, the bound sections sharply delineate the images that eventually will decorate the final woven cloth.

Dyes are important for quality, status, and symbolic value. The major dyes used in *ikat* are a muted blue from the indigo plant and a rust red (*Morinda citrifolia*) scraped from the inner bark of the roots of an indigenous tree. One dye might be applied over another to create wine colors or near blacks. Mud, safflower, a shrub called *Cudrania,* and other plant dyes also come into use. In most places, indigo carries a magical and dangerous quality and often only older women use it. The morinda red in some regions, such as Sumba, is only meant for nobility. Numerous immersions in this red dye produce an intense color. The same applies to indigo, which might require ten to fifteen immersions into the dye pot to achieve a rich, deep blue or a near black. The richer the color, the more valued the cloth.

An *ikat* warp is bound and dyed, then unbound, bound again in other sections and re-dyed until all of the colors and patterns desired appear. This process is extremely time-consuming and in some places, such as Sumba, people tell of particularly complex *ikat* cloths that were 10 years in the making. These fabrics prominently assert prestige, for their creators and eventual wearers. In most regions they clearly mark the social level of the people they clothe. Sumba's intensely pictorial *ikat* cloths reflect skill, imagination, local animist and borrowed foreign motifs, and the dualistic nature of the

One half of a man's *ikat* textile (a *hinggi*) from East Sumba with local motifs of crayfish, crocodiles, roosters, peacocks, birds, and heraldic lions (borrowed from the Dutch) on the borders. The other side of this hanging piece is identical. 1998. Courtesy of Jill Forshee.

island's belief system in its more traditional pieces. These fabrics contain motifs reflecting each other side-to-side and end-to-end (something like a Rorschach print). One scholar concluded that the large cloths worn by men in Sumba (*hinggi*) actually formed a picture of social organization of the region—mirroring villages with houses on either side of a central yard where priests and leaders mediated between two sides.[25]

A good *ikat* features clear, tightly rendered motifs, with little or no bleeding of one dyed area into another. As in other arts of Indonesia, the more complex the design and color variation, the better and often *ikat* pieces are incorporated with other sorts of weaving into one spectacular cloth. Although *ikat* is produced in other parts of the world, such as Guatemala, nowhere does it reach the level of clarity and intricacy of motifs as in Indonesia. *Ikats* from the island of Savu are especially fine, with tightly rendered floral motifs symbolizing clans.

In the 1980s and 1990s, *ikat* was wildly popular with tourists and international collectors. Many outer island people took their *ikats* to Bali to reach tourist markets. In Bali, where people have been extremely innovative for centuries—and very adept at copying—entrepreneurs fashioned outer island cloth into stylish clothing to appeal to foreigners. People from Sumba, Timor, Flores, Savu, and other islands began to design new kinds of ikats to appeal to foreigners. This took place most dramatically in Sumba, famous for its bold, pictorial motifs and history of borrowing from outsiders. In the mid 1990s, one man in Sumba created a "world leaders' series of *ikats* in which he featured then-president Bill Clinton. In the 1980s, another inventive Sumbanese began designing narrative cloths, which told a story from top to bottom, as opposed to the bi-facial format people had historically followed. These fabrics became immensely popular with tourists and eventually entered customary realms in Sumba, such as in bridal exchange and funerals. The man to invent such "story cloths" was also of the first generation generally to become literate in Sumba during the 1960s and 1970s. Reading affected his way of thinking about and designing actual events in real space and time, with distinct beginnings and endings.

One textile scholar considers that "*[b]atik* has become synonymous with Indonesia, the island of Java in particular. It is closely entwined with the other great art forms of Java, the *wayang kulit* shadow plays and the *gamelan orchestras.*" She continues, "Not only did the Javanese *dalang*... preside over the most important of the performing arts, he was also an important source of *batik* patterns. When creating his puppets, he made perforated patterns of what they would wear. These were later sold in the market to eager women."[26]

Batik involves two different methods and produces two distinct types of cloth. The most prized technique employs a tubular *canting* with a tapered copper end (similar in design to an old-fashioned fountain pen) and is called

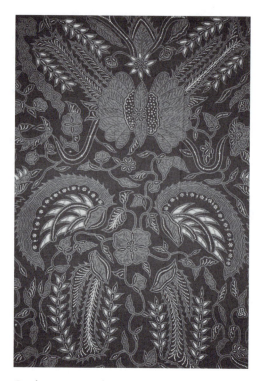

Batik cap pattern from central Java, decorating a long cloth wrapped around the lower body called a *kain.* Courtesy of Jill Forshee.

batik tulis (hand-inscribed *batik*). The *canting* holds hot wax in its hollow tube and the *batik* artist meticulously applies this to cloth to create a design. This method requires painstaking skill not easily mastered (the runny wax is extremely hard to control), yet artists have produced complex, elegant fabrics using this method. *Cap* (stamp) describes the more common *batik* method, whereby a hand-held copper stamp applies the hot wax to the cloth. *Cap* cloth involves a repeated stamping of any number of patterns, requires skill, and can be quite elegant in its own right.

Batik also has become a respected form of painting, and artists in Java and Bali mainly carry this out. A Javanese artist, Mohamed Hadi, became internationally renowned for his elegant *batik* designs, as did a number of artists from workshops in the Yogyakarta-Solo region of central Java. Today *batik* artists produce exquisite pieces on silk or the finest of cotton. In Bali and Java, *batik* paintings of temple rituals, pedicab drivers, and cockfights have become a popular tourist art, though usually lacking the aesthetic fineness and skill of the more developed artists.

Batik carries on as the finest of arts in Indonesia, as does *ikat*. Although greatly boosted by foreign interest, these textiles continue to bear great significance for people throughout Indonesia—for which cloth serves the mundane aspects of life as well as the prestigious and the sacred. Importantly, *batik* creates awe and respect worldwide, as people come to appreciate the tremendous extent of its artistry.

LITERATURE

Early Indonesian Writing

Written script began to appear in the Indonesian archipelago in the fourth century A.D., following cultural and religious influences from India. Pallawa, a script from southern India, spread through the courts of the islands. By the eighth century, this eventually transformed into an "Indonesianized" script called Kawi (although Austronesian in syntax, 30 percent of its lexicon derived from Sanskrit, according to a scholar of Balinese culture and history[27]) used in Java, Sumatra, and Bali. By the fourteenth century, Kawi (meaning "poetic") had become diversified throughout Java, Sumatra, Bali, Madura, and Sumbawa.[28] By the sixteenth century, four distinct families of scripts had evolved to the extent of replacing Kawi: Batak, South Sumatran, Javanese Balinese, and Bugis-Makasar.[29] While these writing systems all bore early Indic influences, they developed distinctly different characteristics to the point of becoming independent regional scripts. Their evolution took place through local ideas, needs, and influences that remain largely unknown. Not much exists of early Indonesian scripts, as they were better suited to palm leaf and paper than to stone carving and have not survived the effects of a tropical climate and time. It appears, however, that these scripts traveled widely through the islands by way of alliances and trade.

In 1930, the Dutch discovered (through a census) the highest literacy rate in the archipelago to be in the Lampung region of southern Sumatra. Despite no formal schooling, nearly half of the population could write and read in the old South Sumatran *ka-ga-nga* alphabet, passed down in the home through generations. The term for this script, *ka-ga-nga,* derives from the first three letters in its alphabet. Young people used such writing to compose flirtatious love notes to each other in the form of four-lined poems called *pantuns*.[30] *Ka-ga-nga* script also spread to Bali, South Sulawesi, and Sumbawa, where people used it in genealogies, histories, literature, and books of divination.[31]

The poetic language of *Kawi* (from old Javanese) long expressed high forms of speech and writing in Bali and Java (and still continues in some settings). Before the spread of Islam, people enjoyed a *Kakawin* (old Javanese romantic poetry) literature—popular for love letters and poems and written on pandanus petals or strips of wood. This held special value in the royal courts, where composing love poems was essential.[32] This script became lavish in its design elegance and used decoratively with visual arts. *Kawi* survives and holds an important function in literary and dramatic forms (often used in *wayang* puppet performances), as well as for religious speech in Bali.

Apart from courtly cultures, poetry developed into a kind of contest in Indonesia (as in much of Southeast Asia), whether written or spoken. The *pantun* poem became central in courtship in Sumatra, Java, and Bali. Islam eventually suppressed such writing, but the popular poetic form persisted in spoken words. However, "Islam took with it to Southeast Asia a very different sexual morality which regarded it as not only unnecessary but also dangerous for women to be able to write."[33] Thus, in much of the Indonesia archipelago:

Prior to the sixteenth century expansion of Islam and Christianity, writing was being adopted by largely animist cultures where women were more commercially and socially active than in other parts of the world. Women took up writing as actively as men, to use in exchanging notes and recording debts and other commercial matters which were in the female domain. The transmission of literacy was therefore a domestic matter, largely the responsibility of mothers and older siblings, and had nothing to do with an exclusive priestly class.[34]

It appears that levels of literacy in sixteenth century Indonesia rivaled any in the world for women and that levels were high by any international standards of the times.[35] Yet the arrival of Islam changed this to a great extent. Islamic practice also specified that its texts be written in Arabic script, which was not well suited to writing Austronesian languages. Thus, various, distinct versions of Arabic script developed in regions of the archipelago. Moreover, the curves and dots of the Arabic writing were difficult to reproduce on palm leaves, so a demand for paper grew. As paper is more durable than leaves, many more texts have survived from the Islamic period than from earlier eras.[36]

Stories called *hikayat* were chronicles in the Malay language written in Arabic script, a type of language called *Jawi*. The *Sejarah Melayu* (*History of the Malay World*) written in 1612, tells of various sultanates and their connections with the Srivijaya and Majapahit empires. *Hikayat*s recorded local tales of sultans across Indonesia along with spoken folklore. A cultural network of such Islamic literature developed based in texts and formal letters, stretching from Aceh in northern Sumatra to Ternate in the eastern Maluku Islands.

Babad tales were a form of literature written in Old Javanese and sung aloud. These were largely chronicles about Muslim saints or kings and their relations to the divine, but this form was also popular in Bali Hindu culture and performed as dance. *Babad*s legitimized religious personages or ruling lineages. Like *hikayat* writing, *Babad* stories recorded political history. These often-romantic adventure stories carried subtle, multiple meanings in manners characteristic of Javanese arts and literature.

Indian epics from Sanskrit, such as the *Ramayana* and the *Mahabharata* entered into the oldest Javanese poetic style (as did popular Javanese stories), which people then considered to be about actual characters and events from the distant past. Indonesians, particularly the Balinese and Javanese, made the Indian stories their own, even placing them in local geographical settings. These tales form a basic theme of the *wayang* shadow play, dance dramas, popular stories, and continue into contemporary comic books, films, and television programs.

The *Mahabharata* (*Mahabarata* in Indonesian spelling) tells of the five Pandawa brothers in tragic and ongoing warfare with parties of the Kaurava family—forming a classic theme of good against evil. The Pandawas align with and receive help from the gods; the Kauravas are in league with evil giants. The five brothers and many diverse characters of this lengthy epic (90,000 verses in Sanskrit) became basic Southeast Asian archetypes of heroicism, vanity, nobility, loyalty, bravery, folly, lust, aggression, duplicity, and other human attributes. As does the *Ramayana,* the *Mahabarata* (Ind.) carries on moral ideals and models of right and wrong behavior for men and women, while permitting complexity.

The *Ramayana* also has been immensely influential and popular throughout Southeast Asia and especially in Indonesia. Made up of 2,774 verses when translated into ancient Javanese from Sanskrit (around the tenth century), this epic centers upon king Rama and his wife Sita, her abduction by the evil Ravana, her eventual rescue by the loyal and courageous monkey king Hanuman, and Sita's wrenching dilemma of proving her fidelity to Rama. From here the tale goes on, as the couple retain their royal position for centuries. Like the *Mahabarata,* this epic evokes the moral precepts listed above, but especially concerns itself with loyalty, most poignantly in Sita's devotion to Rama against all odds.

The tales of the Prince Panji began in Java in the fourteenth century, in settings preceding the Majapahit Empire. The hero of these stories is a prince, who takes on the name of Panji. He travels unrecognized as a royal throughout his adventures, and he eventually proves his valor. While set in Java and reflecting its culture, Panji tales also became popular in Bali (becoming dance dramas). A basic theme of these tales involved the hero appearing unknown at the scene of a battle, conquering women, winning in war, and enjoying thousands of followers—classically important indicators of potency in Indonesia.[37]

Modern Indonesian Writing

In an examination of nationalism, an historian surmised: "Communities are to be distinguished, not by their falsity/genuineness, but by the style in which they are imagined."[38] Following literacy spread by the Dutch, rapidly growing numbers of Indonesians began to think about themselves in relation to unknown, distant others in profoundly new ways. Print-capitalism broadened thinking, that is, newspapers, books, and magazines allowed people to see pictures and read in a common language (either Dutch or Malay) and then imagine themselves as part of a greater community, a nation. Following this, more people enjoyed access to a shared medium of expression—writing in the European Roman script.

Literacy alters the ways that people conceive of time and events and how they imagine themselves and the world. Reading permits pause for mental reflection that listening to a spoken tale might not. Moreover, beginnings and endings become distinct in written form, as events in linear sequence that chronicle the passing of time. Some have noticed that in nonliterate societies, visual and aural memories are extraordinarily acute, because people fully engage their senses for "recording" events and images. Mental retention of sights and sounds creates narratives in such cultures, where people critically rely upon memorization in the passing on of knowledge.

Most places in Indonesia maintain a rich tradition of stories of the past, often spoken in specialized ritual speech filled with symbolic imagery. In their various local languages, people also carry on tales of encounters with foreigners, local battles, witchcraft, tricksters, and catastrophic events. In the past, such speech was indiscernible to outsiders due to language differences and people's inability (or unwillingness) to translate their oral traditions into Indonesian, Dutch, English, or other languages. In more recent times, however, anthropologists and Malay/Indonesian authors have written translations and interpretations of some of these spoken forms. Still, a great many stories and ritual speech modes remain unknown to outsiders. Through literacy, nonetheless, Indonesians have been able to record a number of their own oral traditions.

Modern Indonesian literature began to appear by the 1920s, largely by authors connected to the Dutch managed and highly popular publishing house *Balai Pustaka* ("Bureau of Literature"). The Indonesian literary journal *Pudjangga Baru* ("New Poet") began in the 1930s. Many scholars since have remarked upon the disproportionate number of Sumatran writers represented in the new publications, especially those from the Minangkabau region where the language was closely related to Malay (later to become the Indonesian national language). Because of this, it proved difficult for writers from Java and elsewhere to do creative work in the upcoming national language. Although Malay was the parlance of trade and public organizations (aside from Dutch), very few schools taught it and most people of the archipelago actually did not think in this language.[39] Consequently, early works available in Malay/Indonesian include a predominance of Sumatrans and reflect cultures and values of their places and times.

Some Sumatran authors transformed oral autobiographies and traditional male travel adventures. called *rantau* ("traveling abroad" to gain prestige, wealth, and manhood), into published works in the first half of the twentieth century.[40] These writers published through *Bulai Pustaka* (described above) "an organ for publishing high-quality works of fiction and folklore in refined, grammatically elegant Indonesian," which by the 1920s had become a "major venue for popular literature, particularly 'journey novels' turning on love story themes." Moreover, "[t]he house published works that directly engaged issues of Indies modernity"[41] and thus gave voice to the conflicts and confusion Indonesians were experiencing between modern European and locally traditional values and life choices. Important literature of this time included the works (titles translated into English here) *Me and Toba: Notes from Childhood Times,* by P. Pospos; *Village Childhood,* by Muhamad Radjab; *Sitti Nurbaya* (a girl's name), by Marah Rusli; and *Childhood Experiences,* by Nur Sutan Iskander.[42] *Sitti Nurbaya* told of a young woman forced to wed an evil old man to whom her father owed money. Officially acclaimed as Indonesia's first novel of substance, for decades this book has been compulsory reading for junior high school students.

Before national independence, however, numerous Indonesian elites had received Dutch educations. Now famous among these students was Raden Adjeng Kartini. As a young woman of the Javanese *Priyayi* class, Kartini wrote a series of letters (largely to a friend in the Netherlands) describing her life in colonial Java and expressing a passionate desire to study in Holland and learn more of the world. This became a book years after Kartini's death, *Letters of a Javanese Princess* (first published in English in 1920) and is now classic reading about the life and times of an intelligent, philosophical, and extraordinarily articulate young woman during the Dutch period. Kartini ardently writes of her personal conflicts between Javanese and European values.

Her progressive ideas caused distress within her parental home. Such controversial notions challenged the very definition of propriety and purpose
for women. The final writings of Kartini, who died young after childbirth,
express a resolved re-commitment to Javanese values, especially motherhood
and obedience to family as the central purpose of women. This shift surprises
many Western readers of the book, who expect Kartini to pursue her literary
dreams. They cannot imagine the cultural and moral weight that family expectations and duties had upon the most intellectual of Javanese women.

After national independence, *Balai Pustaka*—begun by the Dutch for
Indonesian elites—became the publishing house of the new Republic of
Indonesia.[43] Growing tensions between the politics of the right and the left
of the new nation hampered the press, however, in soliciting new manu-
scripts of a consistently high standard. After President Suharto took control
of the government in the mid-1960s, the publishing house declined following a total ban on books with leftist themes. The new state publishing house
of the state became *Gramedia,* an adjunct to the *Kompas* daily newspaper.

As recently noted: "For Indonesia's largest commercial publisher the best
investment and fastest-selling products seem to be self-improvement and
business management guides, cookbooks, and translations of foreign popular romance and mystery novel."[44] These included "airport" books by Agatha
Christie, Danielle Steele, Jackie Collins, Sidney Shelton, and the like.[45] Small
publishers, however, became much more important and influential under
the New Order, often defying national policies. Suharto's strict government
censorship upon films and television did not similarly affect book publishing, which the New Order seemed to ignore to some extent. Suharto was
no intellectual and perhaps thought that too few Indonesians read or could
afford books to be of much consequence. Still, the government established
"authorized reading." Yet, despite the controls of its most repressive regime,
the Suharto era was one of Indonesia's greatest literary periods. Some remark
upon this irony:

Ironically, in the final decade of the New Order some of the most acclaimed "high
literature" (such as the works by Pramoedya) [were] also simultaneously *bacaan liar*
[wild writing], in the sense that they remained outside the mainstream publishing industry and transgressed the state's regulation of content and circulation of books.[46]

Pramoedya Ananta Toer remains Indonesia's most acclaimed writer, both
in his own country and internationally. His stories encompass Japan's wartime occupation, the Indonesian national revolution, his years of imprisonment under the colonial Dutch, and then by both the Sukarno and Suharto
regimes. Eventually, with a lessening of political oppression in the late 1990s,
Pramoedya published his most damning book of the Suharto period, while

celebrating intellectual freedom and the human spirit: *The Mute's Soliloquy.* The book echoes ancient Indonesian epic themes of courage, morality, loyalty to one's allies and cause, and unflagging resilience.

As the subject of university courses the world over, Toer holds the reputation as one of the finest and most historically and socially insightful writers that Indonesia has ever produced. During the mass political upheaval across Indonesia in 1965 following the overthrow of Sukarno, Pramoedya (and thousands of others accused of Communism or political dissidence against Suharto's New Order regime) was held for years without charges. Eventually exiled to the remote island prison of Buru in eastern Indonesia, Toer survived whereas many perished of starvation, physical abuses, and diseases.

Yet, during his 11 years on Buru Island, Pramoedya produced major works, including the four novels of the *Buru Quartet*—essential reading for anyone studying Indonesian literature or modern political history. This epic consists of the volumes *This Earth of Mankind, Child of All Nations, Footsteps,* and *House of Glass.* Toer's quartet progressively traces the emergence of Indonesian nationalism, while depicting realities of local life, identities, and thought during the first half of the twentieth century as affected by those in power.

Although government forces confiscated and destroyed much of his work during his internment, *The Mute's Soliloquy,* published in 1999, survived. It describes the Buru penal colony and Pramoedya's memories of his earlier life.[47] While published in 23 countries, Toer's work remained banned in Indonesia. Yet, this prolonged government censorship greatly embellished Pramoedya's celebrity and heroic status among many, who admired his dedication to social justice during the repressive New Order years. Toer became an international literary and revolutionary legend, to the extent that "Pramoedya is the only Indonesian writer to have had the majority of his fictional works published in translation by large international commercial publishers. Around the world his unjust treatment by the Suharto government stimulated interest and sympathy."[48] On April 30, 2006, Pramoedya Ananta Toer died in Jakarta at the age of 81.

Also illustrious and internationally recognized, Umar Kayam is a different sort of literary figure. As a versatile professional writer, Kayam worked as a government official, actor, art and literary critic, columnist, well-known intellectual, and novelist. Widely rumored as engaging in behind-the-scenes politicking against what became the totalitarian rule of Sukarno, Kayam eventually received from President Suharto the position of Director General of Television, Radio, and Film. While part of the New Order propaganda circuit, Kayam permitted private radio stations and advertising in the media to lessen their dependence on state financing. He supported international exchange of scholars and ideas—facilitating a flow of information that likely raised hackles among New Order leaders. Later, the Suharto government let him go. Kayam did not become a controversial political critic, however, but enjoyed elite, urban Indonesian cultural life (with a reputation of a *bon vivant*, delighting in parties and good food). Wielding a peculiar intelligence, he wrote stories in a literary style rich in multiple meanings. Well known for his novelettes *Sri Sumarah* (Princess Sumarah) and *Bawuk* (a woman's name), Kayam remained associated with the Javanese *priyayi* class and values, which he attempted to explain to readers through his tales.

President Sukarno jailed Mochtar Lubis, editor, journalist, poet, and novelist for 10 years following his stance against corruption and insistence upon a free press. Lubis headed a daily newspaper, *Indonesia Raya,* closed repeatedly for subversive writing. Eventually, Suharto closed it for good. Yet courageously defending freedom of the press, Lubis distinguished himself throughout Asia. His best-known works are collections of short stories, *Twilight in Jakarta* and *The Outlaw and Other Stories,* both published by Oxford University Press. In 1990, he published a history of Indonesia entitled, *Indonesia: Land under the Rainbow.* In the Preface, Lubis wrote of the challenges of writing this book as an Indonesian: "and not be overwhelmed by the historical material written by so many Dutch and other European scholars"[49] with their foreign values and stereotyping of Indonesian groups. Lubis approached this book through what he called an "Indonesian optic." Near the end of the volume, the author urges Indonesians to abandon their ancient conceptions of kingship and power. He asserts that in Indonesia's modern society, leaders should all the more receive their power from the people and not the gods. Thus, he poses a challenge to not only classical Indonesian ways of thinking, but "to all humankind."[50]

The Weaverbirds, first published in 1981, is Y. B. Mangunwijaya's epic account of personal struggles from the time of Indonesian independence through an oil crisis of the mid-1970s. It traces the lives of childhood friends who grow up to be on opposing political sides. The book ambiguously casts characters as neither "good" nor "bad"—allowing for a wide range of human motives and interpretations in times of conflict.[51]

Saraswati Sunindyo is a contemporary and outspoken critic of Indonesian sexist roles for women (narrowly generic under Suharto) as primarily wives, mothers, and supporters of the state. Ambiguity aside, Sunindyo addresses the heavy-handed social and political control of women's sexuality, accenting the general practice of defining women as "good" or "bad." In the poem, "City Garbage from the Nongo River,"[52] Sunindyo painfully describes the nightmarish plight of an urban woman who dares to stay alone in a government hotel in a poor Javanese village. The woman is subsequently assaulted by a local official she refers to as "Mr. Rambo," alluding to the macho hero of the Sylvester Stallone films (long popular in Indonesia, where Rambo was lauded as anti-communist in his violent cinematic battles in Vietnam). The aggressive official feels justified in attacking the woman, and the poem follows his rationale. A woman staying alone—particularly a city woman suspected of holding a college degree—is an abnormality, and thus invites deserved sexual abuse. The poem contains powerful imagery of a modern, confused, debased Indonesia: motorbikes roar all night, men force themselves upon women they do not know, and rivers stink with garbage. In such a place, not only has environmental and social balance gone awry, but so has human decency.

Yet, despite official and social pressures upon their conduct and life choices, a number of novels and short stories have compassionately addressed the unfortunate plight of women in Indonesia, most of them written by men. Often these tell of forced or abusive marriages, declines into poverty, cruelly treated servants, wayward husbands, and other sorrows. The widely read novel *Sitti Nurbaya* (written by Marah Rusli and published in 1922) may have set the tone for such tales, but desperate circumstances of many living in wretched poverty without family support have inspired poignant stories from many Indonesian writers.

So far, Javanese writers have dominated this section, but those of other islands have entered the mainstream of modern literature as well. Not all write directly of corruption and violence, but authors like Gerson Poyk, from the small island of Roti in eastern Indonesia, use satire to animate stories and provide messages. Poyk wrote the first published Indonesian story about West Papua (or Irian Jaya to Indonesians) in 1972. "Matias Akankari" follows a man from West Papua who finds himself in an Indonesian metropolitan location and his confused impressions and hapless reactions to his inexplicable experiences. While some viewed this tale as ridiculing the "primitive" Papuans, others regarded "Matias Akankari" as a mockery of incessant Indonesian government folly in trying to "civilize" (i.e., "Javanize") peoples from remote islands in culturally inappropriate ways. This includes societies that never had a say in becoming part of the Indonesian nation, with some even opposing it. Poyk's story tells, with humor, of the vast cultural and perceptual differences of those from Indonesia's peripheries compared to its centers, which the powers in Jakarta refused to fully grasp or leave well enough alone.

The writers discussed so far all have represented literature with a capital "L," termed *sastra* in Indonesian and read by university students and those with a sophisticated degree of literary appreciation. All in all, many have expressed values and provided social exposés that fly in the face of propaganda and policies of those in power. In doing so they have earned a reputation for courageous integrity—using political savvy and symbolic dexterity in their writing.

Popular Literary Culture

Books read by the greater part of Indonesia's population fall under categories of *fiksi* (fiction) or *roman* (referring to romantic pulp novels). Many young women read these formulaic, simple stories, depicting romances between young men and women. There may be handholding, but stories are not sexual. Plots typically center upon distress among couples involving jealousy over a rival or disapproval of their parents.

Remaja (adolescent) is a type of fiction published for teenagers. Among this genre was the popular *Lupus* series, created by Hilman Hariwijaya. *Lupus* books began circulating in 1986, starring a young, mildly rebellious teenager (by Western standards) embodying all symbols of Indonesian youthful "cool" to his readers. Much was based in Jakartan popular culture, with its own distinctive "dialect," peppered with largely American English words and Western consumer brand names, such as Adidas, Pizza Hut, and Walkman. Characters in the *Lupus* series obviously had money and were thus admired and emulated by their young readers.

Along with prestigious brand names flaunted in Lupus, young "hip" Jakartans use terms like, "okay-*lah*," and "That's right-*lah*" ("lah" is a particle of emphasis in Indonesian, used at the end of a word), thus mixing languages to claim their own unique speech style. Indeed, style is at the very heart of popular culture, the latest the better. Some characters in the Lupus books sported blond-streaked hair and familiarity with American fast food chains, like McDonald's. This marked them as well off compared to most Indonesians. These franchises also confer upon their customers the highest prestige marker of popular culture—that of being "modern."

Comic books have fascinated Indonesians for years, with a number of indigenous artists and writers. Newspapers translated foreign comics, such as the French *Asterix* and the American *Charley Brown*. However, through the 1980s and 1990s, Japanese comic books (translated into Indonesian) grew wildly popular, making up about 90 percent of imported comics.[53]

Levels of violence in Japanese comic books appealed to Indonesian youths, accustomed to seeing gory battles and beheadings in their own media. However, the overt sexual imagery of these comics did not sit well with the New Order. Often sections of the books were deleted or blacked out with permanent markers. Today, these comics continue to be sold in Indonesia. Other popular comics feature classical American characters like Donald Duck, Superman, or Archie and Veronica. Indonesian youth notably prize foreign characters and products.

The Indonesian news magazine, *Tempo,* began in 1971, was modeled on *Time* magazine's format and style, and became a national institution. Popular among the middle class, *Tempo* contained witty satire, irreverent cartoons, and lively and hard-hitting investigative reporting on current issues. Banned twice under the Suharto regime for reporting on corruption, political demonstrations, and topics the New Order did not want its citizens to read about, *Tempo* reopened after Suharto resigned. In 2003, however, it faced destruction by thugs working for a wealthy tycoon after the magazine had published an article concerning his corruption. The editor of *Tempo* went to jail for defamation of the businessman. Thousands of Indonesians were outraged, many recalling the darkest days of the Suharto era. An International Federation of journalists wrote letters of protest to President Megawati. *Tempo* now continues under founder and senior editor Goenawan Mohamed, winner of numerous international awards for promoting freedom of expression.[54]

Numerous magazines about business, technology, or fashion circulate in Indonesia. In most urban centers, publications from around the world such as *Elle, Cosmopolitan, The Far Eastern Economic Review,* and *Newsweek* appear at newsstands and bookstores. The popular *Femina* women's magazine largely produces well-designed ads for fashions and cosmetics with articles on beauty and attracting a husband. Yet, it also features stories and interviews regarding successful career women, many of them unmarried.

In 2001, a colorfully *chic* magazine entitled *Latitudes... views from 6° above to 11° below the equator* began publication from Bali, quickly attracting attention. The editors and writers were a mixture of Westerners and Indonesians. With its polished, contemporary look, the magazine featured a range of topics: reports on Jakarta's scavenger community, lesbians on Bali, fiction about Jakarta mall culture by young writers such as Ayu Utami, an essay by journalist Ariel Heryanto regarding a crisis of mood in post-Suharto Indonesia, and a feature report of a West Papuan woman (Yosepha Alomang) fighting for human rights and the environment. Many excellent photos accompanied the stories. While published in English, some articles provided Indonesian translations. Many of the expatriate community in Indonesia (of which there are thousands) subscribed to *Latitudes,* as did Indonesians and foreigners. Contemporary writers such as Agus Noor, Korrie Layun Rampan, and Dewi Lestari set their stories in modern Indonesian environments and experimented with styles of prose. *Latitudes* grew popular through its *panache,* with articles and photo essays (of a never-before-seen quality and breadth) of Indonesian life—from the popularity of instant noodles to horse racing on the island of Sumbawa.

The Internet is a revolutionary literary medium not yet mentioned. Not only has this "information highway" allowed Indonesians to preview and buy books from companies like *Gramedia,* but it also permitted unlimited access to knowledge, foreign literature, and political ideas (along with the global circulation of pornography) formerly unimaginable in Indonesia. The Internet has heralded dire conditions within Indonesia to the rest of the world, such as Suharto's imminent demise and reports from rebel groups fighting Indonesian control in Banda Aceh, Sumatra; West Irian (Irian Jaya); and the now nationally independent East Timor. Through cyberspace, Indonesians began to enjoy for the first time an utter lack of censorship and a dazzling access to massive information.

Following the independence of East Timor, one scholar summarized that "the internet provided a unique opportunity for East Timor to claim 'independence in cyberspace' as part of a spectrum of internet-related activist struggles, sometimes dubbed 'hactivism.'"[55] This uniquely liberated space permitted any type of expression. The Internet now stimulates rapid changes in Indonesia, affecting politics and economics, while offering a new avenue for art and literature. It remains to be seen how Indonesians transform their expressions to adapt to this, as they practice their creativity in an unforeseen dimension.

NOTES

1. Philip Rawson, *The Art of Southeast Asia* (London: Thames and Hudson, 1967), 203.

2. Rawson, *The Art of Southeast Asia,* 203.

3. Rawson, *The Art of Southeast Asia,* 206, paraphrased here.

4. See Alit Djajasoebrata, *Shadow Theatre in Java: The Puppets, Performance and Repertoire* (Amsterdam: The Pepin Press, 1999), 41.

5. See *Latitudes Magazine* (published in Denpasar, Bali) August, 2004.

6. Adrian Vickers, *Bali: A Paradise Created* (Berkeley: Periplus Editions, 1989), 39.

7. See Anne Richter, *Arts and Crafts of Indonesia* (San Francisco: Chronicle Books, 1994), 129. See also Michael Heppel, *Masks of Kalimantan* (Melbourne: Exhibition Catalogue, 1992).

8. See Hildred Geertz, *Images of Power: Balinese Paintings Made for Gregory Bateson and Margaret Mead* (Honolulu: University of Hawaii Press, 1995), 6.

9. For a most readable translation of the *Ramayana* into English, see William Buck, *Ramayana* (Berkeley: University of California Press, 2000). See also William Buck, *Mahabharata* (Berkeley: University of California Press, 2000).

10. See Geertz, *Images of Power,* 1995, 6.

11. See Idana Pucci, *Bhima Swarga: The Balinese Journey of the Soul* (Boston: Littlebrown and Company), 16, paraphrased here.

12. Soedarso SP, "Indonesian Artists: Looking for Identity," in *Modern Indonesian Art: Three Generations of Tradition and Change, 1945–1990,* ed. Joseph Fischer (Singapore: Singapore National Printers, Ltd., 1990), 78.

13. Astri Wright, "Painting the People," in *Modern Indonesian Art: Three Generations of Tradition and Change, 1945–1990,* ed. Joseph Fischer (Singapore: Singapore National Printers, Ltd., 1990), 106.

14 Wright, "Painting the People," 106, partially paraphrased here.

15. See Geertz, *Images of Power,* for many illustrations and detailed discussion of paintings of this time.

16. Joseph Fischer, "Introduction," in *Modern Indonesian Art: Three Generations of Tradition and Change 1945–1990,* ed. Joseph Fischer (Jakarta: Panita Pameran KIAS, 1990–91, and Festival of Indonesia, 1990), 10–41, 10.

17. See Soedarso SP, "Indonesian Artists," 81–82.

18. See Wright, "Painting the People," 115.

19. See Wright, "Painting the People," 106–157.

20. See Wright, "Painting the People," 123.

21. See Jill Forshee, *Between the Folds: Stories of Cloth, Lives, and Travels from Sumba* (Honolulu: University of Hawaii Press, 2001), 162–167.

22. See Forshee, *Between the Folds,* 161–180, for a description of outer island traders and artists within the Bali context in the 1990s.

23. Susan Rodgers, ed., *Telling Lives, Telling History: Autobiography and Social Imagination in Modern Indonesia* (Berkeley: University of California Press, 1995), 27.

24. Forshee, *Between the Folds,* 3.

25. See Marie Jeanne Adams, *System and Meaning in East Sumba Textile Design: A Study in Traditional Indonesian Art,* Cultural Report 16 (New Haven: Southeast Asia Studies, Yale University, 1969).

26. Sylvia Fraser-Lu, *Indonesian Batik: Processes, Patterns, and Places* (Singapore: Oxford University Press, 1988), 3–4.

27 Margaret J. Wiener, *Visible and Invisible Realms: Power, Magic, and Colonial Conquest in Bali* (Chicago: University of Chicago Press, 1995), 82.

28. See Robert Cribb, *Historical Atlas of Indonesia* (Honolulu: University of Hawaii Press, 2000), 38.

29. Cribb, *Historical Atlas of Indonesia,* 38.

30. Cribb, *Historical Atlas of Indonesia,* 38.

31. See Anthony Reid, *Southeast Asia in the Age of Commerce—1450–1680: Volume One: The Lands below the Winds* (New Haven: Yale University Press, 1988), 218.

32. Reid, *Southeast Asia in the Age of Commerce,* 219.

33. Reid, *Southeast Asia in the Age of Commerce,* 220.

34. Reid, *Southeast Asia in the Age of Commerce,* 221.

35. Reid, *Southeast Asia in the Age of Commerce,* 221.

36. Cribb, *Historical Atlas of Indonesia,* 39.

37. See Adrian Vickers, *Bali: A Paradise Created* (Berkeley: Periplus Editions, 1989), 53–56.

38. Benedict Anderson, *Imagined Communities: Reflections on the Origin and Spread of Nationalism* (London: Verso, 1991), 6.

39. See David Joel Steinberg, ed., *In Search of Southeast Asia: A Modern History*, rev. ed. (Hawaii: University of Hawaii Press, 1987), 310, paraphrased here.

40. See Susan Rodgers, ed. and translator, *Telling Lives, Telling History: Autobiography and Historical Imagination in Modern Indonesia* (Berkeley: University of California Press, 1995), especially 9–78.

41. Rodgers, *Telling Lives, Telling History*, 9.

42. See Rodgers, *Telling Lives, Telling History*, for more extensive discussion of these writers and their times and translations into English of *Me and Toba*, as well as *Village Childhood*.

43. This paragraph borrows from Krishna Sen and David T. Hill, "Books: Translations and Transgressions," in *Media, Culture and Politics in Indonesia* (Oxford: Oxford University Press, 2000), 21–50.

44. Sen and Hill, "Books," 30.

45. Sen and Hill, "Books," 30, paraphrased

46 Sen and Hill, "Books," 24.

47. See Pramoedya Ananta Toer, *The Mute's Soliloquy: A Memoir* (New York: Hyperion East, 1999).

48. Sen and Hill, "Books," 41.

49. Mochtar Lubis, *Indonesia: Land under the Rainbow* (Singapore: Oxford University Press, 1990), vii.

50. Lubis, *Indonesia*, 210.

51. See Thomas M. Hunter, "Introduction," in Y. B. Mangunwijaya *The Weaverbirds*, Trans. by Thomas M. Hunter (Jakarta: The Lontar Foundation, 1991), xvi.

52. See Sariswati Sunindyo, "City Garbage from the Nyongo River," in *Fantasizing the Feminine in Indonesia*, ed. Laurie J. Sears (Durham: Duke University Press, 1996), xii–xvi.

53. Percentages and other information are from Sen and Hill, "Books," 30.

54. Due to its concise and informative value, the section regarding *Tempo* magazine borrows from and paraphrases an on-line article by Bill Guerin, "Tempo magazine fights for its life—again," Pacific Media Watch, March 14, 2003, *Asia Times Online*, http://www.asiapac.org.fj/cafepacific/resources/aspac/indon3980.html.

55. David T. Hill, "East Timor and the Internet: Global Political Leverage in/on Indonesia," *Indonesia* 73, April 2002, 25–51.

SUGGESTED READING

Art

Adams, Kathleen M. *Art as Politics: Re-Crafting Identities, Tourism, and Power in Tana Toraja, Indonesia*. Honolulu: University of Hawaii Press, 2006.

Causey, Andrew. *Hard Bargaining in Sumatra: Western Travelers and Toba Bataks in the Marketplace of Souvenirs*. Honolulu: University of Hawaii Press, 2003.

Covarrubias, Miguel. *Island of Bali*. New York: Alfred A. Knopf, 1956 [Reprint from 1937].

Djajasoebrata, Alit. *Shadow Theatre in Java: The Puppets, Performance and Repertoire*. Amsterdam: The Pepin Press, 1999.

Fischer, Joseph, ed. *Modern Indonesian Art: Three Generations of Tradition and Change, 1945–1990*. Singapore: Singapore National Printers, Ltd., 1990.

Forshee, Jill. *Between the Folds: Stories of Cloth, Lives and Travels from Sumba*. Honolulu: University of Hawaii Press, 2000.

Geertz, Hildred. *Images of Power: Balinese Paintings Made for Gregory Bateson and Margaret Mead*. Honolulu: University of Hawaii Press, 1994.

Gittinger, Mattiebelle, ed. *To Speak with Cloth: Studies in Indonesian Textiles*. Los Angeles: Museum of Cultural History, University of California, 1998.

Holt, Claire. *Art in Indonesia: Communities and Change*. Ithaca: Cornell University Press, 1967.

Rawson, Philip. *The Art of Southeast Asia*. London: Thames and Hudson, 1967.

Richter, Anne. *Arts and Crafts of Indonesia*. San Francisco: Chronicle Books, 1994.

Soemantri, Hildred. *Visual Art: Indonesian Heritage Series*. Singapore: Archipelago Press, 1999.

Weitzman, David. *Rama and Sita: A Tale from Ancient Java*. Boston: David R. Godine, 2002.

Wright, Astri. *Soul, Spirit, and Mountain: Preoccupations of Contemporary Indonesian Painters*. New York: Oxford University Press, 1994.

Literature

Buck, William. *Ramayana*. Berkeley: University of California Press, 2000.

———. *Mahabharata*. Berkeley: University of California Press, 2000.

Kartini, Raden Adjeng. *Letters of a Javanese Princess*. Lanham: University Press of America, 1985.

Mangunwijaya, Y. B. *The Weaverbirds*. Trans. Thomas M. Hunter. Jakarta: The Lontar Foundation, 1991.

McGlynn, John. *Language and Literature: Indonesian Heritage Series*. Singapore: Archipelago Press, 1999.

Pospos, P. "Me and Toba." In Susan Rodgers, ed. and trans., *Telling Lives, Telling History: Autobiography and Historical Imagination in Modern Indonesia* (pp. 81–148). Berkeley: University of California Press, 1995.

Radjab, Muhamad. "Village Childhood (The Autobiography of a Minangkabau Child)" In Susan Rodgers, ed. and trans., *Telling Lives, Telling History: Autobiography and Historical Imagination in Modern Indonesia* (pp. 149–320). Berkeley: University of California Press, 1995.

Sunindyo, Saraswati. "City Garbage from the Nongo River," In Laurie J. Sears, ed., *Fantasizing the Feminine in Indonesia* (pp. xii–xvi). Durham: Duke University Press, 1996.

Sunindyo, Saraswati. "Murder, Gender, and the Media: Sexualizing Politics and Violence." In Laurie J. Sears, ed., *Fantasizing the Feminine in Indonesia* (pp. 120–139). Durham: Duke University Press, 1996.

Toer, Ananta Pramoedya. *The Buru Quartet*. (4 Volume Series). Trans. by Max Lane. New York: Penguin Books, 1997.

Toer, Ananta Pramoedya. *The Mute's Soliloquy*. Trans. by Willem Samuels. New York: Hyperion East, 1999.

4

Architecture and Housing

This chapter examines architecture and housing across Indonesia, with an emphasis upon "vernacular architecture," meaning homes in which ordinary people live. Indonesians usually regard their homes in fundamentally different ways than do Westerners. Not only do homes provide shelter and protection from elements, but Indonesian dwellings frequently require the reverence given to animate forms. The specifications of their construction, design, accompanying rituals, building materials, divisions, and locations demand careful attention to *adat* (customary law), ancestral protocol, and local beliefs in spirits. People who eventually inhabit homes, moreover, continuously affect the structures' spiritual well being, creating positive or negative environments.

Besides family abodes, across Indonesia people refer to many types of structures as "houses," including those created and used for specific purposes nondomestic in nature. Recently, a Timor anthropologist listed 32 types of buildings falling under the rubric of "house" (*uma* in the local Tetun language of the Wehali people). These included "the sitting place house," "the birth place house," "the amulet house," "mother elder sister younger sister house," "the sea house," and even "the ugly house."[1] The basic Indonesian word for house, *rumah,* applies to many kinds of structures, but *rumah tangga* specifies a family household. *Tangga* means a ladder, which many once used to enter their elevated family homes (and some still do). Most people, however, simply refer to their house as their *rumah.*

In contrast to Western homes, Indonesians often disperse their households into separate structures for specific functions, the relative status of household members or even buildings, or following beliefs in spiritually auspicious or dangerous locations. The many-layered meanings Indonesians bestow upon places called homes profoundly differs from Western notions of private residences.

The latter section of the chapter briefly examines public architecture, including temples, mosques, churches, graves, monuments, and modern urban buildings. Such architecture tends to either draw Indonesians together (most notably in places of worship) or, in instances of urban development, tear communities apart leaving many with nowhere to go. Aside from considering the history, forms, and cultural and religious symbolism of these larger edifices, this section describes their effects upon Indonesian communities.

COMPARING WESTERN NOTIONS OF "HOME" AND PROPERTY TO THOSE OF INDONESIANS

Regarding Western homes, people often assume that for many centuries they have resembled the private, comfortable, clean, and consciously decorated domiciles owned (or desired) by people today. Indeed, homes in the United States now typically reflect the major expenditure of their owners, as they often undergo remodeling, enlargement, or redecoration to continuously improve upon their domestic function, visual appeal, market value, "keeping up with the neighbors," and showcasing prestige. An entire publishing industry of magazines and books promotes the beautification of the home (as do popular television programs), presenting magnificent residences of celebrities as idyllic examples of "the good life." Indeed, owning a fashionably large or even palatial home has become a consumer imperative in middle-class American society, where conspicuous consumption appears more vigorous than ever in this first decade of the twenty-first century.

A family home as a realm of domestic comfort and pride, nonetheless, was not always so. The European evolution toward the private, aesthetically pleasing home, traced historically—began with a specifically Dutch female attitude toward domesticity and comfortable décor apparent in the sixteenth century.[2] In a Dutch book of photographs of the colonial era, one picture illustrates an interior of a colonial home in 1883 in Medan, Sumatra, revealing a cozily appointed dining room with a bordering sitting area. Carpets soften the floors, mirrors and pictures embellish the walls, dining chairs sit backed with lace, an attractive glass lamp hangs over the table, various small tables display plants and pottery, and thick draperies divide rooms. The home appears lived in, thoughtfully furnished, clean, and comfortable.[3] By contrast, photographs of even the most elite Indonesians pictured in the same volume portray them sitting on chairs in rooms with no other décor, on porches, or on mats outdoors.[4]

A basic contrast between most Indonesians and peoples of more industrialized societies regarding homes and their relationship to nature is summed up well:

The more effort is expended on built forms, the more architecture mediates our experience of the world, even as it may continue to mirror the social construction of cosmological ideas. In modern industrial societies, the process has reached such an extreme that buildings maroon us inside gigantic bubbles of artificial climate, within which we pass our whole lives without ever touching ground or knowing where food comes from. Among the animist peoples of the Austronesian world, however, the fragmenting of a holistic worldview appears to be deliberately resisted. In these cosmologies, humans still participate in nature on very much the same terms as everything else....The house, too, vegetal like its surroundings, shares in the life force which animates the universe; like everything else in the environment, it is viewed as a subjective entity with which interaction and communication are possible.[5]

This universal life force underlies the Indonesian concept of *semangat,* meaning "spirit," "zest," or "soul." People, gatherings, places, music, structures, and so forth can all possess *semangat*—a positive force of vitality. Themes such as spirits, status, ancestors, prominent cosmological principles like *semangat,* and the importance of rituals and *adat* customs interconnect most everything in this book. When these principles and customs undergo serious disruption, social life, individuals, and communities often go awry.

Finally, privacy (*pribadi*) was a nonexistent term in Indonesian language before borrowed from Europeans. Indonesian homes often bustle with family and visitors. One Indonesian author describes what living in a Sumatran communal Minangkabau great house was like as a boy:

My mother occupied one of the cramped rooms, and there I was born. I would say it was like being born in a barracks, since there were more than forty people living in that house at the time. The seven girls all had children, half of them themselves had children, and every night seven unfamiliar men came to the house, that is, the husbands of the seven women. One can imagine how noisy the place was, what with all these individual needs, dispositions, and behaviors colliding. Morning, noon, and night it was one big hullabaloo.[6]

Yet, despite his memories of being crowded, surrounded by household noise, and personal "collisions" of the many occupants, the writer continues:

That house and its surroundings always made me feel extremely nostalgic every time I visited after I was five years old. I do not know why and have never been able to explain it. The sense of yearning was vague, but it penetrated to my very soul.[7]

RESIDENTIAL HOUSES OF COMMON INDONESIANS

The home in Indonesia, historically, not only frames the center of people's social identities and lives, but also embodies a life force and cosmological connections for its inhabitants. Demonstrating aesthetic taste or impressive interior decoration often becomes a lesser concern. This is not to suggest that Indonesians do not care about tidiness, beauty, or comfort in their homes. People wash their floors daily, furnish rooms, display pictures on walls, and sweep their yards of debris. Nonetheless, interior décor devoid of cultural or family meaning, and consistent physical maintenance are nominal concerns compared to Western households. This difference directly reflects economics. Many Indonesians who might wish to buy new furniture or paint their rooms typically cannot afford such luxuries. Yet, charming or lavish home interiors have seldom been status symbols or important concerns of common folk or even many aristocrats. As noted, historically:

The peoples of monsoon Southeast Asia devoted very little of their time and resources to their housing. No doubt the mild climate and the availability of fast-growing trees, palms, and bamboos as building materials were the fundamental reasons for this low priority. Because houses were so cheap to build, they were regarded as impermanent and inappropriate as the place to sink capital.[8]

Indigenous building materials grew everywhere people built houses employing the social custom of *gotong royong* ("mutual assistance" of neighbors and kin involved in helping with sizeable family projects). In a monsoonal, tropical climate, houses of common folk do not survive much beyond ten years and people routinely replace them when they begin to fall into decomposition.

Materials, Methods, Values, Living

Indonesians tend to live relatively close to their natural environments and portions of a house might be open to the outdoors. Building materials derive from local trees, grasses, rocks, clays, and plants. Most homes sit atop raised piers (also called piles), sometimes at precarious height in areas prone to flooding. Post and beam methods of construction create house frames, usually employing joinery, pegs, or lashing instead of nails. Sometimes sizeable gaps run between hand-hewn floorboards, or holes develop in walls of plaited palm leaf, bamboo, or grass. As vertical posts support a home and keep it erect, walls make up the least substantial sections of most types of houses. Rarely load bearing, walls become attached as screens for privacy after the fact of structural building. Chickens, cats, dogs, and occasionally more fearsome creatures like centipedes enter Indonesian interiors through gaps. While swept clean daily, these structures are far from the comparatively sanitized, deodorized abodes many Westerners occupy.

Of the stark contrasts between conventional (and modern) Indonesian homes and those of the West, bathrooms primarily startle and intimidate

Euro-Americans. First, they usually lack decorative appeal and often contain unavoidable tropical mold on walls and ceilings. But beyond that, many foreigners feel revulsion toward the squat toilets used by most Indonesians—although they often consist of the same porcelain material as do Western models.

Many Indonesian bathrooms (called *kamar mandi*, meaning "bathing room" or *kamar kecil*, meaning "little room," a euphemism for "toilet") exist behind a house, often across a yard. If within a home, these rooms typically sit at the back. As a space for defecation and/or bathing (Indonesians wash using a plastic, handled dipper to poor water over themselves from a cistern), these rooms exist for attending to body eliminations and ridding one's self of soil. Indonesians often bathe at least three times a day and value personal cleanliness. Nevertheless, they generally regard their bathrooms as necessary but polluted or embarrassing spaces where people spend time as needed. These rooms remain bare of attempts toward pleasing, evocative "atmospheres," beyond routine cleansing. In fact, decorative features would seem ludicrous to many, except among affluent urban Indonesians following Western models.

Pits in the ground typically provide toilets in rural areas, enclosed within simple huts. A container of water for flushing and washing oneself is always at hand. Rural people often bathe in rivers or haul water in buckets to use indoors, pouring water over themselves and letting it run out between floorboards to the ground below. Women typically bathe this way in the indoor kitchen section of a traditional home.

While rooms with toilets and bathing places of the more affluent usually are tiled and well cleaned, otherwise they remain functional. Many Indonesians fear bodily secretions of others (associated with witchcraft and maladies), so they employ the water dipper to splash and rinse a bathroom before they use it, even if it appears immaculate. As nudity is a disgrace in much of Indonesia, rooms for bathing are extremely private, and often windowless.

Private property and homes became central requisites of modern capitalist ideals of civilization and social status in the Western world. Historically in Indonesia, people were more concerned with bathing (despite their humble bathrooms) and physical cleanliness, perfuming the body or hair, and a neatness and elegance in dress. That is, civility and prestige were born out on the body "in contrast to house and furniture, which earned very little attention."[9] Most believe to the present that water purifies and carries away pollution. Indonesians defecated in rivers, which they believed dissolved filth as it swept it away, while Indians and Europeans were disposing of their excrement in urban streets. An historian remarks that:

Even in the biggest cities Southeast Asians lived in a dispersed pattern of single-story, elevated, wooden houses surrounded by trees. The disposal of household refuse was for the most part left to the pigs, chickens, or dogs which foraged beneath the house, and to the seasonal floods which carried everything away once a year. The open and elevated styles of house at least kept it free of the worst accumulations of decaying debris, in a way which was impossible in the congested cities of Europe, the Middle East, or China before the era of rubbish collection and sewage.[10]

Indonesian kitchens (called *dapur*) typically exist at the back of households. Historically and currently, a floor recession in the center or back portion of a traditional home provides the cooking area, using a wood fire. Smoke rises through openings near the peak of a roof or sometimes seeps through the roof or plaited walls. The Dutch encouraged people to construct kitchens as separate buildings behind homes, to rid households of unhealthy smoke and allow more space for cooking, storage, and cleaning. In traditional homes of eastern Indonesia, some still adhere to the old manner of in-house fire pit cooking. Most Indonesians, however, prepare food in detached kitchens behind their dwellings. Households often use propane cookers instead of wood fires. As are bathrooms, these utilitarian spaces lack decorative attention, serve for cooking only, and people do not usually eat inside of them.

Concerning family life, some have noted that the advent of the detached kitchen changed the focus of houses in Indonesia, causing an increased separation of men and women. This progressed to the extent that now frequently older boys and men eat together in a house or on a porch, while women and children eat behind the house, in or near the kitchen.[11] Numerous Indonesian homes, however, do include a dining area, with a table and chairs or at least a woven mat for people to share.

In regions where households are one structure, homes generally divide into three tiers: The rafter or attic area beneath roofs; the living floor space of the occupants; and the ground under a raised floor where pigs, chickens, cats, dogs, or even water buffalo reside or forage for scraps from the home. Of these tiers, the roof usually predominates in size, as it encloses sacred spaces for ancestral spirits and the storage of family heirlooms, while exuding the homeowner's prestige. Some spectacular examples of homes boasting extravagant roofs shelter the Minangkabau and Batak of Sumatra, the Toraja of Sulawesi, and people in Sumba.[12]

House posts are vitally important in Indonesian construction. Four major, symbolic posts support the central roof sections of traditional houses in Java, Sumba, Sumatra, Timor, Lombok, and elsewhere. These posts each possess unique metaphysical qualities and serve in ritual functions to maintain the well being of the occupants and the structure itself.

In Java, the rites of construction involve a precise, "gendered" joinery of boards, known as mortise and tenon. This skillful wood crafting fits together shaped pieces explicitly symbolizing human sexual relations. The "male" component is the tenon pin, which inserts into the "female" socket. This complementary union of male and female symbolism creates a harmonious arrangement of structural elements, enabling a secure fit. The joinery also brings together paired opposites that resonate with procreation and balance. The sexual nature of this symbolism, carrying on through architecture, may derive from ancient *lingga–yoni* (phallus–vagina) rituals of the Hindu era in Java.[13] In parts of Indonesia not directly influenced by India, however, the male–female dichotomy forms a central cosmological principle of indigenous beliefs.

Relative Status between People

The precedence and priorities Indonesians accord to relative status between people surfaces perhaps most in this chapter—as status determines and continuously motivates the eccentric designs of Indonesian homes. In most regions, when a person of higher or elder status approaches a porch or seating platform (places to entertain visitors), those of lesser rank or age immediately move from benches or central positions to lower or marginal seating levels. Some even descend from the raised platform and crouch upon the ground. At the same time, a chair may suddenly appear for an esteemed person, while other visitors remain seated on a woven floor mat.

The Balinese, for whom caste forms a central means of identity, will tactfully inquire of each other's social levels by asking, "Where do you sit?" implying the actual seating level they would occupy in a group of varying castes. Some Balinese pavilions include a series of steps surrounding the structures, offering seating options to appropriately accommodate people of differing social levels and age groups, and provide a place for all. As emphasized, "That prestige is a profoundly serious business is apparent everywhere one looks in Bali—in the village, the family, the economy, the state. A peculiar fusion of Polynesian title ranks and Hindu castes, the hierarchy of pride is the backbone of the society."[14] This definition of the "hierarchy of pride" could apply to all groups in this volume—often most evidently in their built environments.

In eastern Sumba, where inherited social caste remains among the most rigidly adhered to systems in Indonesia, similar seating divisions apply. Sumba's three-tiered caste system includes nobles, commoners, and slaves. A lower caste person will always sit on a bottom step or at the far margins of a porch of an elite home and some will choose to stand at some distance from the house. Almost never do people of different castes eat in each other's immediate company. In fact, people of lower castes would feel intensely uncomfortable doing so. As in parts of Sulawesi, Bali, Java, Timor, and other regions, people believe in the purity of bloodlines as a basis for nobility. Humans are born into ascribed, lesser castes based in folk notions of biology. Often Sumbanese speak of low caste people as carrying "dirty blood." Thus, occupying space together within a household becomes an uncomfortable matter, and the slave caste typically sleeps in a kitchen outbuilding with few amenities.

Homes in Indonesia (as in much of the world) are clear symbols of stratification, that is, the social and economic inequalities in societies. Through the archipelago, inequality has prevailed for many centuries in thought and practice and persists as a taken for granted reality of the human condition. For Westerners this is hard to understand, much less accept, in principle. However, an oft-used quote considers status relationships in Bali (and could apply to most of the archipelago); such are their importance that "they are matters of life and death."[15]

DESIGNS AND PRIORITIES

Across Indonesia, houses of ritual significance are called *rumah adat,* meaning customary or traditional house—but also implying a ceremonial center. These structures conform to specific (and often ancient) orientations, locations, building techniques, materials, shapes, sizes, and interior layouts. They often contain sacred heirlooms, which further lend power to the structures as clan centers and sanctified places.

Indonesians judge and admire houses by their size, the quality and elaboration of decorative carving or painting of their exteriors, and the eccentric, complex architecture or dramatic stylistic flair of overlapping or tiered roofs. Conversely, interiors serve as the unseen, relatively unadorned domain of the occupants. Although they might include highly sacred spaces and cosmologically significant posts, carvings, heirlooms (*pusaka*), and household divisions, they also delineate the mundane inner dimensions of houses and families. As status symbols, interior styles and decoration of most traditional homes hold less significance than do exteriors.

Further, much remains secret of customary household interiors; such as where people sleep and locations hiding their sacred possessions, family designs for textiles, carvings, and other arts—not to mention unpredictable visits from ancestral spirits watching from high lofts. For such reasons, Indonesians might appear uneasy at visitors "looking around" within their homes and possibly recognizing places hiding heirlooms or upsetting the social or spiritual order of things through hidden intentions or inappropriate behavior.

In many households, people prefer to sit outside on porches, raised plat-forms, or open-air gazebo-like structures generally called *balé* (or *balai* in Indonesian, but with many local names). *Balé* function for entertaining guests, and residents will quickly unfold a woven palm leaf mat called a *tikar* at the sight of approaching visitors.

For decades the national government has been promoting simple, con-crete, new homes. In regions of West Timor, entire villages were moved from their historical settings and housed in these modern homes, following the lin-ear direction of roads. This ended village life in symbolically significant ways radically changing the design and orientation of dwellings. The spread of such houses follows a general policy of modernization that also concerns stan-dards of health. Following this, people call these houses *rumah sehat* (healthy house) in contrast to *rumah adat*.[16] These modern structures usually include a well or running water and a separate kitchen building. The most common type is a single storey building with jalousie or opening windows to permit ventilation. Roofs are low and often of corrugated metal. These dwellings are similar to low-cost tract housing in the United States or Australia, built in the 1950s or 1960s. They usually contain a living room, two or three bedrooms, and a small dining area. Bathrooms often attach to separate kitchen structures behind the homes.

Ornate *balé* seating pavilion in Bali. © Marie Jeanne Adams. Used by permission.

Java

The classical middle-class Javanese home consists of three separate structures, each with its own roof. The *pendapa* (or *pendopo*) at the front of the house is a large, open pavilion and distinctly public space for hosting guests and performances. The second and smallest structure is called a *pringgitan* and is basically an open, rectangular passageway to the back structure of the house, but sometimes functions as a gallery for the performances of *wayang* shadow plays. The third building is the *dalem ageng* (the inside space), and the only section of the property surrounded by a wall and private in design.

This building divides into at least three separate rooms, enclosing the space where a family actually lives. The central room (*krobongan*) is the most sacred in the house, as a reception site for the rice goddess Dewi Sri and a place to honor ancestors. Rituals and the practice of meditation take place in the *krobongan*. Bedrooms adjoin this central space. In this part of the house human affairs manifest life's sacredness.[17] The kitchen (*dapur*) is comparatively insignificant at the back of this structure. A bathroom, or divided toilet and bathing rooms, sit at a far end of the usually long, rectangular kitchen building.

Javanese homes feature three kinds of roofs, each denoting social status. The simplest is the *kampung* (meaning "village" but also a term denoting "commoners" across Indonesia) roof of a basic pitch supported by four central posts. The second type (signifying higher-ranking people) is called *limasan,* which denotes five roof ridges forming a hip roof with an extended peak on top, and including a verandah. The *joglo* roof distinguishes aristocratic homes. Much larger in size than those of lesser status, this style features a hip roof with a tall peak at its summit, supported by four central beams. A *joglo* home often includes tiled steps and a verandah around its periphery and forms the central residence in a family compound of other household structures.

Many Javanese also live in Dutch colonial houses, built across Indonesia before World War II. These are fairly modest but well-made single storey homes, plastered and painted in and out, with European shuttered windows and steep, red-tiled hip roofs characteristic of homes in Holland. In urban *kampung*s, many small, red-tiled homes share walls. Approaching Jakarta by air, viewing the number of such roofs below is remarkable.

In town and country across Java, the modern tract-like house (described previously) appears everywhere. Wealthier people live in larger homes, often of concrete construction and similar to styles in the West. These structures reflect the growing middle and wealthy classes through the 1980s and 1990s. A trend also followed, involving artificially constructed outdoor walls, meant to resemble cliff sides and complete with waterfalls and pools below.

This style subsequently swept across Indonesia, and now on outer islands cement environments adorn walls of public buildings and homes, including sculpted animals and people.

Bali

Balinese persist in the integrity of their customary household designs. Walled compounds enclosing a series of small buildings make up typical Balinese homes. Rather strict rules dictate the location and orientation of household structures. Compounds follow a directional aspect based in the polarity of the concept of *kaja-kelod*. *Kaja* faces the inland, sacred (and sometimes actively volcanic) mountain of Gunung Agung, while *kelod* follows the direction of the sea, which is "downward" in terms of spatial reckoning. People sleep with their heads toward the *kaja* direction and the head of the household resides in the most *kaja* building in a complex. The kitchen is *kelod,* as are rooms with toilets and edges of a yard for housing pigs or dumping garbage. *Kelod* implies impurity, referring to a direction away from the ultimate *kaja* site—the mountain. However, the term denotes a way, not an ultimate destination, as the sea offers purification for Balinese and certainly not a *kelod* realm. Not only are numerous rituals performed at the sea, but people caste the ashes of their cremated relatives into its waters.[18]

At least five distinct sections make up the family courtyard abode in Bali: a tall arched entranceway, at least one bedroom with a front verandah, a kitchen, bathroom, and granary. Some buildings might be without walls on one side and open to a garden. The size and layout of the compound indicate the wealth and social caste of its owner. While not highly elevated Balinese homes do sit on piers on masonry bases, typically with floors covered in ceramic tile. This is likely an influence from India, which directly affected Balinese culture in numerous ways.

Courtyard grounds are swept clean daily, and are lushly planted with flowering shrubs and trees. The northeast corner (the site of the family temple) is the most auspicious, whereas the southeast corner might host evil spirits and usually remains vacant (although these directions might change depending on which part of the island a family lives).[19] Unlike many Indonesian homes, a Balinese kitchen often sits at the front entrance of the compound, usually to the right of the entrance, with an interior visible to visitors through a large, ventilating window. Neighbors freely come to the kitchen entrance to socialize with women cooking within.

Many homes are brick, often finished over with cement. Brick was also a popular building material of the fourteenth century Majapahit kingdom of Java, and likely made its way to Bali centuries ago. Balinese create lavish entranceways with flamboyantly carved, painted, and gilded double doors, framed by wood or surrounding volcanic rock. Extravagant lintels—of wood or volcanic rock carved with floral patterns, animals, or protective spirits—crown doorways. So much design, effort, and material goes into doorway construction that they might function as freestanding structures.

All Balinese buildings of holy character must feature a sacred roof form, like a pagoda. This symbolizes the cosmic Mount Meru of Hindus, thus people term such roofs *meru*. The more sacred the building, the more layers of its roof. Temple structures of a household contain at least four shrines. More mundane structures bear fairly simple hip roofs, covered in grass or tiles.

Paths meander through Balinese compounds like a maze, sometimes following one direction, then suddenly another. These designs intentionally confuse spirits stalking people or finding their way to buildings. As in cremation processions, taking swerves and sudden sharp turns protects the living from unseen evils.

Dayaks of Kalimantan

Homes of the Dayak peoples in the interior region of Kalimantan are of two types: a square, single-family structure or a rectangular communal longhouse. The famous longhouses (*uma dadoq*), contain walled sections of family apartments (*amin*), housing entire villages under one roof. Headmen live in the center beneath a ceiling higher than others. Families regard the back of their *amin* as sacred spaces to store heirlooms and many cook within their apartments. Longhouses are also sites for ritual performances among the Dayak. These windowless structures often continuously lengthen over time with slightly differing materials or heights of piers supporting new additions. Because of this intermittent building of sections, longhouses might present a rambling, uneven appearance. A verandah runs the length of a longhouse as public space for inhabitants (which may number in the hundreds) to socialize and receive guests. Kalimantan communities typically situate along its numerous rivers, with village boats moored below.

A square Dayak home is much smaller and more exacting in construction, occupied by one family. A simple home, however, becomes distinguished by symbolic, elegant outside details. The wooden finials extending off the ends of roofs of Dayak homes are extremely fine and complex in their carving and accentuate the upper tier. Usually a number of such homes surround a central communal open pavilion.

Minangkabau of West Sumatra

The soaring, "saddleback" roofs of the Minangkabau of West Sumatra express the most dignified and graceful in Indonesia. Both the Minangkabau and the Batak of Sumatra have retained sloping roof forms that likely descend from the Austronesians. This style appears through Indonesia and continues out into the Pacific region. Such roofs distinguish Minangkabau "great houses" (*rumah gadang*), which have become far scarcer than in the past.

For many centuries, Minangkabau society has been matrilineal, that is, family lineages descend through women, and husbands move into their wive's houses. Women inherit houses and all ancestral land. While the Minangkabau adopted Islam early—in the sixteenth century—the matrilineal system has carried on uninterrupted into present times.[20] Minangkabau society falls into two social levels of matrilineal clans: aristocrats and commoners. In elaborate homes of the upper class, even the floors tilt up at each end of the building, mirroring the upward arching roof forms.

Historically, newly married women lived in one end of a great house with their husbands, while older women past reproductive age resided at the other end.

Minangkabau house, with multiple gables covered with carved and painted wood panels and upward arching roof ridges. Sections of the wall are still in progress, later to be covered with carved panels. Courtesy of Andrew Causey. Used by permission.

Thus, as women moved through their biological life courses, they also moved through a house. A large central room functioned for all to meet within.

Mingangkabau houses require a mortised post and beam frame construction and include no nails. Pegs or wedges secure the frame in place and houses rest on elevated piers. In some older homes, wall posts actually lean outward to further accentuate the sloping roofline. As elsewhere, customary roofs were thatched, but the Minangkabau used strong, black sugar palm fiber said to last hundreds of years.[21]

As on other islands, today people might maintain a prestigious family great house to perpetuate status and identity but choose to live in a concrete contemporary home. Concerns of comfort as well as being "modern" motivate moves to new homes. Yet, as elsewhere, older prestigious forms have become pronounced again as status and identity symbols in homogenizing modern times. Now numerous Minangkabau people erect *rumah gadang* with money remitted by family members working in urban areas.

According to many, the arching roofs with pointed finials symbolize paired water buffalo horns. The name Minangkabau relates to the Malay/Indonesian term *minang kerbau,* meaning "winning water buffalo." These valuable animals live beneath houses and signify wealth while holding ritual significance. Symbolic images of these creatures, however abstract, carry meaning in design. However, some have suggested that a particular duality, or incompleteness, shapes Minangkabau cosmology, taking physical shape through architecture. The half circle formed by roofs (through upward curving arches at each end) may symbolize the seen and unseen worlds. That is, the invisible arc of an invisible, upper realm might complete a full roof circle.[22] Minangkabau roofs thus may carry double meanings, simultaneously symbolizing an important animal and the cosmos.

Batak of Northern Sumatra

An Indonesian author who grew up in the Toba Batak region describes something of his family house and those of the more wealthy in the early part of the twentieth century: "Our house was a *balebale,* so we were obviously not rich. It was all black inside from the smoke."[23] He continues:

That is, no more than a hut on four poles. Its walls were made of beaten bamboo and its roof of paddy stalks (the floor was changed every year so it wouldn't get holes in it). The other houses were called *sopa* and *ruma,* which were much larger and more beautiful; they were the houses of rich people. The ruma, for instance, had eight pillars. Its walls were made of carved wood planks and its roof was of black sugar palm fiber. These houses had a single room, in which people ate, slept, and received guests. The pillars were very tall, so that the space underneath the house could be used as a pen for livestock, which made it rather "fragrant."

There was also a new type of house, usually called an *emper* (verandah). Its structure resembled the sorts of houses we see in large numbers in the city today.[24]

The new houses were likely, at that time, bungalows introduced by the Dutch. The Batak include seven different regional groups, all of which cannot be discussed here. The elite homes of Batak also boast impressive saddleback roofs with outward leaning gables. Construction techniques resemble Minangkabau methods, using posts and beams fastened by pegs or notches and built atop piers. The Batak largely converted to Protestantism in the nineteenth century, abandoning clan house rituals and instead building smaller, single family homes. The *rumah gorga* (carved house) is the most prestigious structure among the Toba Batak. Entered from beneath, these homes are exquisitely carved and painted with deities and mythical creatures. Carving on the exteriors is especially fine and difficult to carry out, using a mallet to tap a razor sharp carving knife. Most *gorga* work consists of three parallel grooves and requires master carvers.[25]

As elsewhere, *rumah adat* went into decline as people moved into simpler or more modern houses, following modern trends and pressures. However, as recently described:

In the early 1980s, there was a resurgence of interest in traditional house carving among urban Bataks, many of whom worked for the provincial and national government. Several public works projects in the towns and cities incorporated the traditional *rumah adat*-style architecture, which necessitated the production of huge carved facades.[26]

These facades primarily adorned hotels and vacation homes in the Toba Batak area. The quote above reflects two relatively recent trends in Indonesian architecture. First, the national government has funded projects to revive or at least present imitations of older regional styles to attract tourists and capitalize on "ethnicity." Second, groups throughout Indonesia have been returning to some of their customary forms because modern designs lacked deeper meaning. These older structural designs not only signify revived status symbols, following their increased scarcity. They also proclaim tangible ethnic, clan, gender, religious, and class identities and pride in a country plagued by political and economic woes.

Toraja of Sulawesi

The Torajan homeland is a mountainous interior region of South Sulawesi, long isolated from the dominant ethnic groups of the greater region—the Islamic Buginese and Makasarese peoples of the lowlands. Traditionally, the Toraja lived in scattered mountaintop households and although they maintained relationships through ritual exchange, Dutch colonial forces annexed the region under one political authority in the early twentieth century. As in other regions, particularly eastern Indonesia, Torajan society consisted of three social levels, nobility, commoners, and slaves. After independence, many Torajans converted to the Dutch Reformed Church, following remaining missionaries from Holland. Today, although perhaps 80 percent are Christians, they continue with elaborate sacrificial ceremonies and the construction of fantastic clan homes.[27]

The Toraja *tongkonan* (meaning "sitting place") of the nobility are among the most dramatic of Indonesia's vernacular architecture. These are "origin houses," places where relatives sit together to discuss matters such as disputes, marriages, or inheritances. The upturned, soaring rooflines at the front of these homes present an extraordinary structural achievement, seeming to defy gravity. Among the Toraja, an accelerated effort has produced the elaborate slope and height of frontal roof eaves, which require a freestanding outdoor post for support. The extensive height and mass of these protrusions and the interior support structures they require reduced the usable living space of Torajan homes. Further, exteriors, especially the frontal northernmost walls of *tongkonan*s, became effusively embellished with carved and painted designs, communicating wealth and prestige.

Although the majority of Torajans are Protestants, many still follow or combine their faiths with their ancestral religion, *Aluk to dolo,* meaning "rituals (or ways) of the ancestors." This is one of the few indigenous faiths that the Indonesian government has recognized as a valid religion—largely because of the value Toraja culture offered for tourism and the resulting revenue. As do the Minangkabau and others, Torajans follow the male custom of *rantau.* Many young men migrate to cities in Sulawesi or other areas of Indonesia to work. These far-flung sources of remittances have generated much wealth for the people of Tana Toraja (Toraja Land), reinforcing their way of life. Families receiving money from distant relatives put it to use in constructing or maintaining their *tongkonan*s and ceremonies. Thus, Torajans have prospered both from modern and customary phenomena.

Beginning in the 1970s, the Toraja attracted many international tourists with their impressive and eccentric architecture and rituals. In fact, they became a sort of celebrity culture during the last three decades of the twentieth century, as busloads of foreigners arrived to marvel at their dwellings and witness their fantastic pageantry at times of funerals.[28] Tourism infused Torajans with a stronger sense of their unique cultural value and stimulated a boom in ceremonial life and house building. Today, people may live in more spacious, modern homes, but still maintain their *tongkonan,* which may sit uninhabited. Even for those working far from their clan house, this remains at the center of their ethnic and class identities.

Traditional Toraja *tongkonan* house. Courtesy of
Kathleen M. Adams. Used by permission.

When families from groups throughout Indonesia move into modern homes
(sometimes following government pressure), they often persist in building elaborate, carefully constructed, ritually sanctified houses right next door to their
comparatively bland, tract-like homes. Many Torajans have done just this.

Some Torajans now use their architecture and its related carvings in attempts
to achieve higher positions for themselves in local class, rank, and ethnic
hierarchies in their homeland. Following turbulent political–economic times
in Indonesia, artists now produce a new form of "carved paintings" calling
for peace between different communities (alluding to Christians, Muslims,
Chinese, and other Indonesian groups).[29] In this way, elements of symbolically charged, customary Torajan architecture become expressive media for
personal strategies and contemporary political messages.

Grass "Beehive" Homes of Timor, Flores, and Savu

In contrast to elaborate homes, some abodes in regions of Timor, Flores,
and Savu are basically windowless, grass roofs extending below the floor

platform to the ground, with virtually no other visible materials or design. These houses resemble beehives, are extremely dark within, typically smoky, and residents regard them as womb-like enclosures for living in safety and privacy. Such homes bear sanctified posts, altars, and heirlooms representing and honoring ancestors. In their interior obscurity, they appear unwelcoming and indiscernible to outsiders, but familiar to those within. In the centers of these dim, conical structures, women conventionally tend to forever burning fires, as pivotal and stable household presences—as within some traditional homes of Atoni or Tetun peoples of Timor Island. Platforms of varying sizes, heights, and significance either form seats for men or bear heirlooms and altars.[30]

Houses of eastern Indonesia adhere closely to principles of dualism—forming opposing, paired concepts signifying cosmological thought and symbolism of local belief systems. The most predominant and recurrent dualism is male/female. While organizing much of life, this paired opposition also maintains a mystery and tension between its differences. Among the Atoni people of western Timor, house centers or entire interiors are symbolically female, whereas exteriors represent males. Women, however, may not sit upon male platforms within the house. As elsewhere, roof peaks or attics hold sanctity, where agricultural altars reside with heirlooms. The Wehali people of central Timor divide their homes into male and female spaces—both in terms of inside and outside, and with posts marking boundaries between the realms of men and women within a house.[31]

Indonesian Chinese Homes

Indonesian Chinese homes often differ from those of indigenous Indonesians. Those called "shop-houses," accent the merchant class status of Chinese in Southeast Asia, especially in Indonesia. As noted by Jacques Dumarcay, in *The House of Southeast Asia*: "In Southeast Asia, the Chinese house is essentially urban and its plan is thus dependent on the layout of the town."[32] Since cities are crowded, so is housing and commercial spaces, which Chinese often combine. Many live above or behind their businesses in long, narrow structures resembling urban shops in the West. Often family members wander in and out of the commercial and living spaces, and many will sit in front of their shops in the evenings to socialize with neighbors or enjoy cool air.

When not too limited by space, Chinese homes include an open-air central outdoor courtyard surrounded on four sides by rooms. These dwellings provide a pleasant sense of natural space and often caged songbirds, flowering plants, vegetable gardens, or even fruit trees enliven these family enclosures. Households might shelter several family generations and contain considerable floor space. Because these are walled environments, people live in relative privacy from the outside.

Chinese Indonesians also occupy homes like those of others, such as Dutch colonial houses and the common, modern types already described. In urban areas, many wealthy Chinese live in newer, expensive homes in upscale sections of town. Their homes can be lavish, surrounded by high concrete walls embedded with broken glass at the top to keep robbers at bay. Similar walls provide protection for most urban residences of the middle- or upper-classes, along with foreigners living in Indonesia.

THE LIVING HOUSE[33] AND HOUSE SOCIETIES

Bali: The Living House

The house as a living, breathing, and feeling entity embodies animist concepts of the world, including how sections of houses represent animate body parts. As indigenous people and ethnographers have explained, houses from a variety of regions possess parallels to human or animal anatomy, such as a head, backbone, face, eyes, legs, vagina, a section that allows it to breath, and so forth. This physiological symbolism characterizes houses in Savu, Timor, Lombok, Bali, Sumba, and elsewhere.[34]

In 1937, the artist Miguel Covarrubias expressed of the Balinese house concept:

The Balinese say that a house, like a human being, has a head—the family shrine; arms—the sleeping quarters and the social parlour; a navel—the courtyard; sexual organs—the gate; legs and feet—the kitchen and the granary; and anus—the pit in the backyard where the refuse is disposed of.[35]

Balinese consider themselves as living microcosms of the Hindu–Balinese universe. This view also applies to villages, household compounds, and buildings, which all follow a tripartite division: an upper world of Gods, a middle world of humans, and the underworld. Pertaining to humans, divisions become head, body, and feet—with the head always supreme. (Likewise, households of vastly differing types throughout Indonesia frequently contain architectural anatomies analogous to the three basic levels of the human body and of the universe.)

All structures in a compound correspond to the physical proportions of the owner. The distance between the hands of outstretched arms on each side of the body forms a basic construction measurement. Others include the distance from elbow to tip of the middle finger, the hands in various positions, and the feet. These measurements are marked onto sticks and used through out building and spacing between structures. Thus, the body provides the basic units of proportions within a family compound, creating similar, but unique differences between households within a neighborhood.

Sumba: Persistent House Societies

Across Indonesia, especially the eastern islands, homes define the center of people's moral universes and identities. These regions fall under a type of social system described as a "house society."[36] Such homes link directly to the inhabitants' ancestors and enclose their own sanctity, revered as places that ensure the safety, stability, and health of a family or clan. Sacred wooden posts (each of cosmological significance) support these homes and sections of the buildings symbolize male, female, public, private, forbidden, and sacred spaces. As noted, "Ethnographies of South-East Asian societies ... provide evidence that ritual functions are inseparable from the house's identity. What are sometimes referred to in older literature as 'temples' were, in fact, simultaneously inhabited houses of a kin group."[37] In house societies one's home is indeed one's temple.

In these Indonesian dwellings, people believe that ancestral spirits periodically inhabit spaces under roofs and critically observe their descendents below. This is eminently so in Sumba, where inhabitants seldom risk improper behavior beneath the eccentrically high-peaked roofs (described by an American tourist visiting Sumba in 1990 as resembling "Pizza Hut").[38] Propriety especially applies to sexual trysts. Extramarital or pre-marital sexual activity usually occurs in socially neutral and spiritually unsanctified spaces. These are simple, isolated garden huts, or even in the midst of high fields of maize, as those involved would feel shame and even fear in their visibility to ancestors.

In East Sumba, districts contain major villages of nobility and heads of large kinship lineages, which include clan households, important megalithic graves, and ritual centers. Despite more than five decades of belonging to a nation—with its national leaders, regional officials, modern institutions, and ostensibly democratic ideology—Sumbanese have steadfastedly maintained their caste and prestige systems. Usually at least four high-ranking families occupy major villages, frequently located on hilltops. Noted for its high-peaked ancestral clan houses (*uma bokulu*), Sumba remains a characteristically animist island, although there is much overlap between Christianity and the local *Marapu* faith. It was estimated in the mid-1990s that about one-half of the population still followed animist practices, and yet more if including Christian converts.[39]

Four ritual posts support the tall peaks (*tiku*) of roofs, which contain offering places for ancestors, family valuables, and male and female ancestral figures. These pinnacles also periodically host spirits of ancestors during ritual events. Sitting on floors beneath roof peaks, skilled speakers employ sacred ritual language (spoken in poetic, paired couplets), calling *Marapu* spirits down to hear needs or witness important ceremonies of the living.

Sumbanese perceive some clan homes as so forbiddingly potent with ancestral powers and life force (*ndewa*) that they fear living in them. A low caste person then often becomes the sole caretaker. In Sumba and neighboring islands, the concepts of "hot" and "cool" represent spiritually menacing or safe environments. Clan houses and the grounds surrounding them at times become hot and must be cooled by rituals, usually involving the blood of sacrificed animals. In a real sense "hot" implies forces of nature and the supernatural while "cool" relates to local culture and the human realm. The living must make their environments safe (or cool) by ritually appeasing the spirits and the dead.

Opposing concepts (such as hot/cool, male/female, bitter/sweet, dark/light) categorize and organize parts of a house. The masculine, right side of a house remains reserved for the rituals and public matters of men. Women's domains occupy the left portion of a house, which include a bedroom, weaving areas, and often spaces behind the home.

High-peaked traditional homes in West Sumba, surrounding megalithic graves in a central yard. 1990. Courtesy of Jill Forshee.

A clan house roots a cosmological center for its members, providing a shared physical building and genealogical identity for a social group (even if uninhabited), while signifying "the starting point for each individual's location in time."[40] The term for Sumba's animist faith, *Marapu,* signifies ancestral roots. In a highly stratified society of three distinct castes (similar to Torajans), the clan house is one way in which "hierarchy and equality are created, imagined and maintained by reference to ideas of origin and ancestry as a 'founding' ideology."[41] Following this:

An apparently universal rule in South-East Asian societies is that house posts always be "planted" (literally the term used in most instances) with their root or base end down, the same way as the tree originally grew. Symbolism of "base" and "tip" is highly elaborated in some Indonesian societies, and rules may even apply to the placing of horizontal members.[42]

Torajan people of Sulawesi consider the southernmost room of their homes as its root and a place to store their heirlooms.[43] The Nuaulu people of the eastern Indonesian island of Seram plant their house posts along with sacred shrubs "always according to their natural orientation, that is, root end first ... the house is thus considered to be, in a very real sense, 'living.' This aliveness is often expressed in anthropomorphic terms."[44] On the eastern Indonesian island of Buru, people express ideas about origin and cause based on imagery of living plants or trees. Roots and trunks of trees and the young leaves at the tips of branches form culturally significant reference points for these metaphors.[45] Throughout Indonesians societies, this idiom of life parallels dualisms of near and far, sacred and profane, and ancestors and descendants, and defines various parts of a home.

In Eastern Sumba, distinctions between "trunk" and "tip" shape a dynamic polarity in thought for a number of things, including households and lineages.[46] While relative to concepts of "center" and "periphery" or "inner" and "outer," the trunk and tip notions also coordinate with values of time depth. Thus, a trunk or old, established clan home holds eminence through its age.

During construction, the four sacred posts supporting a Sumbanese roof peak become erected in a fixed order in a "movement to the right," with each bearing a specific function. The first pillar to be set is at the right front, the site for divination. Here priests interpret signs through the organs of chickens and pigs, then offer the animals to the ancestors.[47] The post conducts information between two realms.

Noble clan heads bear the utmost responsibility for house maintenance. Throughout Indonesia, roofs in particular but also floors or entire structures need replacement about every 10 years. This obligation also falls to the people regarding the clan home as the basis of their lineage, even if they live far from it. As on other islands, descendants working in distant regions typically remit money to their families in Sumba in support of keeping a clan house standing. This also perpetuates the contributors' inherent identities and ongoing psychological well-being, perhaps all the more needed if they reside at great distance from "home." In fact, nobles may play upon their ranks while living abroad, if to their advantage. Such posturing carries a doubled importance, as conspicuous social status crucially concerns elite Sumbanese, wherever they are. Following a revival in prestige of older status symbols, some clan homes have been rebuilt grander than ever.

Common people of Sumba dwell in modest, single story houses with plaited palm leaf or cement walls, both types typical throughout Indonesia. These are conceptually "cool" without spiritual significance. Although grass roofs have historically sheltered homes across the archipelago, now many people use corrugated zinc or iron. Metal roofs, however, radiate heat into buildings and do not allow ventilation as does grass. These newer roofs result in much hotter homes and the sound of rain on metal becomes extreme. Nonetheless, such roofs are longer lasting, impermeable to rats and insects, and appeal to many as low maintenance. For a time, even some large clan homes underwent repair with metal roofs. These generally are falling out of favor, though, due to increased household heat, an unaesthetic rusty appearance, and lack of customary value.

Tanimbar: The House as Status and Memory

The islands of Tanimbar, located among the Maluku chain (sitting between Timor and West Papua) historically contain a sort of "ultimate house society." Marriage and descent on this island has been varied and confusing, thus houses mark clan identities more than do people. Tanimbar dwellings customary sit in long rows, the most important of these called *lolat. Lolat* designates structures defined by the women from these homes given out in marriage, typically in earlier times. That is, women who left their natal homes to live elsewhere with husbands still remain the most important ancestors in their houses of origin. Thus, a certain female ancestor defines a row of houses, as bloodlines flow from mothers and create connections between homes. These female bloodlines carry names and only named houses may be part of *lolat* rows. Greater and lesser rows exist in terms of social status. People once believed that house rows could stretch to ancestors and the next world; the sources of life. The house in Tanimbar society thus became the focus of importance.[48]

Homes stand on piers and relatively simple, pitched roofs comprise almost the entire structure. Buildings lack much adornment but customarily contained valuables within. *Lolat* homes once possessed exquisitely carved wooden altars, as complex, abstract human figures with out-stretched arms. These symbols of ancestral status are almost lace-like in curving detail and were made nowhere else. Christianity caused people of Tanimbar to abandon such altars and now most survive in foreign museums.[49] Moreover, much has changed regarding cosmological ideas, and many customary rows of homes have fallen into decay. Yet, these unique structures and intricate marriage patterns still persist to an extent and notions of social status and lineage identity are likely still important.

Savu: A Living, Nautical, and Shifting House Society

On the small island of Savu, between Timor and Sumba in eastern Indonesia, houses consist of three platform levels, as is common elsewhere. They also divide into parts named after those of living beings, such as a head, neck, cheeks, a space for breathing, a chest and ribs, and a tail (implying beings may always not be human). Like other Indonesian houses, those in Savu possess spiritual force. Although most people of the island are Protestant converts, a Savu home (*amu*) is bestowed with *hemanga* (*semangat* in Indonesian, signifying life force and spirit) through a series of ceremonies during its construction. After these are complete, people regard the house as a living entity, comparable to people, animals, or plants. A family house grows and multiplies through its descendents.[50] Homes contain, foster, and emanate life. People of Savu also liken their island to a living being, with its "head" to the west and its "tail" to the east. The geography of the island thus divides into sections analogous to physical anatomy.[51]

The symbolism of the boat (*perahu*) also applies to Savu house layout. Customary homes follow the shape of a bow and a stern and are called by these terms. Thus, "like the members of a village, the members of a house form a group of passengers on a perahu."[52] Savunese historically have believed that their ancestors arrived from the west and that after death they will journey in that direction by boat to the next world. People orient the heads of deceased people and even sacrificed animals to the west—the direction of both origins and ultimate endings. Savu houses also follow a "base" and "tip" orientation, as in neighboring islands. The nautically symbolic "bow" of a house form is also its "base," associated with men—whose patrilineage descends from its founder. The "stern" is like a "tip," and relates to women, who move to their husbands clan homes from elsewhere after marriage.

Savu houses divide into male and female sections, reflecting a basic principle in eastern Indonesia. Household members all follow the founder's patrilineage, and any may enter the male half of a home. Relatively open and light, this section offers a place for entertaining visitors. The female household portion, however, is not visible from the male section and is dimmer inside. Customarily, ceremonies held in its especially dark loft (storing food and weaving yarn) remain exclusively and secretively female. All house posts fall under male and female classification, following their position.

Many Savu homes now follow the Indonesian modern, tract-like style. As long-standing Protestant converts, many Savunese have abandoned or neglected their former house forms and related cosmology to a good extent. Still, ideas integral to time-honored houses might apply in various degrees and manners to these contemporary residences, as clan identities go on.

The House as Boat

Boat symbolism dominates homes and grave stones in diverse regions of Indonesia. The meaning behind houses, that is, whether or not much of this architecture literally intends to replicate a sea vessel, or whether boat-like houses exist as metaphorical forms, has created controversy. Many if not most Indonesians descend from ancestors who journeyed to their present islands on boats. Seafaring vessels thus became visual symbols of origins along with folklore of former homelands.

The Muslim Bugis, originally from Sulawesi, choose to live by sailing and trading throughout the archipelago and beyond. They have been renowned seamen and boat-builders for centuries. The Bugis in parts of Sulawesi follow a three-tiered system of social levels, as in many parts of Indonesia. This system remains more established in their homeland than after they migrate to other islands. In Luwu, Sulawesi, houses contain central posts—points of power (*sumange*, the local word for "spirit" or "liveliness," similar to Indonesian *semangat*) regarded as "navels," paralleling the point of power in humans. These must be guarded from harm.[53] Thus, houses—most powerfully clan homes of nobles—possess potency. Where Bugis have formed settlements on other islands, however, the concept of *sumange* is less invested in a clan home (and reflects that Bugis in these settlements were not likely migrants from Sulawesi nobility). In simpler homes, and far from their homeland, their *sumange* might be centered individually or even within separate parts of a person and can be volatile and fly off.[54]

The fiercely independent Bugis maintain strong notions of autonomy, independent of a nation-state or province. Sea-faring Bugis long traded in slavery, sea products, weapons, and bird's nests (for soup). They historically practiced the *rantau*, venturing afar, sometimes in permanent migration. For many, their boats have become their only meaningful homes, allowing them a certain freedom through mobility.

Bugis fishing boats sail the Savu Sea, eastern Indonesia. 1994. Courtesy of Jill Forshee.

Bugis invest effort into boats (*perahu*) as they would homes. Built of teak or ironwood, some tightly crafted vessels serve as cargo schooners (*pinisi*) reaching 70 feet in length. These typically carry eight or more people and might boast up to four sails. Elegant, sturdy, and meticulously made, they signify pride and independence. Bugis also regard the sea as spiritually potent and make ritual offerings to the aquatic realm before fishing or setting out on a journey. Throughout the wide Austronesian region, boats and homes typically command similar metaphysical and ritual value among people who sail the waters.

People originating in the Philippines and referred to as the sea-gypsies, or *Badjau* (often *Bajo* in Indonesian) sail their boats over thousands of miles, through the Sulu Sea (between the Philippines and Indonesia) into eastern Indonesia. Some Badjau still live an aquatic, nomadic life, but others have settled near the sea on numerous islands. Wherever these people locate themselves, however, they continue with their boat building, which requires sophisticated craftsmanship. So often at sea, the Bajau hold specific ideas about human orientations within their boats, such as sleeping crosswise rather than lengthwise, for the dead are buried lengthwise in a coffin made of a boat sawn in half.[55] As in Bali, associations with "right" and "wrong" directions of orientation position a dwelling or the way one sleeps. Bajau imbue their boats with similar values of a clan home, including a "navel" or spiritual center.

A journalist recently characterized sea gypsies of the Sulu Sea region as modern buccaneers: "Modern buccaneers, they recognize no borders and no rule but that of the open sea, as they smuggle goods and guns across pirate-infested waters that form a sort of Silk Road of the Sea."[56] While this swashbuckling portrayal is colorful, the Indonesian waters are rife with piracy in some regions, and smuggling has characterized maritime life for centuries. Imaginably, as economic conditions have worsened in Indonesia, this commerce has gained momentum. Thus, sea people sail through routes and moorings to sustain their living and provide islanders with goods otherwise unavailable.

Homeless People of Indonesia

In urban areas such as Jakarta, homeless people make up a substantial proportion of the population. These may be roadside food vendors who sleep under their tables at night, pedicab (*becak*) drivers using their vehicles for shelters, or at the most impoverished level, those surviving beneath bridges, under plastic scraps, or at garbage dumps. Many of these people suffered displacement through community-insensitive urban renewal projects and others migrated to cities to find work (unsuccessfully). Some descend from families trapped in conditions of urban poverty for generations. Drugs now pose a social problem in Jakarta as they do elsewhere in the world, involving crack cocaine, methamphetamines, heroin, or sniffing chemicals (this, despite the fact that possession or sale of illegal drugs carries the death penalty in Indonesia). Drug use has led to further homelessness and mental illness, leaving people destitute. Worsening this dilemma, drugs and prostitution have facilitated a growing aids epidemic in Indonesia, largely in urban and tourist regions.

Under President Suharto's New Order regime, "development" and "modernization" schemes and methods reached scandalously impractical and corrupt levels. In Bali, plans for mammoth resort complexes of hotels, golf courses, condominiums, the biggest luxury housing project in Asia, and "entertainment parks" wreaked havoc upon the environment and disenfranchised sizeable local communities. These visions of modern grandeur and prosperity completely ignored the wellbeing and rights of common, local people. As during old Indonesian kingdoms (and by Indonesia's first president, Sukarno), the erection of grandiose structures and monuments by those in power took precedence over the interests of the general population.

An immense luxury housing project devouring the land of many farmers had barely begun when the New Order ended. Water was to come from draining Bali's mountain lakes, which would have caused severe irrigation shortages for rice farmers, disrupting their sustenance and culture in many places. At one point, a plan for the biggest statue on earth was underway. Conceived of as the center of an entertainment park on the Bukit Peninsula, Bali's dry southern coast, this was to be higher than the Statue of Liberty and plaited in gold—representing the Hindu god Vishnu riding on the back of the mythical bird, Garuda. The economic crisis of 1997–1998 put an end to the frivolous project. However, the Bukit peninsula's limestone base has been excavated and permanently disfigured by many such New Order follies. Moreover, money from these extravagant ventures was not destined to benefit local people, but to fill the coffers of the national government and its cronies.[57]

Jakarta has been rampant with socially devastating grand schemes. According to one report, between the years 2000 to 2005, the city evicted almost 64,000 urban poor for public–private projects and was threatening to evict almost another 1,600,000.[58] Earlier, in 1989, a community of 5,000 households—perhaps 30,000 people—received eviction notices, in order that their neighborhoods become the site for the largest international trade center in Indonesia. Although people protested, many moved. The government offered them flats that they could not afford to rent, so many became homeless. The *kampungs* (village-like neighborhoods of small homes) of central Jakarta took on the appearance of bombsites, according to one report, once housing an average of 1,000 to 2,000 people per hectare. Seventy percent of the city's inhabitants had been living in *kampungs*, yet hardly one such neighborhood remained unscathed.[59]

In Jakarta and other cities, communities of people permanently live at mountainous garbage dumps, where they scavenge for food, resalable items, or rags. Such communities had become so commonplace and established that one popular Indonesian television soap opera in the late 1990s dramatized the lives and travails of a family desperately trying to survive at a city dump. These dwellers of "garbage villages" were subsisting upon the refuse of the more affluent. The program became controversial as it highlighted the vast differences in wealth in Indonesia. Further, garbage dumps had become entrenched Jakartan communities to the degree of providing valid settings for televised dramas.

The governor of Jakarta called for a "clean up" campaign in 2001, targeting thousands of poor street workers, such as pedicab (*becak*) drivers (vehicles increasingly illegal in much of the city), sidewalk vendors, street musicians, as well as many families from impoverished makeshift settlements along rivers. By 2003, as many as 34,000 pedicab drivers lost work, as their vehicles were systematically destroyed, depriving them of livelihood and shelter. Carts and wares of 1,525 vendors were confiscated, and the number of demolished street side stalls serving food rose to more than 21,000. By this time, more or less 50,000 people had been evicted from their shelters.[60] The poor in cities across Indonesia have endured similar miseries, which no longer can be blamed upon the New Order regime. In fact, despite its many faults and excesses, the New Order regime at least maintained some basic forms of infrastructural support for Indonesian people (such as clinics, bridges, and sewers), which have disappeared or fallen into neglect in the years since Suharto's resignation.

As of February, 2006, many left homeless by the tsunami of December, 2004 in Banda Aceh remained in tents or without shelter, despite international aid. This echoed the situation of poor coastal people in Maumere, Flores, devastated by a tidal wave in the early 1990s, but never receiving sufficient help (or internationally contributed funds) to rebuild. Moreover, in remote regions of Kalimantan or West Papua, large-scale, often multi-national logging or mining operations have forcibly relocated many indigenous people, sometimes by violent means. In West Papua, or Irian Jaya, this has further fueled long-standing movements for national independence from Indonesia.

In the wake of this type of blind destruction of habitats and lives, an insight by a poet from the other side of the world comes to mind: "Progress might have been all right once, but it has gone on too long" (Ogden Nash). This aptly applies to ill-conceived and corrupt schemes of "progress" across modern Indonesia and much of the world, especially regarding common people and their dwellings.

MOSQUES, TEMPLES, AND CHURCHES

Mosques

In predominantly Muslim Indonesia, the melodic call to prayer from the summits of mosques (*mesjid* in Indonesian) fills the air five times a day, all the more in cities where multiple calls from all directions resonate at once. Like other religious architecture, mosques include design principles combining Islamic and indigenous concepts of sacred structures. Modern, grand mosques designed by Indonesian and European architects stand in major cities, as do older ones echoing European colonial influences. The national mosque is the Istiqlal Mosque in Jakarta, built in 1984 as the largest mosque in Southeast Asia and able to hold a congregation of more than 120,000 people. This mosque reflects urban modern architecture of the period in many ways, except for two domes at the top: one a minaret and the other a voluminous spherical structure covering the main prayer hall building.

The Minangkabau of Sumatra construct mosques with the exquisitely carved walls and the "horned" roof designs of their homes. Yet these always feature a minaret or spire of some sort on top. Four pillars support a central area, except in the simplest of mosques in small communities, which might be one room. There must be clean water outside of any mosque, provided by a pool or at least a water spigot, in order that worshippers wash their feet, hands, and faces before prayer.

Following the tsunami of 2004, which left perhaps half a million people homeless in the Banda Aceh region of northern Sumatra, the number of mosques that survived devastation, including the Grand Mosque, stunned many. Aerial photos of completely washed away communities show a number of mosques apparently standing intact. Regarded by many of all religions as miraculous, this tremendously boosted the faith of Muslims in Indonesia and the world over.

As the Koran does not specifically prescribe the architecture of mosques, throughout the Indonesian islands they became locally interpreted structures, eclectic mixes, or humble buildings, yet with a dome and minaret and an amplifier for the prayer call. A mosque must provide enough space to gather the surrounding Muslim community within it. People enter the side of the building in the opposite direction of Mecca. Facing this entrance, marks upon a wall indicate the direction of Mecca and worshippers orient themselves so that their heads face this way. If a Muslim prays away from a mosque, and many do as prayer occurs five times daily, he or she will always orient the head toward the proper direction. This orientation is similar to Balinese concepts of sacred and less-than-sacred in ways they build residences and temples—looking to a spiritual center and away from its peripheries.

Temples

Temples in Java are called *Candi*. In Bali people refer to them as *Pura* or *Candi*, although the latter often signifies the entranceway. Classical Hindu and Buddhist temples—and sometimes a combination of the two faiths in one structure—follow models of Mount Meru, the Hindu center of the universe and home of the gods. Hindu temples contain a *lingga* (phallic symbol) at its sanctified core, while Buddhist temples enshrine a statue of the Buddha. The earliest temples in Indonesia were Hindu, built high upon volcanic mountains in central Java. Symbolism of the mountain or the stupa (an up reaching, conical structure) resonated with indigenous notions of the piety of mountains and ancestors. The number of ancient Indonesian Hindu and Buddhist temples is too great to even mention here. Most exist in Java; others in Sumatra, Bali, and Kalimantan.

Some time in the eighth century A.D., the world's largest Buddhist shrine of Borobudur began to rise in central Java. This finally reached completion in the ninth century, under rulers known as the Sailendras of Central Java, allied historically with Sumatran Srivijaya. This extravagant and immense tiered "mountain"—embellished with miles of intricate bas relief Buddhist scenes, countless carved panel depictions of everyday life, and impressive stupas—still stands intact and visible across the plains for miles. At its base it measures more than 370 feet and rises to 114 feet. The hundreds of engraved stone panels of Borobudur document in detail how Javanese looked and lived in ancient times. Many of these images appear astonishingly similar to dress and activities in Java to this day, from market scenes to cock fights.

The architectural and artistic mastery of Borobudur arguably surpasses any structures produced in Europe in the same era. It remains Indonesia's ultimate temple and one of the most impressive religious edifices in the world. Borobudur was dedicated to telling visually of the many lives of Buddha (*Jataka* tales) and architecturally symbolizing the path to enlightenment. The monument expressed this journey through an ever-rising walkway circumventing the entire structure in several tiers. Walls border this upward route, meticulously chiseled with episodes of Buddha's various incarnations, the glories of local kingdoms, and all aspects of human activities. The most profane views of life border the bottommost level. The episodic progression of stories ends at the ultimate open-air plane of Borobudur. Here, all imagery subsides except for stone Buddhas sitting within bricked stupas facing out at the vast landscape.

Borobudur, the world's largest Buddhist monument, central Java. Courtesy of Jill Forshee.

Unique among temples, Borobudur encases the top of a hill, originally augmented by filled soil to support the temple foundation. While the monument provides entrances on all four sides, the main entry stands on the eastern section, leading into walls of bas-relief narratives. Borobudur was designed as a ten-stepped ascending pyramid culminating at the top. This follows Mahayana Buddhist scriptures—ten stages of lives on earth following moral and compassionate ways of living embodied in the ideal of a "Bodhisattva"—and depict Buddha's own succession of incarnations. Coincidentally, the Sailendra king at Borobudur's inception was the tenth in his dynasty.

Numerous magnificent temples stand in central Java, such as at Prambanan, Mendut, and the Dieng Plateau, and in Bali, such as Besakih, influenced by Buddhism and Hinduism. Like Borobudur, they often contain richly illustrative carvings and symbolic, upward-reaching architectural details, visually striving toward enlightenment. These skyward arches, profusely detailed architecturally and decorative carvings, were commissioned by various rulers and tell different stories of Buddha and Hindu gods and goddesses.[61]

Many Indonesian and foreign visitors travel to these temples and carved images, including tourists and religious pilgrims. Some monuments retain their spiritual function and likely hold greater significance in a nation currently weakened by economic woes, political instability, natural disasters, and recent terrorism.

Rulers originally constructed temples of stone, but later of brick and tile beginning in the fourteenth century Majapahit era. These holy structures not only proclaimed devotion of kings, but also asserted their own divine authority. Impressive architecture then legitimized or extended their power by attracting larger followings. While temples followed Indian influences to an extent, much of the design and carved imagery was vividly Javanese. Otherwise, the impact of these sanctuaries, however impressive they might have appeared, would have been far less powerful among the population.

A crucial aspect of these structures was that "[t]he architects who designed and built the great Hindu and Buddhist temples of eastern and central Java were masters of perspective effects. They manipulated changes in scale and the positioning of architectural elements to create an illusion of great mass and structure."[62] This especially applied to the imposing temples at Prambanan and the Dieng Plateau, Java.

In Bali, temples stand at the very heart of society, culture and history.[63] Estimates of the number of temples in Bali exceed 20,000. For this reason, any visitor to the island can usually see people carrying offerings, colorful processions, or even elaborate ceremonies such as cremations. Each village contains at least three temples, and larger villages often hold many more.

There are also special temples for different organizations—neighborhoods, state temples, rice irrigation societies, and so forth. These structures are repaired or rebuilt following strict specifications. When a group of Balinese resides away from their island, such as policemen or civil servants, they will usually construct a temple for themselves.

Most of Bali's temples are not old, but amid the humid, tropical climate and monsoonal rains, they quickly appear so. Depending upon the type of rock, brick, or cement used for temples and their carvings, erosion can be rapid and carved figures may appear ancient when they are 10 to 20 years old. As so much in Bali includes carved lintels and guardian figures, a general appearance of antiquity (which charms foreigners) pervades the island's architecture.

The most revered temple in Bali is Besakih, sitting nearly 3,280 feet above sea level, on the southwest slope of the holy mountain, Gunung Agung. This mountain was also the realm of departed ancestors for Bali animists before Hinduism arrived. People called the Bali Aga still practice a pre-Hindu belief system and some live near this mountain region. Besakih includes a dramatic stairway to its open-topped, imposing tiered gateway. The complex within contains approximately 30 pagoda-like temples (*meru*). The Dutch restored this temple in the early twentieth century, after years of neglect by warring kingdoms.

Balinese also chiseled temples and shrines from solid rock walls, such as the famous "Elephant Cave" (Goa Gajah), perhaps originally a site for Mahayana Buddhists by the eleventh century or local Balinese priests. Buddhist or

Tanah Lot, Bali's sea temple. Courtesy of Ian Fischer-Laycock. Used by permission.

Hindu hermits may have used these caves for solitude and meditation, but much of their history remains a mystery. Goa Gajah's spectacular rock face features a large demon-like creature (likely to repel menacing spirits), whose mouth becomes the cave. Fantastic animals and plants etch deeply into the surrounding wall. This is one of Bali's most flamboyant religious sites.

The fifteenth century temple, Tanah Lot, perches on a rock outcropping in the Indian Ocean off southern Bali, accessible only at low tide. Legend has it that a traveling Hindu priest founded the temple for privacy, permitting him to carry out spiritual practices undistracted by local fishermen. One of Bali's holiest sites, this small temple draws many pilgrims and tourists. Tanah Lot has become an icon of Bali internationally, with photographs of its *meru* roofs against an ocean backdrop.

Churches

According to one scholar, in 1854 the Dutch Governor General divided up the Lesser Sunda Islands of eastern Indonesia for the missionaries. The Catholics were permitted Flores and the middle region of Timor. The Protestants got most of the rest of the archipelago, including Bali.[64] As most of the population of Indonesia by that time had adhered to Islam (or in Bali Hinduism) for centuries, missionaries faced an easier task converting animists of outer islands. Nonetheless, Christianity did take hold in parts of Java, Bali, and Sumatra.

Approximately 10 to 13 percent of Indonesians are Christians, following numerous denominations. The Protestant majority, belonging to the Dutch Reformed Church, adapted the new faith to local cultures. Catholic congregations exist on most islands, especially Flores. More recently, other Protestant denominations have spread, such as Lutherans, Methodists, Evangelicals, and others. The number of Evangelical, Fundamentalist, and Mormon missionaries from the United States is a more recent phenomenon, resulting in many new churches.

Churches throughout Indonesia tend to resemble either the European or American types of architecture of a founding missionary or the religious buildings of indigenous people. Some village churches are simple wooden structures with a cross on top while urban regions contain large, impressive constructions. The Catholic Church in Denpasar, Bali features many basic elements of a Balinese temple, including carvings and a tiered, *meru* roof. The Bali Protestant Church in Seminyak, however, follows a more European design, without any of the usual Balinese embellishments. In fact, the church bought a bordering tourist resort and replaced many of the Balinese stone carvings of gods and creatures with cement deer and decorations decidedly not local. In Sumba, a Catholic church consists of modern, concrete architecture but displays a cement statue of a beckoning Christ near the roadway, clad in local *ikat* costume.

PUBLIC BUILDINGS AND MONUMENTS

Public Buildings

The colonial bureaucracy introduced public buildings to Indonesia that were not of a religious or aristocratic nature. These include any number of buildings like those in Europe. Architecture of government offices, banks, post offices, schools, hospitals, and so forth throughout Indonesia tend to be either of Dutch colonial style with red-tiled roofs and concrete walls (and often in states of disrepair) or generic single or multi-storied concrete structures built between the 1950s and the present—resembling mundane urban architecture in much of the world. Much construction after independence reflected Dutch modernism of the times. Yet many older buildings remain, such as Chinese shop-houses and Dutch colonial structures on commercial or residential streets in cities, typically alongside newer buildings.

In appearance, the skyline of Jakarta could be almost anywhere. During the 1990s, an immense amount of large structures rose, including shopping malls, government buildings, expensive and largely multi-national hotels, office buildings, and high-rise apartments. At the same time, infrastructure did not keep up with building, causing frequent power blackouts and flooding. The boom in urban building made an immense amount of money for favored businessmen and contractors, while taking little else into account—such as traffic problems, air pollution, waste disposal, the demise of *kampung* communities, and the costs of maintaining these enormous new monuments to Indonesia's modern face. Building got far ahead of itself, and some of the high-rises remained at least half vacant or began to deteriorate.

Defining one particular style of Indonesian urban architecture is impossible. However, an Indonesian scholar notes, "the 'International Style' continues to prevail resulting in the suppression of local elements, which are all too often entirely absent from the most prestigious sectors of modern Indonesian cities. Critics have referred to this as a 'crisis of cultural identity.'"[65] While sometimes of prize-winning design, the modern urban architecture of Indonesia also provides an immediate and graphic contrast between the rich and poor.

Public Monuments

Many Indonesian public monuments celebrate heroes of liberation or religious figures and on some islands these might be locals. Others take form as realistic policemen at intersections to remind people of traffic laws. In Bali, a giant concrete baby was constructed near a road intersection, following years of reports by local people of the sounds of crying children from the small, vacant lot. Recent Balinese monuments (intentionally visible on route from the airport) are immense, baroque affairs celebrating ancient Hindu gods.

After national independence, older monuments in Jakarta came down and new ones went up, in the crude style of Soviet realism. President Sukarno was exceedingly fond of statues and ordered one built that mimicked the Washington monument. As his popularity waned from his extravagances, people referred to it as "Sukarno's last erection." Another monument of liberation in Jakarta distinguishes a busy traffic circle. This "youth monument" portrays an elevated, large, and muscular male peasant holding above his head a large circle, engulfed in flame. Modern Jakartans, especially youth, often irreverently term this heroic image "Pizza Man." People regard the statue as a landmark by which to give directions through the city's traffic clogged streets. This is not to belittle the heroism of the Indonesian national revolution, but to illustrate how political monuments often take on unintended meanings in local, popular culture.

The famous *Taman Mini Indonesia* ("Beautiful Indonesia in Minature") arose through the direction of President Suharto's wife, inspired by a visit to Disneyland. This took place amid great protest, displacing several neighborhoods and countless people whose homes were razed for the project. This was a monument to the New Order slogan "Unity in Diversity," which features miniature ancient and recent Javanese monuments, impressive replicas of the customary styles of homes throughout Indonesia's 26 provinces, an immense pavilion, a shopping center, a small lake, hotel, and a waterfall, among other attractions. The project cost many millions and the opening ceremony in 1975 included Imelda Marcos. The theme park attracts hoards of people each year. As a tourist site, it is a successful monument to Indonesia.

In the small town of Soe, West Timor, a giant monument of a man dressed in government uniform stands by the roadway, with one hand held forward in salute. Painted and resembling an immense mannequin, the figure exalts a recent, regional politician. As did kings of old, this man saw to his enormous effigy to proclaim his power. However, in this case the monument is a personified facsimile, more Stalin-like than Indonesian in style. Leaders across Indonesia have erected similar modern monuments to themselves.

At many small airports of the outer islands, life-size monuments of a man and woman dressed in indigenous garb greet visitors as they enter the terminals. These are often bordered by beds of flowers and serve to represent something of the identity of locals to those arriving to their islands. People fashion monuments of horses, leaders, flowers, or any number of images at village entranceways, asserting local powers and histories.

BURIAL STRUCTURES

The value placed upon ancestors and ceremonies honoring the dead throughout Indonesia surfaces dramatically on landscapes. Graves determine central elements of village design or provide places to visit for spiritual strength. As part of a vast megalithic arch spread by Austronesian culture, Indonesian regions such as Nias (Sumatra), Toba (Sumatra), Central Sulawesi, Sumba, and Flores contain old, immense grave markers. Some are simple table-like structures with four stone legs (dolmen). Others are elaborately designed megaliths, carved with a range of figures and designs. Yet others resemble graves in the Western world. Burial structures reflect the layers of religious thought and diversity of the archipelago.

Islamic Graves

Muslim graves usually consist of stone or cement (and more recently include tiles), with a distinct head marker and an elongated section under which the deceased lies buried. They somewhat resemble graves in Europe and North America. The section over the body may be an elevated block (sometimes resembling a building) or a flat rectangular section near ground level. Depending on where Muslim graves exist in Indonesia, they might lie near mosques, outside of towns in graveyards, or within villages. Styles of head stones differ greatly, from simple rounded pillars, to flat, inscribed tablets, to forms reminiscent of earlier Hindu–Buddhist influences.

Tombs also enclose the Islamic dead. These can be as large as buildings or smaller structures accommodating one person. Denoting people of importance, tombs hold exalted meaning. As noted of tombs on Java, "Tombs embody an authority from the past and through this embodiment offer a source of power. ... Individuals on Java visit tombs with their special intentions, often at times of personal crisis, in order to place themselves in relationship to a personage of the past."[66] Tombs of Islamic saints are great mausoleums, with caretakers and specific practices (such as meditation) required by people wanting to visit them. Numerous religious leaders, devotees, and presidents of Indonesia have visited tombs of certain saints to receive spiritual guidance and renewed power.

The most recent and renowned of these was President Abdurrahman Wahid, who in 2001 visited the tomb of a long-departed spiritual leader before deciding to fire part of his cabinet. Although this caused alarm among politicians, many Javanese understood his actions, some believing that such spirituality signified a true leader. Wahid's frequent visits to tombs and absences from cabinet meetings and government affairs, however, eventually earned him a vote of no confidence, thus ending a short-lived presidency.

Tombs and Graves throughout the Archipelago

The Kenyah people of Kalimantan entomb their dead in structures called *liang*—often mirroring the design of their homes but with more elaborately carved, up-curving wooden extensions along the roof tops and eaves. Some of life's essentials accompany the deceased within these structures, such as salt, a sword, tobacco, and eating implements. Brass gongs and pottery decorate the outside to denote wealth. Kenyah construct *liang* downstream from their villages, to prevent the dead from returning to the realm of the living.

A number of groups erect tombs to resemble clan homes. Some Christian Batak construct concrete tombs, mimicking the details of their traditional homes. These are often deeply etched with patterns and brightly painted, with a cross and name of the deceased in front. Minangkabau of western Sumatra traditionally have built a *rumah gadang* over grave sites, complete with arching, elegant spires on a saddleback roof. In parts of Toraja Land, Sulawesi, miniature *tongkonan* mark burial sites of the dead. Indeed, the dead must be housed in manners similar to the living in these societies.

The famous graves of the Sa'dan Toraja (named after a nearby river) long have been chiseled caves of hillsides, which entomb the departed (wrapped in many *ikat* and silken textiles) and feature his or her carved wooden effigy at the entrance. Some of the caves are sealed with carved wooden doors, often containing imagery of the symbolically important water buffalo. These caves reach soaring heights and transporting a body and effigy to the higher sites requires tremendous group effort and agility.

Grave types have changed drastically with the times in some, if not most, regions. Batak monuments were once as large and spectacular as those of Sumba, with carved figures riding an elephant or lion. These were hewn from quarries and dragged to the burial site, asserting the wealth and power of the family of the deceased. Since conversion to Islam and then Christianity, many Batak have abandoned these sculpted grave markers. Now, from various reports, in addition to their house-like tombs the northern Toba Batak erect tall, concrete *tugu* (meaning memorial monument) in their place, sponsored by relatives working in cities. These appear as modern monuments—geometrical and upright, bearing a statue of the clan founder on top. Yet, they still emphasize wealth and status and even expanded, worldly knowledge in their contemporary design.[67]

The island of Nias sits off the west coast of Sumatra and long maintained a culture that differed from those on the mainland. Megalithic statuary on this island reached immense heights. Sculptors created unique, distinctive stone pieces of all uses that came to designate prestige of the living and fill village grounds. Ancestral effigies, however, held central importance. Some

Nias statues rose more than three meters high, rivaling the stone heads of Easter Island. People also dragged huge, chiseled stone slabs to burial sites. Following conversion to Christianity in the early twentieth century, these arts and practices went into decline in Nias.

Nowhere in the archipelago do graves exceed the effort, expense, and ongoing reverence as in Sumba. These consist of large, chiseled slabs weighing up to 60 tons, dragged to a burial site by great numbers of people, then carved and finished with a curved stele (headstone) called a *penji*. This might symbolize a banner, a sword hilt, or even an unfolding fern. Often finely carved, *penji*s are relatively small in comparison to the megaliths they adorn. Consequently, many have been stolen and sold to international collectors over the past century. Headstones often also include ancestral figures, stylized trees, mythical creatures, or animals. The other end of a burial slab might feature a smaller motif or remain unadorned.

People bury their dead in excavated chambers beneath the gravestones, often large enough to hold many. More than 100 *ikat* fabrics might enfold the deceased, depending upon rank. In eastern Sumba, the ground must be cooled with the blood of a sacrificed horse before a body can be carried safe from evil spirits to the grave chamber. In the west of the island, people sac-rifice water buffalo for this purpose. In recent times, stone dragging carries renewed prestige, leading one anthropologist to note a "'ritual inflation' in the size, decoration and elaboration of new funerary art forms"[68] in Sumba. People will drag a stone for distances as great as 5 miles over hilly terrain. This sometimes involves floating a slab across an ocean inlet atop logs for part of the distance. Sumbanese invest immense amounts of time and expense into funeral markers and their surrounding rituals. These continue to persist and evolve in grandness of scale and elaboration.

In parts of Indonesia, graves consist of simple concrete slabs embedded with relatively cheap commercial blue or white square tiles. These permit comparatively inexpensive undertakings for the less affluent and often sit just outside of households. Yet, however humble a grave might be, it will bear indispensable value to those burying their dead. In the city of Kupang, West Timor, in 1999, several such graves filled the modest yard of a poor trader, the smaller ones memorializing the family's lost children. Crosses and blue tile headstones served as markers for these sites.

NOTES

1. Tom Therik, *Wehali—The Female Land: Traditions of a Timorese Ritual Centre* (Can-berra: Pandanus Books, published in association with the Research School of Pacific and Asian Studies, The Australian National University, 2004), 316–317.

2. See Witold Rybczynski, *Home: The Short History of an Idea* (New York: Penguin Books, 1987). As commerce flourished in Holland in the sixteenth century, men took their business and trade to offices and factories away from their homes. For the first time, homes became solely womens' domain and they proceeded to make them more decorative and comfortable.

3. This photograph appears in *Toekang Potret: 100 Years of Photography in the Dutch Indies* [*Toekang Potret* means "A Photographer" in Indonesian language] (Rotterdam: The Museum of Ethnology at Rotterdam, 1989), 105.

4. *Toekang Potret,* 60, 72, 119, 151.

5. Roxana Waterson, *The Living House: An Anthropology of Architecture in Southeast Asia* (London: Thames and Hudson, 1997), 91–92.

6. Muhamad Radjab, "Village Childhood (The Autobiography of a Minangkabau Child)" in *Telling Lives, Telling History: Autobiography and Historical Imagination in Modern Indonesia,* ed. and trans. Susan Rodgers (Berkeley: University of California Press, 1995), 151.

7. Radjab, "Village Childhood," 151.

8. Anthony Reid, *Southeast Asia in the Age of Commerce—1450–1680: Volume One, The Lands below the Winds* (New Haven: Yale University Press, 1988), 62.

9. Reid, *Southeast Asia in the Age of Commerce,* 51.

10. Reid, *Southeast Asia in the Age of Commerce,* 51–52.

11. Waterson, *The Living House,* 42, paraphrased here.

12. See Gunawan Tjahjono, ed., *Indonesian Heritage: Architecture* (Singapore: Archipelago Press, 2001) for many fine illustrations and explanations of numerous types of Indonesian houses.

13. Tjahjono, *Indonesian Heritage,* 20, paraphrased and expanded upon here.

14. Clifford Geertz, "Deep Play: Notes on the Balinese Cockfight," in *The Interpretation of Cultures* (New York: Basic Books, 1973), 447.

15. Geertz, "Deep Play," 447.

16. See Therik, *Wehali,* 150.

17. Joseph Prijotomo, *Ideas and Forms of Javanese Architecture* (Yogyakarta, Java: Gadjah Mada University Press, 1988), 40–41, See p. 56 for an illustration of a Javanese house floor plan.

18. See Fred B. Eiseman, Jr., *Bali: Sekala and Niskala, Volume I, Essays on Religion, Ritual, and Art* (Denpasar, Bali: Periplus Editions, 1990), 2–10 for extensive explanation of these terms, partially paraphrased here.

19. See Jacques Dumarcay, *The House in Southeast Asia* (Singapore: Oxford University Press, 1987), 43–48.

20. See Tjahjono, *Indonesian Heritage,* 26.

21. Tjahjono, *Indonesian Heritage,* 26, paraphrased here.

22. Craig Latrell, personal communication in 2005, based in fieldwork with the Minangkabau. For more on this cosmological concept, see Latrell's "Widening the Circle: The Refiguring of West Sumatran Randai," *Asian Theatre Journal* 16, no. 2 (Fall 1999): 248–259.

23. P. Pospos, "Me and Toba," in *Telling Lives, Telling History: Autobiography and Historical Imagination in Modern Indonesia,* ed. and trans. Susan Rodgers (Berkeley: University of California Press, 1995), 81.

24. Pospos, "Me and Toba," 81, footnote.

25. See Andrew Causey, *Hard Bargaining in Sumatra* (Honolulu: University of Hawaii Press, 2003), 250 n.4.

26. Causey, *Hard Bargaining in Sumatra,* 115.

27. Kathleen Adams, "Taming Traditions: Torajan Ethnic Imagery in the Age of Tourism." in *Converging Interests: Traders, Travelers, and Tourists in Southeast Asia,* ed. Jill Forshee, with Christina Fink and Sandra Cate (Berkeley: Center for Southeast Asia Studies, University of California, 1999), 251–252, from which I borrow here.

28. See Adams, "Taming Traditions," 249–263. See also Eric Crystal, "Tourism in Toraja," in *Hosts and Guests: The Anthropology of Tourism,* ed. Valene Smith (Philadelphia: University of Pennsylvania Press, 1989), 109–125; and Toby Volkman, "Visions and Revisions: Toraja Culture and the Tourist Gaze," *American Ethnologist* 17 (1990): 91–110.

29. Kathleen Adams, personal communication, January 30, 2006.

30. For more information on the Atoni, their unusual homes, and culture see Clark Cunningham, "Order in the Atoni House," *Bijdragen tot de Taal-, Land-en Volkenkunde* 120 (1964): 34–68.

31. See Therik, *Wehali,* 165–176.

32. Dumarcay, *The House in Southeast Asia,* 62.

33. This borrows from the title of the book by Waterson, *The Living House,* cited in full above.

34. See Waterson, *The Living House,* 131–132.

35. Miguel Covarrubias, *The Island of Bali* (New York: Knopf, 1937), 88; also cited in Waterson, *The Living House,* 130.

36. See Claude Levi-Strauss, *The Way of the Masks* (London: Cape, 1983), 185–187, for ideas of the French anthropologist who developed this social category.

37. Waterson, *The Living House,* 46, paraphrased here.

38. Jill Forshee, personal observation during fieldwork.

39. Jill Forshee, *Between the Folds: Stories of Cloth, Lives, and Travels from Sumba* (Honolulu: University of Hawaii Press, 2000), 18, 208 n.10.

40. Janet Hoskins, *The Play of Time: Kodi Perspectives on Calendars, History, and Exchange* (Berkeley: University of California Press, 1993), 14.

41. James J. Fox, "Introduction," in *Origins, Ancestry and Alliance: Explorations in Austronesian Ethnography,* ed. James J. Fox and Clifford Sather (Canberra: The Australian National University, Department of Anthropology, 1996), 2.

42. Waterson, *The Living House,* 124.

43. See Toby Volkman, *Feasts of Honor: Ritual and Change in the Toraja Highlands* (Urbana: University of Illinois Press, 1985), 47.

44. Roy Ellen, "Microcosm, Macrocosm, and the Nuaulu House: Concerning the Reductionist Fallacy as Applied to Metaphorical levels," *Bijdragen tot de Taal-, Land-en Volkenkunde* 142, no. 1 (1986): 2–30.

45. Barbara Dix Grimes, in *Origins, Ancestry and Alliance: Explorations in Austronesian Ethnography,* ed. James J. Fox and Clifford Sather (Australian National University, Department of Anthropology, 1996), 199–215.

46. See Gregory Forth, *Rindi: An Ethnographic Study of a Traditional Domain in Eastern Sumba* (The Hague: Martinus Nijhoff) for a detailed description of values placed upon sections of an East Sumba home.

47. See Tjahjono, ed., *Indonesian Heritage,* 43.

48. See Susan McKinnon, *From a Shattered Sun: Hierarchy, Gender, and Alliance in the Tanimbar Islands* (Madison: University of Wisconsin Press, 2001).

49. See Waterson, *The Living House,* 161–163.

50. See N. L. Kana, "The Order and Significance of the Savunese House," in *The Flow of Life: Essays on Eastern Indonesia,* ed. James J. Fox (Cambridge, MA: Harvard University Press, 1980), 228–229.

51. See Kana, "The Order and Significance of the Savunese House," from which I draw from here.

52. Kana, "The Order and Significance of the Savunese House," 228.

53. See Shelly Errington, "Embodied *Sumange* in Luwu," *Journal of Asian Studies,* 42, no. 3: 545–570. Also quoted in Waterson, *The Living House,* 115.

54. See Waterson, *The Living House,* 115–116 (paraphrased here).

55. Waterson, *The Living House,* 94, noting personal communication from Clifford Sather.

56. Ron Gluckman, "Waterworld," http://www.gluckman.com/Waterworld.html (accessed January 29, 2006).

57. See Diana Darling and Bodrek Arsana (photo essay by Obro Markoto), "The Morning After the New Order," *Latitudes* 43 (August 2004): 56–65. I borrow from this article here.

58. Urban Poor Linkage in Indonesia (UPLINK), http://www.habitants.org/article/articleprint/1502/-1/395/.

59. Lea Jellinek, "Big Projects, Little People," Inside Indonesia, Edition No. 50, On-line, http://www.insideindonesia.org/edit50/lea.htm, paraphrased here.

60. Urban Poor Asia, On-line (2003) http://www.achr.net/indonesia.htm (accessed August 2005).

61. See Phillip Rawson, *The Art of Southeast Asia* (London: Thames and Hudson, 1967), 203–272.

62. Tjahjono, *Indonesian Heritage,* 58.

63. See Hildred Geertz, *The Life of a Balinese Temple: Artistry, Imagination, and History in a Peasant Village* (Honolulu: University of Hawaii Press, 2004), xv.

64. See Eiseman, *Bali,* 46.

65. Tjahjono, *Indonesian Heritage,* 134.

66. James J. Fox, "Interpreting the Historical Significance of Tombs and Chronicles in Contemporary Java," in *The Potent Dead: Ancestors, Saints and Heroes in Contemporary Indonesia,* ed. Henri-Chambert-Loir and Anthony Reid (Crows Nest, Australia: Allen & Unwin; and Honolulu: University of Hawaii Press, 2002), 160.

67. See Edward M. Bruner, "Megaliths, Migration, and the Segmented Self," in *Cultures and Societies of North Sumatra,* Veröffentlichungen der Universität Hamburg, Vol. 19 (Berlin: Dietrich Reimer Verlag, 1987), 133–149.

68. Janet Hoskins, "The Stony Faces of Death: Funeral and Politics in East and West Sumba," in *Messages in Stone,* ed. Jean Paul Barbier (Milan: Skira, 1999), 169.

SUGGESTED READING

Barbier, Jean Paul. *Messages in Stone: Statues and Sculptures from Tribal Indonesia in the Collections of the Barbier-Mueller Museum.* Milan: Skira, 1999.

Dumarcay, Jacques. *The House in Southeast Asia.* Trans. and ed. by Michael Smithies. Singapore: Oxford University Press, 1987.

Eiseman, Fred. B. *Bali: Sekala & Niskala: Essays on Religion, Ritual, and Art (Volume I).* Hong Kong: Periplus Editions, 2004.

Feldman, Jerome, *The Eloquent Dead: Ancestral Sculpture of Indonesia and Southeast Asia.* Los Angeles: UCLA Museum of Cultural History, 1985.

Geertz, Hildred. *The Life of a Balinese Temple: Artistry, Imagination, and History in a Peasant Village.* Honolulu: University of Hawaii Press, 2004.

Rawson, Philip. *The Art of Southeast Asia.* London: Thames and Hudson, 1967.

Rybczynski, Witold. *Home: The Short History of an Idea.* New York: Penguin Books, 1987.

Tjahjono, Gunawan, ed. *Architecture, Indonesian Heritage Series.* Singapore: Archipelago Press, 2001.

Waterson, Roxana. *The Living House: An Anthropology of Architecture in South-East Asia.* London: Thames and Hudson, 1997.

Wijaya, Made. *Architecture of Bali: A Source Book of Traditional and Modern Forms.* Honolulu: University of Hawaii Press, 2003.

5

Cuisine and Traditional Dress

Cuisine and traditional dress across Indonesia share clear similarities and remarkable differences. As people increasingly migrated between islands over the past century, now eateries serving distant cuisines appear by the sides of roads on remote islands. Regarding dress, people buy Javanese factory-made *sarungs,* shirts, slacks, skirts, or blouses in markets across the archipelago. Many men and women wear *sarung*s at home, as they are inexpensive and comfortable. Urban Indonesians have adopted modern dress for many decades, and denim jeans and T-shirts are established casual wear among young people everywhere. Yet local cuisines and dress still thrive and even have resurged in many places. Traditional dress and food have gained renewed distinction in modern times, as people strive to maintain their ethnic, clan, gender, and class identities.

Bali, Java, and Sumatra, influenced by India, court cultures, Hindu-Buddhism, and Islam early on, offer some of the most sophisticated, subtle, and spicy foods of Indonesia. These islands also produce elegant and refined fabrics for clothing, including silks and weavings of silver and gold. Ceremonial costumes in Bali or Sumatra may be multi-layered and splendid, comparable to the archipelago's finest cuisine. In some places, traditional dress involves complex textiles whereas food remains simple, receiving relatively minimal attention. For example, many eastern islands maintain highly developed textile traditions and people take special care in ways of making and wearing cloth. Yet local foods frequently offer little diversity or flavor in these regions—likely because these were not court influenced societies. As times change everywhere, so do ways of dressing and eating. While essential for survival, food and clothing fundamentally denote social rank, wealth, and more recently a modern savvy following global fashion trends. This chapter will describe customary ideas and manners of cuisine and dress in contemporary Indonesian contexts.

CUISINE

Most foreign visitors to Indonesia vividly remember their first "sense" after arrival—the multiple and exotic aromas of foods wafting through the air from houses and open-air eateries. Reflecting centuries of incoming influences, many ingredients flavoring Indonesian cuisine originated from around the globe. The hot chili made its way from Mexico through Spanish conquest in the Philippines, along with green beans, tomatoes, maize, and potatoes. Portuguese introduced peanuts and sweet potatoes from colonies in Africa and Brazil, along with papayas and pineapples. Dutch brought cabbage, carrots, and cauliflower. Centuries before, Chinese imported soy products, stir-frying, noodles, and domestic pigs. Earliest known influences arrived from India, introducing onions, garlic, eggplant, and spices like coriander, cumin, and ginger. Most notably, India also brought the fine culinary art of making curries, which Indonesians adopted and recreated with ingenuity and zest. Living amid native and abundant coconut palms, people could freely access milk forming the basis of curry sauce.

Apparently, Indonesians used turmeric, coconut, cassava, palm sugar, salt, tamarind, and fish paste before the introduction of other foods. Fruits grew far more abundantly than vegetables, including mangoes, bananas, durians, jackfruits, rambutans, citrus fruits, and mangosteens. Some fruits, however, functioned as vegetables, as people ate them green. Indonesians flavor and cook un-ripened jackfruits, papayas, bananas, and mangoes as they would vegetables. Many enjoy the sautéed, bitter flowers of the papaya plant and believe they prevent malaria. Fish may have been the most common meat-like protein of early Indonesian diets, along with wild pigs, dogs, and chickens. Austronesians probably introduced wet rice farming to some islands as far back as two to three thousand years ago.

As the staple grain of Indonesia, rice feeds millions three times a day and carries immense religious importance. In most of the eastern islands, cassava (*ubi kayu* in Indonesian) formerly provided the main carbohydrate, and people still mix bits of this root into the rice they now eat. Many believe this enriches the grain, but often mixing cassava or maize (corn) enables people to stretch a rice supply until the next harvest or to when they can afford to buy more.

Rice and Life

During its many centuries of association with man, rice in raw and cooked form has assumed special meanings, much as in the Occident, bread has become "the staff of life," the food to be ceremonially "broken."[1]

Rice represents a fundamental spiritual, social, and nutritional basis for much of Indonesia. Balinese wear small dabs of rice on their temples and foreheads after prayer. Life's passages inspire festive accompanying rice dishes or sculptures, and most everywhere rice carries spirit. Indeed, Bali's complex irrigation systems for growing rice shaped land and culture, while sustaining strongly cooperative communities for many centuries. Likewise in Java, wet-rice cultivation involved tightly functioning political systems early on, developing into great polities such as Majapahit. Dewi Sri, the rice goddess recognized in Bali, Java, and places beyond, holds prominence among deities. Balinese honor Siwa (adopted from the Indian god Shiva) as god of the soil, supporting the growth of everything, including rice. Siwa and Dewi Sri work in complementary balance with one another.

While the "Green Revolution" (launched in the mid-twentieth century) allowed far more rice production throughout Indonesia, it also created problems for numerous farmers. Suspecting Dewi Sri's disapproval, President Suharto went to the extent of modifying national policy toward new pesticides, banning the most toxic following reports of their poisonous environmental effects. Pesticides often destroyed creatures (such as ducks, frogs, shrimps, and minnows) integral to fertilizing rice paddies and controlling crop-eating pests and malarial mosquitoes. The expense of chemical fertilizers, moreover, was beyond the means of the poor, who had formerly relied upon manure and composted plant material in fields.

Nonetheless, Indonesia is now self-sufficient in rice whereas it once was the world's largest importer of the grain. In many regions people follow modern agricultural methods and plant imported, high-yielding rice hybrids. Yet farmers in some areas maintain their time-honored methods and plant varieties. Many people express that they do not like the texture nor taste of the newer rice hybrids and much prefer their older types. This echoes older values upon precedence and origins, as in clans, houses, metaphysical beliefs, and personal identities.

In the minds of most Indonesians, consuming rice is essential to living. Many regard a meal without rice as nonsustaining and incomplete. People often express that they will weaken and become sick if deprived of rice and complain that they do not feel "satisfied" (*kenyang*) after any type of meal excluding it. They marvel at how Westerners might ever become *kenyang*, as they see them eating small portions of rice or none at all. For the Indonesian majority, rice bears crucial cosmological significance. Regarding culinary etiquette, some advise that it is acceptable if guests leave other sorts of food uneaten, but not to consume all of the rice on a plate is next to sinful.

As so much effort goes into its planting, growing, harvesting, husking, and accompanying ritual offerings, rice maintains a position of sanctity among foods. Likely for reasons of fertility, rice carries an association with women in much of Indonesia, who often plant and then harvest the grain, using small, curved knives. These cutting devises take different forms across the islands. Women cup them within their hands while cutting so as not to cause shock and fear among the rice sheaves. This method also respects the rice goddess and related spirits.

Rice paste forms the sculptural medium for brightly dyed and detailed Balinese offerings at ceremonies. It also becomes the basis for sweets eaten at these events. During a cremation procession, family members sometimes throw rice toward by-standers to ensure good feelings along their passage. In Java, a cone-shaped rice form called *nasi tumpeng* ("mountain-shaped rice"), communicates passages in life—such as the seventh month of pregnancy, weddings, and birthdays. Any number of adornments or dishes may surround this cone. After a death, relatives serve the dish sliced in half down the middle, then reorient the sections to symbolize that life and growth have come to an end. In many parts of Indonesia, fertility of rice crops connects to dead relatives and pageants honor rice and ancestors in specific ways. People symbolically feed the dead through ceremonies (including rice offerings), and in turn receive their blessings through fertile crops.

Rice marks important times of the year for people, and countless beliefs and rituals correspond with its planting, growth, and harvesting. In West Sumba, people fear that others can steal the souls of their growing rice by dancing and singing with magic baskets. Describing this belief, one account also remarks that "[f]or this reason, the months when the young rice crop is growing are shrouded in a strict silence."[2]

Types of Indonesian rice include natural colors of black, red, and white. Indonesians also like to tint rice using the turmeric root, producing *nasi kuning*, or "yellow rice," favored at festive events. The Balinese specialize in a rich pudding made of black rice, coconut milk, and palm sugar. Red rice holds special value in drier, less fertile parts of Indonesia, where people believe it provides greater nutrition than other types (likely true, as it remains un-husked).

Flavorful Fare

Popular almost everywhere, people prepare noodles (*mie*) in a number of ways. Unlike rice, they do not carry religious significance. Consisting of rice or wheat flour, Indonesian noodles might be very fine or similar to fettuccine in shape and size. Rarely served without seasoning, noodles become bases for stir-fried dishes mixed with bits of meat or vegetables. Noodles also make for filling, economical soups. Often they appear in mixed forms as side dishes with rice. *Mie goreng* (fried noodles) is one of Indonesia's most widespread simple dishes, along with *nasi goring* (fried rice). These fast, wok-cooked, economical meals typically include inexpensive ingredients or leftovers to enhance them.

Often a molasses like sauce, called *kecap manis* (sweet sauce) flavors these dishes, or else a spicy hot sauce called *sambal*. The word "ketchup" in English comes from the similarly pronounced Indonesian word *kecap* ("sauce"). In recent decades, monosodium glutamate (MSG), has become popular across Indonesia. This ingredient now goes into many foods, especially those stir-fried. Many simply call it *rasa* ("flavor").

As does Thai cuisine, the finest of Indonesian cooking requires subtle combinations of flavors and complementary dishes. Seasonings include lemon grass, ginger, shrimp paste, chilies, pureed peanuts, coconut milk, lime leaves, lemon juice, garlic, shallots, tamarind, *laos* root, cloves, nutmeg, coriander, salt, and a variety of ready-made sauces. Indonesian meals at their best offer a wide and colorful range of distinctively different dishes, always served with an abundance of rice. Curries and soups carry explicitly Indonesian tastes and scents, often including chicken, goat, beef, or seafood. For non-Islamic peoples, pork is a favorite meat. *Kangkung*, a common Indonesian vegetable served with meals stir-fried or stewed, is an aquatic green like watercress. Shrimp crackers (*krupuk*), stir-fried peanuts, along with small potato or corn fritters embellish many plates. In fact, condiments and side dishes pull together all elements of meals.

Sauces called *sambal* are one of Indonesia's extraordinary culinary art achievements. Of endless variety, many people make their own favorites. Preparing *sambal* involves pounding chilies with oils, shallots, garlic, sugar, salt, shrimp paste, and other seasonings using a mortar and pestle. Some prefer to fry pounded pastes to deepen their flavors. *Sambals* can be sweet, salty, sour, garlic-seasoned, or extremely hot with chilies. They may be smooth or chunky with ingredients such as shallots, chilies, tomatoes, and orange peel (similar to Mexican *salsa*).

Indonesians make brilliant use of soybeans, producing both tofu (*tahu*) and *tempeh*. *Tempeh* is a Javanese invention of fermented, compressed soybeans. Typically sold in public markets by the slice off of a long rectangular block, this soy product far surpasses tofu (and meat) in protein content. *Tempeh* is cheap and often referred to as "poor people's meat." However, it incorporates well many spices and sauces, is especially good fried, and people of all classes enjoy it in Java, Bali, and beyond. *Tempeh* often becomes a condiment, in small pieces deeply fried with shallots and bits of potato. Also inexpensive and available in public markets, *Tahu* (tofu) develops from fermented soybean paste and originates from China. Like *tempeh,* cooks primarily fry *tahu,* serving it with other dishes. Many eat both *tahu* and *tempeh* as snack foods sold in stalls or from small carts, often with a bit of *sambal* or a few small chilies. As walking while eating constitutes rudeness in much of Indonesia, people usually consume snacks on the spot where they buy them or take them to where they can sit.

Certain renowned recipes please locals and foreigners with their unique flavors and visual appeal. These largely originate from the western islands. Pungent, curry dishes might contain any number of combinations, such as chicken, beef, fish, eggplant, beans, or young jackfruit, and are among Indonesia's tastiest foods. Usually made with beef, *rendang* originated in the Minangkabau region of West Sumatra. Part of an intricately spiced, piquant cuisine called *Padang* (after the port city of the region), richly seasoned *rendang* becomes tender through stewing in coconut milk and appears at special events. Of course, rice, vegetables, and condiments round out this dish. Balinese *gado-gado* (meaning "mixture") consists of a salad of greens, compressed glutinous rice slices, cooked vegetables, peanuts, bean sprouts, *tahu, tempeh,* and so forth—covered with puréed peanut sauce containing coconut milk and spices. This usually includes no meat. *Saté* is Indonesia's answer to the Turkish *shish kebab* but includes only meat. Most frequently chicken or beef coated with a spicy peanut sauce and impaled upon a slender wooden skewer, this quickly cooks on open grills. *Saté* ranks among the most popular of street foods.

Then there are limitless variations upon rice dishes, a few of which follow. *Nasi campur* (mixed rice) offers a mound of white rice surrounded with a mixture of meats, seafood, vegetables, potato or corn fritters, *sambal, krupuk* crackers, peanuts, and *tahu* or *tempeh*. This attractive dish displays a medley of Indonesian foods and condiments. *Nasi Padang* also provides ample white rice with blends of spicy, curried meats and vegetables distinctive of West

Sumatran food. *Nasi goreng* (fried rice) incorporates almost any ensemble of palatable ingredients fried in a wok, flavored and colored with red *sambal*. People in Flores, Sumba, and Timor eat *nasi jagung* (corn rice), a simple rice dish cooked with bits of ground maize. *Lemper* consists of glutinous rice simmered in coconut milk, steamed with meat and spices, and then wrapped in tubes of banana leaf. These resemble small, green Mexican *tamales* and vendors sell them in Java and elsewhere. For take-away meals, people eat *nasi bungkus* (wrapped rice), containing any mixture of rice and foods in a large banana leaf package. These often include a "spoon," also fashioned from banana leaf.

Martabak stands offer a sort of large crepe enfolding spicy meat or sweet peanut and coconut fillings. They open in the evening and their food descends from recipes introduced by Arabs. While usually a snack, people might take several portions home to add to a meal. *Martabak* offers variation from rice, as it often includes wheat flour and Westerners frequently enjoy this food.

Places to Eat

While in urban regions some middle-class people have taken to Western fast foods, most still prefer Indonesian diets and never seem to abandon rice. Throughout Indonesia the most common eating-place long has been the *warung*. This is a small, inexpensive, streetside food stall where cooks quickly prepare meals, often in a wok. Common fare also includes soups and curries stewing in large pots and ready to eat. Customers typically share benches at simple tables set with condiments such as salt, *kecap*, chilies, and *sambal*. Awnings or tarps shelter these small eateries from the elements. *Warungs* range in size, quality, specialties, and remain popular places for all sorts of people to eat quickly and even very well. Most provide take-out food wrapped in banana leaves.

Warungs often serve cuisine from different regions, such as Padang food from Sumatra and Javanese dishes. Padang *warungs* attract people through the diversity and flavor of their dishes. Commonly, Indonesian bus stations feature bordering Padang *warungs*. Prepared early in the day and then served at room temperature, Padang food is always ready to eat. These modest eateries appear in the most remote places of Indonesia, as do small stalls called *kios* (borrowed from the word "kiosk"), selling soft drinks and packaged snacks. Individual vendors on most islands also sell food in the evening, as they squat beside small lanterns—offering simply peanuts, roasted corn, or fried bananas. "Fast food" is not a new phenomenon in Indonesia but centuries old.

In Java, modest hand-pushed food carts called *kaki lima* (meaning "five legs" of supports when standing still) travel residential streets. Their vendors sell soup, fried noodles or rice, sweets, fruit juices, sodas, ice cream, and so on. Each peddler emits a uniquely identifying sound to broadcast his arrival and fare. Thus, bells, drum beats, twangs of metal wires, horns, gongs, or distinctive vocal chants enliven streets and lanes—notably after dark or early morning. Often people await signals of specific carts to buy breakfast, snacks, or an evening meal. Indonesians comment that they realize the time of day by the sounds of specific *kaki lima,* heralding their specialties through neighborhoods.

As Indonesians love snacks, they also like sweets. Some *warung*s specialize in *es* (ice) dishes. Composed of finely crushed ice mixed with fruits and colorful bits of sweet agar jelly, sweetened, canned condensed milk drenches all ingredients, adding richness. *Es* dishes are Indonesia's version of ice cream sundaes and the young flock to these stands. Vendors and kiosks also sell candies, cookies, ice cream, and batter-fried bananas.

A *kaki lima* food vendor in Yogyakarta, Java selling fruit and ice dishes on a residential street. 1993. Courtesy of Jill Forshee.

Many *warungs* serve neighborhoods as social centers to meet and talk. People exchange local gossip, discuss rising prices, and express political opinions. During the 2004 political campaigns, one determined candidate opened *warungs*—bearing his name on the front awning—in every Indonesian province; thus, they were called *Warung Wiranto*. *Warungs* now cater to separate social classes. The more upscale resemble outdoor restaurants, with private tables, chairs, and elevated television sets. Some *warungs* play lively, popular music to draw in fans.

A restaurant in Indonesia is a *rumah makan* (eating house) and some *warungs* catering to the middle class resemble them. *Rumah makans* can be humble places to eat, but many are beyond the means of common people. Indonesian Chinese families often run restaurants serving a mixture of Chinese and Indonesian dishes. *Rumah makans* are common in cities and towns but rare in village or rural regions. *Warungs* and kiosks, however, seem to exist wherever there are people.

Food, Beliefs, and Behavior

Everywhere cuisine interconnects with metaphysical and practical beliefs and social behavior. Throughout Indonesia, people talk about food often, sharing recipes, expressing likes and dislikes, comparing ritual feasts, discussing crops and livestock, or complaining of high prices. The sheer number and variety of roadside food sellers reflect the paramount concern of eating in Indonesian daily life. Preparation, tastes, and customs of eating vary across the islands, as do the values placed upon certain foods. Sociability connected to food also ranges from communal events to singularly private acts.

Families might normally eat an evening meal together or separately in different parts of a household. Lunch is usually an informal affair—to the extent that in some areas individuals simply will grab a handful of cooked rice from a kitchen and eat it immediately. Formality or shared activity of eating relates to each society and class. In many areas people eat with their right hands, but most Indonesians use a tablespoon. Breakfast often consists of rice porridge with coffee or tea. Indonesians do not usually linger over meals as do Westerners, and often conversation waits until after eating.

When eating together, custom frequently determines that the head of the household or oldest male initiate dining. When guests are present, etiquette requires that the host or hostess express, "Please eat" (*Silakan makan*) before anyone makes a gesture toward doing so. Some Indonesian families share meals around a table, some dine together on a *tikar* mat, and some eat alone in private at the back of a house. Moreover, food and eating can relate to real or metaphysical dangers, as people fear poisoning, curses, or spirits entering their open mouths. Many Indonesians do not speak while eating for such reasons, and sometimes water must wait until after a meal.

Food throughout the islands incorporates greater systems of belief. As discussed, offerings and rituals ensure fertility and all crops rely upon the good will of ancestors, nature spirits, or deities. So with livestock, which affords both sustenance and status to owners. Many island people use metaphors of plants or animals as concepts—in house design, clan organization, ritual prayers, and the reckoning of space and time. Elderly people without birth records typically estimate their age by events such as the year a certain mango tree was planted. In Sumba, water buffalo correspond with their owners' biographies. The animals a man begins to raise after marriage represents the moment in time in which he reached adulthood.[3]

Certain taboos apply to foods, the most common one upon pork for Muslims. In animist regions, people often follow strictures against eating particular "clan animals." Following these ideas, creatures historically assisted the living or were even original ancestors. While not forbidden, other foods may bring on disease or relapses in malaria, if too cold or too hot. Foods might also transmit dangerous curses, and people will avoid anyone rumored to have caused illness repeatedly through offering meals or even water.

Various food taboos apply to pregnant women. In parts of Timor, expectant mothers must refrain from eating hot meals and goat meat, also classified as "hot" and thereby dangerous in Tetun society.[4] In some regions, any food held too close to a pot of indigo dye then becomes "hot" and perilous to pregnant women, as is the dye itself. In eastern Indonesia, new mothers avoid spiritually "hot" foods, yet often sit for days warmed by a household fire. On the other hand, in central Java during the *slametan* ritual celebrating the seventh month of pregnancy, the expectant woman ceremoniously eats a hard-boiled egg as a symbol of the actuality and health of her unborn child. Thus, certain foods might ensure healthy reproduction.

At funerals in many regions, all attending must have eaten to their contentment before a body can be carried safely to its grave. This relates to the Indonesian concept of *kenyang,* or satisfaction mentioned above. To leave anyone at critical ritual events unsatisfied with the food might cause bad feeling, arouse harmful spirits, and invite supernatural problems. Sumba funeral fare includes boiled pork and rice, distributed in deliberately generous servings. Feeding guests and spirits is a serious matter across Indonesia. At shamanic ceremonies of the Meratus Dayak of Kalimantan, people prepare sweet rice desserts to host the spirits, shaped into boats, airplanes, flowers, and lines of uniformed soldiers to represent both pleasant and powerful possessions. In this way, fearsome spirits (*dewa*) are appeased.[5]

To refuse hospitably offered food constitutes a grievous insult in Indonesia. Among the Meratus Dayak people of Kalimantan, "[b]y refusing food—and by extension, social connection—one becomes vulnerable to accidents, such as bites by poisonous snakes or centipedes, as well as to illness."[6] A visiting European "eco-tourist" to Sumba in 1994 created alarm and fears of witchery in several villages where she camped in her tent. A vegetarian and fearful of germs, she firmly refused all food and drink from villagers, while shunning interaction. Her inexplicable unsociability gave rise to suspicions of madness or sorcery. This tourist entered local folklore, as "the women who would not socialize."[7]

Foods also carry political functions, sometimes for the better, but also creating unforeseen problems. As the national government centers in Jakarta, Java, it attempted for decades to deploy Javanese models of "civilization" by establishing wet-rice agriculture throughout the islands. In some regions this worked well, but in others environmental and social conditions were most unsuited to this farming method. This policy accompanied the New Order's transmigration (*transmigrasi*) of people from over-crowded Java to less populated islands. Despite the use of pesticides, the introduction of wet-rice farming in some regions significantly increased incidences and strains of malaria, encephalitis, and dengue fever through the amount of standing water rice required. This provided ideal breeding environments for mosquitoes carrying these diseases. Unlike Balinese, many peoples unaccustomed to growing wet-rice were unaware of how to control mosquitoes through animals suited to rice paddies.

In the Tetun region of Timor, the *gebang* palm feeds people and carries ritual value, while the *sago* palm is the food of nobles. In this dry, mountainous region, people prefer dry-rice growing to wet-rice methods promoted by the national government. Tetun claim that the latter method is not the way of their ancestors, thus locally invalid.[8] For these people, dry rice holds precedent ritual significance while wet rice does not. Indigenous farming methods carry on through the long-standing spiritual value of foods and the practicality in producing them. As do local lineages, so do native plants carry on metaphysical worth. Likewise in Sumba, the more recently introduced white Brahmin cattle carry no ritual value, as compared to long-established species of horses, pigs, chickens, and water buffalo.

Recent Food Trends

In modern Indonesia, many have taken to fast foods and especially to instant noodles called "Super *Mie*" (*Mie* means "noodles"), similar to "Top Ramen" available in the United States. Sold everywhere, Super Mie crosses all ethnic and class boundaries and feeds urbanites and rural villagers. Now other noodle brands compete and offer a plethora of "flavor packets," some catering to more elite customers by offering "gourmet" varieties. As noted in a June 2001 article in *Latitudes*, "[m]ore than the national anthem or even the national language, the instant noodle unites."[9]

Modern notions of fashion and global influences stimulated new ideas of prestigious eating in Indonesia. In numerous urban settings, American fast-food restaurants became elevated locally to status domains of young elites. Well-dressed, dating couples frequented McDonald's and Kentucky Fried Chicken in Jakarta. In Java and Bali, Indonesians dining at such franchises often demonstrated *savoir-faire* to others in ordering and eating American "junk" food. Moreover, the bright lights and sterile, plasticized interiors of these restaurants exemplify an international standard of modernity.[10] The seductive lure of "being modern" (*moderen* in Indonesian) in Indonesia especially entices the young and the upwardly mobile. Yet, as Adrian Vickers notes in *Being Modern in Bali*: "In Bali, as in most of Southeast Asia, the desire to embrace the new [is] not new."[11] So with cuisines, as people select from incoming foods and build upon what has sustained them.

In recent times of political and economic crises, numerous Indonesians have returned to farming and raising animals with renewed vigor. Realizing the dangers of over-reliance upon tourism, foreign aid, modern global trends, or their own government, many now increasingly value their customary foods and ways of producing and preparing them. Further, following extensive international disdain of the Bush administration, Indonesians have become far less admiring of things "American." Thus, McDonald's, Kentucky Fried Chicken, Pizza Hut, and the like may come to bear different symbolic meanings than in the past. It remains to be seen how the international chaos following the terrorist attack on New York's World Trade Towers in 2001—and the United States' subsequently controversial invasion of Iraq—will reshape Indonesian ideas and trends regarding the Western world. In particular, the United States, Australia, and Britain may come to bear an altered status compared to previous years.

DRESS

Everywhere in Indonesia, manners of dress carry fundamental social importance. Even as customary dress currently wanes in some regions, people aspire to appear clean, neat, and fashionable. The Indonesian term *rapi* means "neat" but also implies a modern sleekness in dress. In cities, people typically wear contemporary, factory-made clothing, similar to styles in the West, albeit comparatively conservative. Indonesian women dress modestly and normally do not wear sleeveless blouses or short skirts. The Muslim female custom of covering the hair by wearing a *jilbab*—a cloth leaving only the face exposed—has grown in popularity in recent decades in parts of Indonesia. This may be in response to perceived excesses of modern popular culture and a renewed ethnic and religious identity. The custom has recently increased in Indonesia, reflecting attitudes of Islamic peoples toward the Bush policies in the Middle East.

Nevertheless, numerous urban youth (male and female) sport jeans, T-shirts, body piercings, tattoos, and spiky dyed hair, and they attend rave parties. In fact, T-shirts and jeans constitute standard youthful garb throughout the archipelago and have for some time. "Style" has been called a visible reference point for life in *progress*.[12] While styles of traditional dress still integrally link to prestige and power, knowledge of "newness" in an expanded, volatile world often matters most in recent status contests.

Yet style might arise and proceed from any direction, and novelty does not necessarily issue from the Euro-American world. Diversely modern Asian trends affect Indonesians: from heroes of Hong Kong martial arts action films; to songs, dances, and fashions of India's spectacular Bollywood movies; to head wraps worn by Indonesian youth following the contemporary dance style called *joget. Joget* moves to the lively Indian and Arabic inspired rhythms of *dangdut,* a Malay/Indonesian pop music craze. Through mass media and ever changing fashions in urban centers, more than ever before Indonesians enjoy access to stylistic trends from both hemispheres.

People throughout the islands proclaim identities through their dress, involving deeper personal and social meanings. Traditional garb has not remained static in design, but reflects individual choices in aesthetics and lives revealing changing

University students wearing *jilbab*s in central Java. 1990. Courtesy of Jill Forshee.

times. This likely always was so, although to a far lesser extent than in today's world. Across Indonesia, many dress in combinations of new and old ways: selectively modern while retaining essentials of their homeland customs.

Where Threads Still Bind

Customary dress across Indonesia communicates binding cosmological principles, group identities, and local systems of meaning and power. It enhances cultural ideals of masculinity and femininity, in multiple ways. Still thriving through the islands, some traditional styles gained renewed value in recent times. However, as textile scholars note: "Precisely because it wears thin and disintegrates, cloth becomes an apt medium for communicating a central problem of power: Social and traditional relationships are necessarily fragile in an impermanent, ever-changing world."[13]

Traditional Indonesian apparel chronicles people's histories, secures social relationships, and communicates to others. Such dress widely ranges between islands in specific motifs and techniques, but most always emerges from local designers, weavers, and dyers. In some regions, imported cloths, such as ancient Indian trade fabrics (*patola* cloths) or Javanese *batik* head cloths, became adopted into costumes regarded as locally traditional. These may symbolize formerly prestigious foreign trade connections or assertions of descent from royal courts on other islands.

Still, "tradition" usually survives through changing—incorporating aspects that update and enhance its current relevance. Traditions rarely function over time as rigidly inadaptable dogmas. As does life, they constantly undergo flux. Otherwise, old ways die out, as they have in much of the world. In so-called developed countries, people tend to regard "traditional societies" as completely static—following resolutely ancient, unalterable forms of culture. Moreover, when such societies demonstrate creative innovations reflecting their current ideas of the world, outsiders might then label them as "spoiled" or "no longer authentic," as though they must remain frozen in time to be genuine.

Romantic or stark definitions of the traditional give short shrift to non-Western peoples, whose lives are as dynamic and innovative as people elsewhere (not to mention "modern," which carries unique interpretations the world over). The difference in customary societies lies in certain tenacious principles that maintain traditions. These include reverence toward ancestors, belief in the metaphysical, and the successful carrying on of clan lineages—values that have lapsed in much of the industrialized world. Precisely because Indonesians have remained so continuously adaptive and ingenious, they have been able to brilliantly maintain traditions important to them in the face of modern pressures. This applies to all aspects of cultures but becomes visible and individual through manners of dress.

Clothing throughout the archipelago historically derived from local plants and barks. Thus, cloth, dyes, and looms intricately connected with indigenous ecologies and cosmologies. Manners of dress long have signified people's identities, their comings and goings, what they regard as meaningful, and diverse social interactions with outside peoples throughout the past. Traditional dress also reflects ongoing tensions between the past and the present. In recent times, customary dress interweaves and convolutes the traditional and the modern, blurring these categories. As surviving traditions are never inert, so it goes with Indonesian clothing.

Most customary Indonesian dress bases upon a *sarung* or a *kain. Sarung*s are cloths sewn together at either end to form a tube. People then step into, pull

Girls in West Timor stand before a "beehive" house, wearing finely woven *buna sarungs. Buna* is a unique, painstaking weaving method resembling embroidery, mastered by women in certain regions of West Timor. 1999. Courtesy of Jill Forshee.

up, then wrap and tuck this cloth around their waists, sometimes adding a sash. *Sarungs* and *kains* always extend to the ankle, except when worn by men on certain islands, where they reach the knees. In Java, Bali, and other islands both men and women wear *sarungs*, which vary in their patterns and manners of fastening. On islands like Sumatra, Sulawesi, Flores, Sumba, Timor, and beyond, traditional *sarungs* differ. Of heavier, handwoven textiles, they are narrower and longer in shape. Only women wear these tubular garments— long enough to pull up over the breasts and fasten, or to draw up to the waist and tuck.

Kain means simply "cloth" in Indonesian. In dress it refers to a lengthy stretch of unsewn fabric, typically 3 meters in length. This might be wrapped and cinched in multiple ways and worn by men or women in many places, involving all levels of formality. Women often wear a *batik kain* with a matching *selendang*—a shawl draped over one shoulder. They use *kain* for practical needs, like carrying babies by tying the cloths into a sling across their shoulders. *Kain* often functions as backpacks, as women carry purchases from the market in them, or female vendors bundle their goods to market in this cloth.

Traditional wear visibly accentuates cultural ideals of masculinity and femininity across the islands. Women's hips become emphasized and attractive to men through the way they appear in *sarungs* or *kains*. Men in diverse regions express that they only appreciate a woman's figure if clad in local dress. This follows the ways a garment fits and hangs, as well as how it flows in movement. Following customary poise, women throughout Indonesia should be slow and graceful (*halus*), and clothing accentuates their movements. Most traditional wear inhibits long strides affecting a woman's poise. Some have interpreted this as constraining women's mobility in a larger sense, notably in Java where women's tightly wrapped *kain* can be especially binding.[14]

Regarding this *kain*, one argues that, "restrictions on the behavior of women symbolized by 'traditional' Javanese clothing were actually an innovation of the 1950s and 1960s and are kept in place by oppressive government programs and policies circulated throughout Indonesian society by modern media."[15] In fact, the national government deployed images of the ideal Indonesian woman as primarily those of "motherhood" (*keibuan*)—the foundation of home life and nationalism. It follows that inflated emphasis upon binding, traditional female dress was part of these programs and policies.

Batik often epitomizes "Indonesian-ness," carrying the status of the national costume, yet also providing everyday wear as *sarungs* and *kains*. *Batik* is mandatory formal wear in Java. The finest cloths of silk adorn men and women in assorted styles and colors. Javanese men don distinct *batik* headpieces for ceremonial wear, folded and shaped in complex ways to construct a classical, pleated cap (called *iket*, meaning "bundled" or "bound," relating to the word

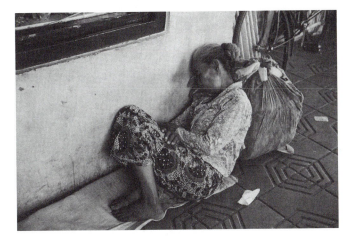

A market woman in Java takes a midday nap, wearing a commercial *batik kain,* resting against her backpack of wares bundled in an old *kain.* 1994. Courtesy of Jill Forshee.

ikat). The traditional *iket* descends from court cultures and indicates refinement. Male headpieces express cultural and individual notions of status and masculinity throughout the archipelago and range widely in style.

Better *sarungs* or *kain* are of silk or fine cotton decorated with elegantly precise handcrafted *batik.* This wax-resist dye method (described in Chapter 3) lends status to clothing through the time and skill involved in its patterns. Internationally, *batik* represents the quintessentially Indonesian textile. Elegant and inexhaustible, its motifs take natural forms like birds and flowers, but also contain abstract, symbolic designs from diverse courts and regions. Altogether, approximately three thousand *batik* patterns are on record.[16]

Although originally and still predominantly a Javanese art, this cloth long ago traveled to outer islands, where *batik* headpieces worn by men still denote their standing. Women on various islands proudly don their best *batik kains* and *selendangs* for special occasions. In many regions of Indonesia, wearing their finest *batik* clothing is how people "dress up."

With a *sarung* Indonesian women usually wear blouses called *kebayas*, of silk, voile, or nylon. These form-fitting, long-sleeved garments resemble sheer jackets, delicately embroidered down the front panels and the wrists. As they do not include buttons, women secure them with broaches (or often simply safety pins) to keep them closed. These came to Indonesia via Malaysia, following religious conversions of Indonesians to Islam or Christianity. Formerly, women of most islands went bare-breasted or wore simple cloths across their chests, leaving their shoulders and arms free. Dutch further encouraged modesty in unconverted societies, and women complied by wearing cloth or blouses. *Kebayas* also took long, shapeless forms and women have worn loose tunics (*baju*).

Minangkabau women wear a spectacular head cloth called a *tengkuluak* ("head cloth") often folded around a crescent-shaped form. At formal events, these textiles go on display as women form a parade and represent their matrilineal descent groups. The long *tengkuluak* contain intricate patterns of finely woven gold threads. Motifs evoke key Minangkabau tenets of spiritual and behavioral righteousness, including ceremonial foods and esteemed animals. The wealthier the woman, the more intricate and multiple the designs on her headpiece, along with its increased size. In bulk and elaboration, the *tengkuluak* communicates the weight and complexity of women's responsibilities in this persistently matrilineal society. These headpieces mirror the shape of Minangkabau roofs, as they form upward-curving crescents suggesting water buffalo horns. As do roofs, they also may imply spiritual notions of an invisible realm, required to complete the arcs to form full circles. The women also wear silken shoulder cloths, long-fitted tunics, and *sarungs* containing gold threads and mica or *sarungs* of fine *batik*.

In the Lampung region of South Sumatra, gold threads, embroidery, and mirror-like mica sequins adorn some of the most splendid and intricately patterned traditional clothing of Indonesia. *Tapis* (meaning "wrapped cloth") skirts worn by women display elegantly curving, labyrinthine designs. Gold threads are laid upon sections in patterns and then hand sewn into a woven cloth by a technique called "couching." Further embroidery and sequins of varying sizes render these pieces spectacular. Viewing a *tapis* is like seeing countless possibilities in art and life portrayed in cloth. International museums and collectors especially seek and prize *tapis* pieces.

The island of Timor produces textiles using a broad scope of techniques and motifs, some solely specific to regions. Moreover, "one of the delights of the textiles on Timor is that they are still very much a part of a living tradition."[17] Across its length, Timor's peoples might employ the most varied scope of techniques of all the Indonesian islands, including *ikat,* embroidery, couching, twining, supplementary warps and wefts, floating threads within a weave, and so on. Motifs across this island differ tremendously. Cloth of some regions bears no resemblance to that of not-so-distant parts of the same island. The history of mountainous Timor Island is complex and particular and vividly emerges through the range and intricacy of its woven clothing. Indigenous dress has maintained in Timor to a far greater extent than other traditional forms such as houses.

Ikat textiles represent an older type of fabric that for centuries has clothed the royalty of some islands. Torajans of Sulawesi, Sumbanese, Bataks of

The *Raja* of Boti, West Timor, wearing clothing from cotton grown, spun, dyed, and woven by his village. 1999. Courtesy of Jill Forshee.

northern Sumatra, Dayaks of Kalimantan and peoples of Flores, Lembata, Timor, Savu, Solor, Adonara, Lamalera, Tanimbar, and other islands have long produced distinctive patterns using the *ikat* technique. Entire books have been written on the *ikat* cloth of just one island region, and this section only can attempt a general description of this important fabric. Many *ikats* contain symbols from animist iconographies such as plant forms, animals, and amphibians or human figures representing ancestors. People have borrowed motifs from many incoming sources and *ikat* pieces contain images from Indian, Dutch, Chinese, or Portuguese encounters. These include ancient Indian trade cloth patterns, Chinese dragons, heraldic lions from colonial coins and seals, European floral designs with vases, and winged cherubs. The late queen Wilhelmina of the Dutch colonial era became a standard, localized motif in East Sumba. Helicopters and the likenesses of President Bill Clinton also appeared in eastern Sumba *ikat* in the early 1990s.

Larger, blanket-like *ikat* pieces wrap the lower bodies of men, sometimes with matching shoulder cloths. *Ikat* also decorates head cloths for men, worn proudly in diverse manners. Women wear *ikat* as tubular skirts and shawls. In Sumba, 100 *ikats* may enfold a dead body—the motifs of the outermost fabric identifying the deceased to ancestors in the next world. People use the best cloths possible for burials. The departed family member and ancestors directly affect well-being of the living so must receive due honors. These tenacious beliefs, more than anything else, maintain local quality control in textiles.

Ikats also are essential in bridal exchange. In the eastern islands of Indonesia (sometimes called the exchange archipelago), typically a new wife's family gives textiles to that of her husband's, who reciprocate with animals such as water buffalo, horses, and gold pieces of jewelry. In fact, to be marriageable, women of some islands must be appropriately skilled in the arts of creating *ikat* and other fabrics. Daughters in this part of Indonesia, however, hold immense value for their parents, due to the wealth they are able to bring in through their bride price.[18]

Ikat cloths for men are generally called *selimut* in Indonesian (meaning "blanket") but hold specific names in every regional language. These wrap lower bodies in multiple styles but usually extend no longer than knee length. Men of Timor, Sumba, Flores, and elsewhere still commonly wear these garments. Many ride horses between villages clad in *ikat* cloths. People wear their best *ikat* fabrics for ceremonies. Indispensable head cloths mark men's rank or ritual function, proclaim their masculinity, and assert their personality. In recent years, the head cloth might be the sole element of a young man's attire marking his historical identity. Ironically, jeans and a T-shirt further accentuate a traditional cloth wrapped about the head. Head cloths consist of pounded bark, *batik,* a bright solid color, the finest *ikat,* or other esteemed types of fabric. Men in some areas fashion these in individualistic ways.

In Sumba, a wrapped head cloth characteristically features a starched, upright, protruding end. This resembles a cockscomb (of a rooster) or pompadour when worn at the front, though some wear them to one side. Terms for "cock" bear the same double entendre in Indonesian as in English (as well as in some local languages of the archipelago). Following this, a jauntily stiff, upright portion of cloth suggests a phallus. Remarkably, Elvis Presley, with his trademark hairstyle, has been a hero for decades in East Sumba. Such was his popularity that for a number of years an annual "Elvis Impersonator" contest took place on the east coast of the island. The Elvis frontal pompadour, stiffened with pomade to remain erect and distinctly masculine, incited a multi-cultural overlapping of style in Sumba—with the head cloth symbolizing similar attributes. Thus, cultural ideals of masculinity become enhanced through traditional dress, which paralleled more recent trends from afar.

For women of Sumba, *ikat sarungs* (*lau*) of finer style include other methods of complex weaving, embellished with shells and beads. *Lau hada* ("*lau* with beads and shells"), display decorative images solely through densely clustered beads and shells sewn onto black woven cloth. *Lau hada* contain the oldest of Sumba's motifs, from times before people used the *ikat* technique. Women's traditional cloths more often feature older indigenous motifs than do men's (which might include the old with the new). This secures these ancient symbols and provides women with the role of safeguarding patterns of the distant past. Adornments on fine clothing further advertise a woman's social standing or "worth" in terms of a bride price. Thus, clothing signifies much for the family of a marriageable girl and considerable effort goes into what a daughter wears at a ritual event. This extends to gold jewelry.

Today, many Indonesians wear factory-made *batik* or plaid cloths throughout the islands. *Ikat* also issues from factories in Java and beyond but never approximates the look of handmade textiles. Most Indonesians resist wearing cheap renditions of their own traditional clothing—and always mark important life transitions with the best of customary cloth and dress. In the words of one young women of Sumba, "[t]o not wear our finest tradition cloth at funerals or weddings would be like saying that we don't know where we come from. Like saying that we don't know whom our parents are. This would be a great shame upon us, no matter how modern we may think that we are. No matter if we have converted to being Christians."[19]

NOTES

1. Lucien M. Hanks, *Rice and Man: Agricultural Ecology in Southeast Asia* (Honolulu: University of Hawaii Press, 1972), 20.

2. Janet Hoskins, "Doubling Deities, Descent, and Personhood: An Exploration of Kodi Gender Categories," in *Power & Difference: Gender in Island Southeast Asia*, ed. Jane Monnig Atkinson and Shelly Errington (Stanford: Stanford University Press, 1990), 286.

3. See Janet Hoskins, *The Play of Time: Kodi Perspectives on Calendars, History, and Exchange* (Berkeley: University of California Press, 1993), 110, paraphrased here.

4. See Tom Therik, *Wehali—The Female Land: Traditions of a Timorese Ritual Center* (Canberra: Pandanus Books, 2004), 190.

5. Anna Lowenhaupt Tsing, *In the Realm of the Diamond Queen: Marginality in an Out-of-the-Way Place* (Princeton: Princeton University Press, 1993), 94, paraphrased here.

6. Tsing, *Diamond Queen*, 189.

7. See Jill Forshee, *Between the Folds: Stories of Cloth, Lives, and Travels from Sumba* (Honolulu: University of Hawaii Press, 2001), 148–151.

8. See Therik, *Wehali*, 38, 40.

9. "Let Us Now Praise Instant Noodles," *Latitudes* 5 (June 2001): 58–60.

10. Forshee, *Between the Folds,* 228 n. 28.

11. Adrian Vickers, "Modernity and Being *Moderen:* An Introduction," in *Being Modern in Bali: Image and Change,* ed. Adrian Vickers (New Haven: Yale University Southeast Asia Studies, 1996), 9.

12. Stuart Ewen, *All-Consuming Images: The Politics of Style in Contemporary Culture* (New York: Basic Books, 1988), 33.

13. Jane Schneider and Annette B. Weiner, "Introduction," in *Cloth and Human Experience,* ed. Annette B. Weiner and Jane Schneider (Washington: Smithsonian Institution Press, 1989), 6.

14. Widespread wear of these garments came about in the late nineteenth century, with the invention of metal printing stamps to produce *batik* quickly. Thus, common women were able to afford them.

15. See Laurie J. Sears, "Introduction: Fragile Identities—Deconstructing Women and Indonesia," in *Fantasizing the Feminine in Indonesia,* ed. Laurie J. Sears (Durham: Duke University Press, 1996), 38. See also chapters by Sylvia Tiwon and Sita Aripurnami in the same volume.

16. See Anne Richter, *Arts and Crafts of Indonesia* (San Francisco: Chronicle Books, 1994), 90–91.

17. Mark Ivan Jacobson, and Ruth Marie Yeager, *Traditional Textiles of West Timor: Regional Variations in Historical Perspective* (Jacksonville, Illinois: Batuan Baru Productions, 1995), ii.

18. A bride's family also has the upper hand in requiring much more in "payment " than does the groom's to secure a marriage. Moreover, the groom's family will always be called upon to help out the family of the bride (such as in repairing a house), whereas the opposite is not true. Thus, " bride-givers" enjoy continuously higher status than do "bride-takers."

19. Told to Jill Forshee by a woman in Rindi, East Sumba in 2000.

SUGGESTED READING

Cuisine (Including Ecological and Social Aspects of Food)

Fox, James J. *Harvest of the Palm: Ecological Change in Eastern Indonesia.* Cambridge, MA: Harvard University Press, 1977.

Geertz, Clifford. *Agricultural Involution: The Process of Ecological Change in Indonesia.* Berkeley: University of California Press, 1963.

Hamilton, Roy W. *The Art of Rice: Spirit and Sustenance in Asia.* Los Angeles: The Fowler Museum of Cultural History, University of California, 2004.

Lansing, J. Stephen. *Perfect Order: Recognizing Complexity in Bali.* Princeton: Princeton University Press, 2006.

Miller, Keith Ruskin. *Indonesian Street Food Secrets: A Culinary Travel Odyssey.* Portland, OR: Hawkibinkler Press, 2003.

Von Holzen, Heinz, Lothar Arsana, and Wendy Hutton, eds. *The Food of Indonesia: Authentic Recipes of the Spice Islands.* Singapore: Periplus World Food Series, 1999.

Traditional Dress

Adams, Marie Jeanne. *System and Meaning in East Sumba Textile Design: A Study in Traditional Indonesian Art.* New Haven, CT: Yale University, Southeast Asia Studies, 1969.

Adams, Marie Jeanne, Jill Forshee, Alit Djajasoebrata, and Linda Hansen. *Decorative Arts of Sumba*. Amsterdam: The Pepin Press, 1999.

Barnes, Ruth. *The Ikat Textiles of Lamalera: A Study of an Eastern Indonesian Weaving Tradition*. Leiden: E. J. Brill, 1989.

Elliot, Inger McCabe. *Batik: Fabled Cloth of Java*. rev. ed. Hong Kong: Periplus, 2004.

Forshee, Jill. *Between the Folds: Stories of Cloth, Lives, and Travels from Sumba*. Honolulu: University of Hawaii Press, 2000.

Fischer, Joseph, ed. *Threads of Tradition: Textiles of Indonesia and Sarawak*. Berkeley: Lowie Museum of Anthropology, University of California, 1979.

Fraser-Lu, Sylvia. *Indonesian Batik: Processes, Patterns and Places*. Singapore: Oxford University Press, 1988.

Gittinger, Mattiebelle, ed. *To Speak with Cloth: Studies in Indonesian Textiles*. Los Angeles: University of California, Museum of Cultural History, 1989.

Hamilton, Roy W., ed. *Gift of the Cotton Maiden: Textiles of Flores and the Solor Islands*. Los Angeles: University of California, Museum of Cultural History, 1994.

Hitchcock, Michael. *Indonesian Textiles*. New York: HarperCollins, 1991.

Niessen, Sandra. *Batak Cloth and Clothing: A Dynamic Indonesian Tradition (The Asia Collection)*. Oxford: Oxford University Press, 1994.

Yeager, Ruth Marie, and Mark Ivan Jacobson. *Textiles of Western Timor: Regional Variations in Historical Perspective*. Bangkok: White Lotus Press, 2002.

6

Gender, Courtship, and Marriage

Gender, courtship, and marriages take varied forms across Indonesia—not always following one another in predicable ways. The Indonesian language contains no pronouns denoting gender, such as "he" or "she." This trait extends to other indigenous languages throughout the archipelago (and across Southeast Asia). Following historical accounts of many centuries back, hairstyles and dress of men and women did not emphasize sexual distinctions. Dressed in *sarung*s or wrapped cloth, people went bare to the waist, and wore long hair.[1] New religions, colonialism, and popularity of world fashion changed this. However, early markers of masculinity and femininity were likely borne out in ways too subtle for outside observers to recognize, thus much remains unknown. Foreign chronicles of early Indonesian customs inevitably reflected the biases and cultural unawareness of their authors. This chapter provides glimpses of a recent range of moralities, courtships, sexualities, and unions among Indonesian peoples.

GENDER ROLES AND SOCIALIZATION

Early visitors to Indonesia noted a relatively high level of autonomy of women. One historian remarks:

It would be wrong to say that women were *equal* to men—indeed there were few areas in which they competed directly. Women had different functions from men, but these included transplanting and harvesting rice, weaving, and marketing. Their reproductive role gave them magical and ritual powers which it was difficult for men to match. These values may explain why the value of daughters was never questioned in Southeast Asia as it was in China, India, and the Middle East.[2]

This still holds true to a great extent, as women maintain family social and economic control. Yet handling money is not a prestigious activity in most of Indonesia and considered beneath the concerns of men. Market women are among the *kasar* (coarse) of society and Indonesians often refer to low levels of speech as "market language" (*bahasa pasar*). While women may direct the public scene through commerce, men control it through political prestige, such as higher-level jobs or ruling positions.

Still, power maneuvers through sinuous routes and one must live among Indonesians to understand social forces directing households and societies. Women's reproductive and magical powers play out in daily life through birth, agriculture, textile production and dyeing, and cooking. Importantly, women control the social information and tone affecting family and community relations.

Traditional Ideals of Masculinity and Femininity

Ideals of masculinity contrast across Indonesia. In Java, masculine models follow principles of refinement and stoicism. Such traits characterize the Javanese *wayang kulit* shadow play, where heroes are small, elegant puppets in stark opposition to villainously large, vulgar giants. The *halus* (refined) champions of manhood win in the end through guile, connections, and magical powers. Thus, physical might does not make right in Javanese displays of manhood. The status of a powerful man rests upon historical notions of potency. This (often volatile) force provides grounds for political authority, sexual capacity, material wealth, or social control—in a word, power—in the world.[3] To lose one's temper or behave aggressively marks a man as low in character and devoid of true potency. This explains why Indonesians become shocked and confused by how quickly Westerners rise to displays of anger—a long-standing basis of cultural misunderstandings.

Ironically, as pointed out, "Javanese have many of the same kinds of fears and fantasies about 'Kalimantan' that North Americans have about the jungles and headhunters of "Borneo."[4] On islands besides Java, people might prize open fierceness as an attribute of masculinity—yet within controlled contexts. This notably applies to former headhunting or war-like societies. Simultaneously, men also adhere to local notions of propriety and etiquette in presenting a favorable male image. Across the archipelago contests such as cockfights, boxing matches, battles on horseback with lances, and other demonstrations of bravado draw audiences and assert male prowess. These displays now include *karaoke* performances or showing off on motorbikes.

Other archetypal modes for the sexes manifest across Indonesia: for men, *berani* ("bravery" or "boldness") and *kejantanan* ("roosterish," "virile," or "brave") and for women, *lemah* ("weak" but also "supple" and "graceful"). In their bodily strength, men have symbolized power and its justification through heroics. This surfaces through Indonesia's many modern monuments (echoing a global visual cliché). While bravado characterizes battles or competitions, men typically do not conduct themselves in "macho" like manners in normal social circumstances. A rude man will repel women, who will label him as *kasar* or worse—*kurang ajar* (literally "without learning," meaning "ignorant,"—the strongest Indonesian insult implying an animal state of being).

Following custom, women across the islands appear languid in movements and facial expressions. People often remark that females tire easily and cannot walk long distances. (This, despite the reality that common women walk with heavy loads for miles to and from market or carrying water. In Bali, women labor on grueling road crews, unloading and carrying heavy rocks for hours). Yet through graceful, subtle gestures, women exhibit attractive feminine demeanors. Both sexes frequently cover their mouths in laughter, as showing teeth connotes animal-like behavior. Women's hair should be clean, combed, and worn in a ponytail or bun, depending upon age. Long, uncontrolled hair signifies wildness or insanity—the ultimate disorder.

Notions of Sexual Morality

The language of everyday moralism is shot through, on the male side of it, with roosterish imagery. *Sabung,* the word for cock (and one which appears in inscriptions as early as A.D. 922), is used metaphorically to mean "hero," "warrior," "champion," "man of parts," "political candidate," "bachelor," "dandy," "lady-killer," or "tough guy."[5]

Indeed, it appears that as sex is forbidden, it becomes an even more seductive creature.[6]

Indonesians do not openly discuss sex. While terms for "rooster" or "cock" (as in the quote above) signify male powers, a general term for both male and female sexual organs is *kemaluan,* meaning "shame" or "embarrassment." This does not mean, however, that Indonesians engage in sex less frequently or with less fervor than do people anywhere else. In some regions, they carry on more sexual dalliances and extramarital affairs than do average Americans. Further, moralistic prohibitions regarding homosexual relations typical of Euro-America have never guided most customary Indonesian ideas.

Among animistic societies unconverted to world faiths, concepts such as "original sin" or "asceticism" bear no meaning. Sex among such people does not carry pious stigmas like those in many parts of the world. In fact, men often prefer wives with sexual experience, though this might relate to fears of hymeneal blood in defloration. However, serious rules, taboos, and norms still apply to sexual and marital relations. For example, everywhere incest taboos exist, although cross-cousin marriage long was encouraged to ramify lineages. In recent times, this occurs less frequently. Other rules define conduct during pregnancy, after birth, modes of marriage, and treatment between spouses.

Context determines sexual talk and behavior in Indonesia. Women bathing together in a river often joke candidly about their sex lives or a group of male friends may boast of conquests. Still, casual sexual references in mixed company are rare. Raucous sexual banter among same-sex friends also employs euphemisms avoiding reference to genitals by direct, anatomical names.

Across Indonesia, male and female sexual organs possess a mystical dualism—simultaneously sacred and profane. In some regions, this descends from ancient Hindu concepts of *linggam-yoni,* that is, the coupling of phallus and vagina as a central religious principle organizing the universe. In animist societies, genitals are sites of potency through which ancestors direct their forces along lineages. The name for Sumba's animist faith (*Marapu*) also denotes genitals in some regions. This implies ancestral transmission and inheritance through sexual organs of the living. Thus, genitalia become essential conduits for religion, humanity, and reproduction—centers of cosmological and personal potency. Yet, when spoken of or displayed in a vulgar manner, private parts of the body symbolize the socially shameful—reflecting lowly character on the part of the offender. This dualism carries through much of Indonesian culture, while reinforcing ideal social behavior.

Yet life everywhere finds outlets in defiance of the forbidden. Indonesians at times speak with as much bawdiness as people anywhere and sex becomes a covert matter of what one can get away with. Tensions between the ideal and the real provide hidden sparks to sexual life.

COMING OF AGE AND COURTSHIP

Relationships Traditional and Modern

Indonesian courtship extends to flirting or forming relationships not leading to marriage. Conventional modes and mores differ between islands, classes, and religions. Nonetheless, male suitors almost always require approval of a female's family, while a male's parents usually must accept his marital choice. In Muslim societies in Java and beyond, young women's sexual purity reflects upon family honor; people expect virginity at the time of their marriages. In outer island regions where Islam and Christianity are not entrenched historically, sex becomes less an issue of morality than one of social rank—where women receive a return for their sexual favors acknowledging their "worth."

Traditionally, conjugal matches took place through family go-betweens and often followed ideals of cross-cousin marriage in many areas. Where arranged marriages still occur, nonetheless, parents commonly allow the prospective couple to meet and decide whether or not they like one another. Unless a family is very poor and seeking higher connections or greedy for bride price, they will rarely force a girl into a marriage that she does not want. Men sometimes wed to suit their parents, then give their wives minimal attention and continue to philander. Recent ideas of equality and compatibility between men and women have affected many of the young, leading to new types of relationships and marriages. Yet families frequently maintain great influence in their children's lives and choices.

In light of new times and popular cultural influences, many younger Indonesians emulate foreign ideas of romance. Pop music croons longings of young love and single people desire sentimental marriages. Yet, flirting, ballads, and romantic poetry express nothing new. Indonesians have mastered such forms of sexual communication for centuries, like the flirtatious *pantun* poetry discussed in Chapter 3. Major differences in customary Indonesian marriages (compared to those in the West) include the primary involvement of family in choosing or approving mates and the practicality rather than the romanticism of matrimony.[7]

Still, many have defied families in the face of love, while others have committed suicide when forbidden to wed those they desire. Suicide is not uncommon in caste-conscious Bali, when someone suffers a broken heart (*putus asa,* also meaning "loss of hope") after denied marriage for love. Suicidal practice reflects the tragic side of ultimate parental control. Following this, despondent youth commonly drink insecticide to end their lives.

Further, some families have forced young women into marriages they did not want. One report from eastern Indonesia describes a young woman hog-tied and carried to the home of a local schoolteacher against her will. The teacher had paid her father many animals in bride price, but the girl loved another young man. At her new "husband's" house she was "broken" through rape, and locals reported hearing her screams. The indigenous term for first-time sex for a girl means "mixing" of the couple involved. Now the term frequently borrows from the Indonesian word *rusak* ("broken"), in breaking a girl's hymen (and in some cases her spirit). This contrasts drastically with former local notions where premarital sex was accepted, as long as parents approved of the boy.[8] Such relations changed following a Javacentric view of virginity and lack of choices for women, cast across the islands by the New Order national regime.

Displaying Oneself—Male and Female Attractiveness

Besides following norms of beauty, Indonesians everywhere seek herbal or supernatural ways of enhancing their sex appeal. Popular potions called *jamu* offer a wide range of herbal elixirs and remedies for illness. These are sold in packets, served at pharmacies, or concocted individually. Men across the islands drink *jamu* for virility, along with the more recently sold "energy drinks" (often containing caffeine and nicotine) to increase their drive. In parts of Java, women drink an herbal mixture to make them vaginally "dry" and tight during sexual intercourse to please men (though often causing pain for women). In some regions, women use *jamu* to shorten their menstrual periods, as men tend to fear and loathe uterine blood. Indeed, body fluids carry negative supernatural associations, involved in the workings of "black magic" (*gaib hitam*).

As both sexes display themselves through appropriate manners of grace, they also adopt newer fashions to attract attention. Young women in many places now wear skirts to the knees (or above), showing off their calves. As women's legs customarily remain hidden under ankle length clothing, the sight of thighs, calves, or even ankles arouses Indonesian men. In most places long, shiny hair adds to a girl's beauty, though now many wear their hair chin length and shorter, following fashion. Young men ideally dress in clothing deemed neatly fashionable (*rapi*). Most wear jeans or slacks. Rarely do Indonesians of either sex wear shorts in public, except in tourist regions like Bali. Even in grass huts without electricity, old-styled irons containing hot coals ensure that residents emerge in neatly pressed clothing.

Cleanliness is fundamental to physical attractiveness and scented bath and beauty products are immensely popular in Indonesia. Women love cosmetics and Indonesia produces several lines of quality lotions, shampoos, and so forth. These days, both sexes value Western toiletry brands, much as Americans prize such products from France. Sensitive to aroma, Indonesians often complain that Westerners rarely bathe and emit an unpleasant body odor. Across the islands, one's scent signifies personal essence. Offensive body odors might incite suspicions of evil character. Cleanliness and sweet scents denote humans, while the opposite evokes beasts.

Over the past decade, the media increasingly have emphasized the beauty of white skin, through advertisements for lightening creams. This mostly applies to women, as those light of complexion have long held esteem. A preference for paler skin results from class biases of those not forced to work outdoors. Most western Indonesians view darkness as unattractive and often denigrate more swarthy peoples as "primitives"—such as those of West Papua and the eastern islands.

Indonesians disdain anything animal-like in human physicality or behavior. Thus, as in Bali, many undergo ceremonial tooth filing at puberty, making their pointed canine teeth even with the others. Some animal metaphors, such as the rooster, importantly apply to ideal male dispositions, like bravery and virility. Still, the bravest of men will not impress the opposite sex if unwashed and coarse in dress and manners.

For centuries men demonstrated courage by traveling to other lands, such as the *rantau* previously discussed. By bringing back goods and new knowledge from afar, men thus gained prestige in their homelands. This practice never ceased, but took on modern forms. Worldly sophistication has accelerated as an attractive male attribute—as expertise regarding foreign ideas and contemporary world fashions especially impresses young women. Throughout Indonesia's history, men have introduced new styles, ideas, foods, and so forth to their home regions. Imaginably, a desire to impress women has continuously motivated their far-flung quests for the new. Thus, many stylistic and conceptual changes have come about through men's displays of their worldly wise qualities in attempts to attract women.

Courting and Dating

Young people in Indonesia usually socialize in groups and romantic interests develop at around age 16, although dating may happen later. A girlfriend or boyfriend (both termed *pacar*) frequently belongs to an extended circle of friends, including siblings. Within these circles, much banter and laughter goes on between the sexes. Girls often tease boys, and some show their interest by slapping them in fun. Young couples rarely socialize alone, although a boy may visit a girl on a front verandah or pavilion. Still, he will often bring a male friend.

Generally, couples do not touch or sit close together and almost never show affection when out in public. Recently, this has changed somewhat and *pacar*s might hold hands as they walk. Yet Indonesians never exhibit public displays of affection common to Euro-Americans. Groups including "couples" visit each other's homes, play guitars and sing, go to movies, stop at *warung*s, or walk around town.

In village areas, a boy will visit the village of a girl he likes, often initially appearing nonchalant and observing her from a distance. Messages pass back and forth between the couple through friends or siblings, and eventually a suitor might be invited to make an appearance at the girl's home. Much then transpires through family channels on both sides. Eventually, a girl may be allowed to go out for a walk with a boy or ride somewhere nearby on the back of his motorbike. Botanical euphemisms abound for a girl's coming of age, such as becoming a "ripe banana."

Dating also happens on the sly, as couples secretly meet to flirt and talk. Depending upon region, religion, and social class, such liaisons may progress to sexual adventures. In rural areas, couples carry on affairs at night, hidden in high cornfields or inlets of beaches. Young men at times sneak into a girl's room under cover of dark. This does not necessarily result in sexual intercourse but, rather, simply lying together for a few hours. In some places, parents permit engaged young couples to spend trial evenings together in a girl's bed. Nuptial negotiations usually are well under way for this to happen.

Betel nut (*pinang*) is a historical elixir of choice across Southeast Asia. In terms of sexual symbolism, the sexes chewing betel together is loaded. In most places, people do not partake of this practice until they reach sexually maturity. Sharing betel insinuates much for a man and woman. Flirting and innuendo accompany the preparation and chewing of this mild narcotic. In many areas, the betel nut process involves placing a bit of the dried nut (of the areca palm) in one's mouth, then dipping a long, solid catkin from the piper plant (*sirih*) into a bit of powdered lime (*kapur*) cupped in the left hand. People then bite off this lime-coated section and chew as it breaks down the nut in their mouths. The catalyzing moment begins when all ingredients mix. Thus, betel is termed *sirih-pinang*—implying a complementary dualism of phallic catkin and feminine nut. Things begin to happen when the mouth turns red and fills with saliva. At this point, a chewer spits the red liquid (often with neat precision) while continuing to munch and chat. After a few moments, a sense of mild euphoria takes over. *Sirih-pinang* is an eminently social substance, facilitating relaxation and conversation. Some chew betel with tobacco or use a leaf from the piper plant to wrap the entire combination.

Customarily, men became excited at the sight of a woman's red-stained lips. The eventually black-stained teeth *sirih-pinang* caused were a sign of beauty for centuries. In eastern Indonesia, if a man dips his stick of *sirih* into a woman's hand for lime powder, this constitutes a sexual proposition. Through consistently bringing a woman *sirih-pinang*, a man signifies a relationship. Courtships and affairs (including extramarital) often begin with betel nut.

Virginity and Premarital Sex (When *Sarungs* Go Up)

Apart from strict Islamic societies, female sexuality outside of marriage seldom carried the moral censure as in much of the world. Under the New Order, however, women's sexual conduct became a central government concern. Government organizations and policies arose to sublimate women into one realm—as wife and mother. For men, sexual models were looser. Issuing from Jakarta, Javanese Muslim values upon female virginity were disseminated through national discourse throughout Indonesia. Reflecting ascetic notions, most Javanese customarily engage in sex fully clad, including married couples. While *sarungs* may go up for a sex act, people of Java can be exceptionally "straight-laced" about their bodies and usually perform in the dark (at least following custom). Thus, traditional Javanese sexual models issued from Jakarta likely did not take hold on other islands to a significant degree.

Regardless of policies, across Indonesia married and unmarried women joke about sex and compare experiences. Butts of jokes become men, whose penises and sexual aptitude undergo scrutiny. When women share secrets of pleasures in sex acts, they often use metaphorical terms to discuss such things—such as "coconuts" "bananas," "cakes," or "mangoes" and term sexual phenomena as "peeling a fruit" or "flowering."

In societies of outer islands, sex between unmarried couples can be common. Some families permit young people to experience "trial marriages" while living in a girl's family household. Should pregnancies occur, children resulting from such arrangements belong to the girl's descent group. In many societies, girls hold high value for parents through their eventual bride price. In these areas, bride-givers carry more authority and higher status than bride-takers.

Same-sex experimentation long has been normal throughout Indonesia. Young friends will simulate sex acts between men and women to "practice" for the future event or to experience pleasure. Usually such relations represent a passing phase in the lives of Indonesians, although some develop homosexual preferences. Public touching between members of the opposite sex rarely occurs in Indonesia, but same-sex friends and relatives of all ages hold hands, rest their arms upon a companion's leg, or even sleep with arms across each other. Such intimacy provides opportunities for sexual experience. Usually not regarded as homosexual behavior, people instead view this as adolescent play. In Java and Bali, many have noted this tendency among the young.

With the growing availability of pornographic images via media and the Internet, Indonesian men have broadened their notions of sexual activities, although many likely persist in fears regarding facial proximity to female genitals. In fact, kissing on the mouth is a relatively new phenomenon in Indonesia and yet unpracticed in many regions. The term for "kissing," *cium*, means to sniff (and thereby take in) another's essence and forms a standard greeting among family and close friends across the islands, as they "kiss" each other's cheeks. In some places, people rub noses among family to show affection. Rubbing noses also becomes foreplay, as opposed to mouth kissing. Sexual intercourse can be fast in Indonesia, and only recently has much general discussion developed regarding female orgasm. Yet one cannot know the practices among people of such a large, diverse country. It may be that in regions people have attended well to the pleasures of sex for men and women for centuries—practicing far more sophistication than outsiders can imagine.

Views on Women's Sexuality and Emotional Control

Often when a seduction takes place without family approval, people consider the man at fault—although in stricter Muslim communities, views toward women can be harsher and based in family honor. Nonetheless, usually a girl will be chastised but not harshly punished, as most Indonesians consider women vulnerable (and even irrational) in the face of male advances. An extension of the *lemah* feminine composite of grace, suppleness, and weakness, people customarily regard women's sexuality as passive and compliant. Therefore, in some regions a girl's family will demand a payment for her seduction. Often male kin will pressure a young man to comply, to the extent of using physical violence.

The opposite archetype of female sexuality creates myths, beliefs, and accusations of witchery. Ancient tales from Java tell of a seductive women wandering at night, with a hole in the middle of her trunk. Similar myths pervade the islands, in which such women will lure men to possession or death. At night in some regions, men are more afraid at the sight of lone women than women are of men. As women traveling alone are rare sights across the archipelago, they appear abnormal or dangerous when they do so—particularly in the dark.

Thus, opposing images of female sexuality shape ideas of the feminine. One is compliant and gives life; the other is predatory and takes away life. Men fear women's sexual fluids, and the dark, visceral mysteries of fertility and reproductive power. Thus, blood of the womb represents a perilous substance to men—in its inexplicable difference and uncontrollable nature. Many tales across the islands express such fears, telling of men going mad from contact with uterine blood or losing their virility.

Indigo dye used for textiles often corresponds to women's fluids. In most places, men will avoid an indigo dye pot like the plague. Fermented and odiferous, people liken liquid indigo to uterine blood. Control over this colorant is a realm where women wield uncontested power.[9] Still, the blue yarns of indigo weave through most of Indonesia's customary fabrics, clothing both sexes for centuries. The dye only carries danger in liquid form.

It may be that ideals of passivity and weakness in women developed not only in response to men's fears of their elusive powers, but of their real behavior in the world. That women ever willingly yielded all power seems unlikely. Rather, they asserted themselves through possible circuits in daily life. Imaginably, men felt impelled to cast them as the weaker sex, to curb their activities and influence. World religions, colonialism, and nationalistic ideals further established male dominance.

Views on Male Sexuality and Emotional Control

In Java control over passions marks a customary ideal of manhood and a refined character, but men do "lose control" (*hilang kontrol*). Sometimes they blame this on love magic by women but often they admit to their own desires. Javanese possess a two-sided ethic of masculinity. One demands ascetic control of sex urges while the other champions virility and seduction. Men generally emulate the latter qualities. The term *jago* ("rooster") characterizes a man successful with woman. President Sukarno married several times while renowned for numerous affairs. To many Indonesians this was laudable conduct, confirming that their leader was a *jago* in many realms. Indonesian men often admire the philandering reputation of U.S. President John Kennedy. Further, most were baffled as to why Americans made such an obsessive moral issue of U.S. President Bill Clinton's indiscretions in the oval office. To them, such censure contradicted the normal privileges of power and made Americans appear naïve.

Indonesian women typically regard men as powerful in "vitality" (*semangat*) when young, but as untrustworthy and less committed to family than themselves after marriage. They expect or suspect sexual infidelity and respond to this in various ways, from ignoring it to leaving a marriage. Men often assert their daring through gambling and risk-taking. Sexual dalliances fall within the seductive realm of risk, while gambling is a ubiquitous male preoccupation across Indonesia. Thus, men generally hold less reliability at handling family finances than women, who therefore usually handle the money. Still, men typically enjoy far less social control than women, regardless of female economic competence.

Traditional Beliefs Surrounding Menstruation and Venereal Disease

In effect, the dangerousness of female fertility for men and society is the other face of its enormous importance.[10]

Most men in Indonesia fear menstrual blood and sexual relations cease with women until days after bleeding stops, often followed by ritual cleansing. In some regions, women must leave their homes and live in special dwellings during menses. People consider menstruation as a form of pollution, dangerous to men and their powerful possessions—such as weapons. In former headhunting societies of eastern Indonesia, some regarded menstruating women as more dangerous than warring men. Yet, on islands such as Seram, while superior in their powers of destruction in terms of positive value, men accorded women inferior value.[11] This echoes ideas throughout Indonesia, suggesting reasons and meanings behind taboos. In many parts of the world, that which is ambiguous and uncontrollable becomes taboo. Taboos maintain differences and boundaries while reinforcing them. Fluids by nature are uncontrollable if not contained. Menstrual fluids represent a unique power (reproduction), a female mystery, and a process beyond male command. Consequently, these fluids incite fears, prohibitions, and myths.

Historically, many eastern Indonesians believed that gonorrhea and syphilis passed to men through women. When men experienced discharge associated with certain sexually transmitted diseases, they believed that they had absorbed the uterine blood of a woman through intercourse. The remedy was to find a "clean" (i.e., virgin) woman and return the malady to where it belonged. The sexual diseases did not exist as such in women as they always contained these liquids, but only manifested in men through their contact with feminine blood—causing their own bloody discharge.[12] Such belief and practice spread sexual disease to an epidemic proportion in some regions.

MARRIAGE ACROSS THE ISLANDS

Let him taste greener pastures as long as he doesn't bring a goat home.[13]

The influence of blood cannot be denied. I attach a certain value to the descent of everyone around me, and I have an idea that I will be blessed by the ancestors of those persons whom I love and honor.[14]

Marriages

Following conventional thinking, to be unmarried in Indonesia is to remain a child, regardless of one's age. Marriage is a pivotal rite of passage by which people reach adulthood and become recognized community members. To remain single constitutes a social aberration for most Indonesians, who wonder how lone people in the world find any human joy or meaning to life. Moreover, to exist without children is a tragedy. Indonesians regard childless Westerners with sadness, remarking "*Kasihan*" ("What a pity").

Notions of customary marriage across Indonesia contrast with romantic unions people seek in the West. Often arranged by family or requiring their approval, ideal marriages cement partnerships in which women handle finances and raise children while men hold the (at least public) role of power. Passionate or affectionate marriages, nevertheless, certainly exist. International media also have influenced current notions regarding love and marriage, especially through films. Yet romance and sexual desire seldom represent primary nuptial necessities to many. In fact, Javanese societies regard passion as disruptive—a fleeting, volatile force inevitably causing marital disharmony.

While polite conduct smoothes attraction between the sexes and enables parental approval, social levels hold utmost importance to families. The terms *tinggi* ("high") and *rendah* ("low") become essential in marriage negotiations among class-conscious Indonesian kin. In many places, a man may marry a woman of lower rank, but the reverse rarely occurs. In areas where a bride price forms the crux of a nuptial agreement, some high-ranking women remain single their entire lives. As their marriages require so many water buffalo, horses, gold items, and so on, few men of any standing can ever afford such costs. Further, as men currently move to other islands for education and work, they often marry women away from their homelands. Off-island marriages might demand far less expense for the groom and his family but also reflect changing ideas of choice in love and marriage.

Particularly in Java, people have valued asceticism for many centuries (beginning with Hindu–Buddhism). This informs ideas about marriage. Javanese tend to regard sex and sleep as necessary to a point but profane indulgences if not practiced with control. Passions, however, emerge in other ways and Indonesian men (and women) enjoy discreet sexual dalliances. Some men even take more than one wife. Islamic law allows a man to have four wives, but he must be able to support them all equally (which is a difficult undertaking). In current times, this has become far less common, following women's resistance and economic impracticalities. In some animist societies, men persist in taking multiple wives.

Ceremonies vary throughout the islands, from exorbitant ritual pageants to elopement. In Bali, eloping (called *nganten*) is the most common form of marriage and parents are aware of it beforehand. Ceremonial weddings of Bali are characteristically lavish and expensive. They include a priest and may be held in a temple. Parents are frequently relieved at avoiding such costs through the elopement of their children. Javanese marry by meeting at a bride's home and participating in an elaborate *slametan* (ceremonial meal) involving all families. Then the couple must go to a district religious officer to undergo an official Muslim marriage. In some regions of Indonesia, a marriage ceremony is a simple event conducted by a shaman, priest, or senior family member at a bride's home. The groom's kin group then often takes her away (sometimes by truck carrying many people in the back). People in some villages feign anger at the loss of the bride and ritually throw dirty water, dung, and other refuse at the departing family. Western-style weddings with white bridal gowns and veils are now popular and prestigious among Christians. The weddings are held in churches and then celebrated with receptions and food at halls or family homes.

Marriage essentially carries on lineages and ensures the soundness of family descendants. Caste or class concerns create major qualms in matrimonial

agreements as the "quality of blood" takes precedence over other consider-
ations. People in some areas speak of clean or white blood as a biological
reality and an inherent attribute of high rank. For elites, maintaining their
bloodlines becomes a paramount concern. Thus, blood trumps all other
values in marital arrangements.

Men's Family Roles

Men across Indonesia maintain the position of head of household and the
main providers for wives and children. Even in matrilineal societies such as
the Minangkabau of Sumatra, public power and decisions frequently fall to
husbands—if only on the face of things. In many areas, wives address their
mates with a degree of formality, calling them *Bapak,* or the shortened *Pak* in
deference to their standing as fathers and married men. Yet men will also address their wives as *Ibu* or *Bu,* denoting their status. Not infrequently, fathers
maintain some distance from their children, who approach and address them
formally. Often a mother's brother assumes the role of disciplinarian and
protector of her children, becoming a major negotiator in their marriages.

In public, wives and families must show respect to men. In private, all sorts
of conduct might occur. A man may dominate the front stage of a household,
receiving guests and appearing in command. Yet his wife may hold ultimate
authority behind the public eye. Where women are particularly clever in handling and earning money, their power in the family tends to increase. Personalities and relations among Indonesian men and women vary as much as
anywhere else. In reality, some wives are domineering and ambitious while
some husbands are passive and lacking enterprise.

Men, however, generally enjoy more freedom of mobility and when not
working might ride off on motorbikes to visit friends or gamble. As married
adults, they often still socialize with old male friends. Women principally
devote their attentions to family, though many visit each other to mingle and
share confidences. In many villages, men appear to do little actual work and
spend much of their time as they please. By contrast, women care for children, cook, clean, husk rice, pound coffee, garden, go to market, and often
weave and dye cloth.

Women's Family Roles

As noted of the Sumatran Batak culture (by Susan Rodgers in *Power &
Difference*), "Women are the pivot around which kin relationships and politics turn."[15] Aside from state policies of *ibu*ism, Indonesian women usually
take motherhood and the home most seriously. While often supported by

husband's salaries, they nonetheless manage the money, budget, and shop for most everything needed for the home. Children typically feel close emotional attachments to their mothers, extending into adulthood. In many areas, Indonesians do not spank their children and attitudes toward the very young are indulgent and loving.

Most influentially, women control social discourse through talk—sharing secrets among themselves, ridiculing others, berating or praising their husbands, censuring neighbors' conduct, and teaching their young. While men maintain a public image, women produce social reality within and between households. This becomes political on the ground level and, indeed, women engineer most family and community relationships and the directions they take. Female communication circuits often form the hidden yet predominant power in communities.

As fertility in most things crucially concerns Indonesians, so with women. Most desire children and many resist birth control to have several. In outer island regions the death of children remains frequent and women fear the limitations of birth control in the event of the loss of a child. Among the islands of Indonesia where set marriage exchange between regions takes place, a woman's reproductive powers come at a price. Thus, bride price will pay her family for losing her in movement to her husband's village and providing children to his kin group.

While many arranged marriages work out as well as any other types of unions, frequently women find themselves in unsuitable or even physically abusive relationships. If these become unbearable, some women take to "running back" (*lari kembali*) to their parents' homes. If the abuse has been severe, a wife's father, uncle, or brother might exact a fine or physical punishment upon the husband, and the women will never return to the marriage. Moreover, bride price will not be returned to the man's family.

Government-Fostered Ideals Regarding Marriage and Male and Female Propriety

Initial principles for the Indonesian Constitution came about in 1945, emphasizing society as a whole made up of groups and individuals. Neither communistic nor democratic, this model grew out of Javanese ideals of power, which were basically feudalistic. The Constitution did not include human rights provisions, although President Sukarno's Vice-President, Muhammed Hatta, had originally proposed them.[16] This constitutional vacuum concerning rights of the people resulted in the arbitrary use of political authority.

Under President Suharto's New Order regime (1966–1998), all wives of civil servants became obligatory members of the state-sponsored *Dharma*

Wanita (Women's Association). This organization pressured women to behave as submissive wives in service to their husbands and the national government—based in exaggerated "traditional" feminine models of Java. Stemming from Indonesian military thought, Dharma Wanita espoused conformity and obedience, while regimenting the conduct and image of women.[17] Thus, an archetype of "housewife," in conservatively binding traditional Javanese dress, became a nationalistic icon.

Simultaneously, following ancient notions of potency in Javanese culture, the possession of women persisted as a natural attribute of male power, and among bureaucrats and technocrats, sexual access likewise symbolized success.[18] Eventually, women of Dharma Wanita mounted organized protests concerning their husband's sexual indiscretions, freedom to divorce them, physical abusiveness, and lack of sufficient financial support. Even Suharto's wife (perhaps fearing the possibility of a second presidential spouse) supported a law protecting women, enacted in 1983 on Kartini Day.[19]

However, the New Order continued to regiment marriage and family life through its encompassing economic power over civil servants. Many wives remained trapped in marriages for the sake of children, financial support, or social appearances, especially those at upper levels with the most to lose. Reflecting employee attitudes toward male bosses in Indonesia, an adage developed—*Selama Bapak senang*—meaning "As long as the boss is happy." This further fostered corruption and extramarital infidelity as perquisites for men in power.

During the 1999 Indonesian Presidential campaigns, a contingent of the national political party long in control—Golkar—held a convention at a hotel in the city of Kupang, West Timor. Scores of men appeared in party colors of yellow and black in hotel restaurants. One evening, a Golkar jaunt to a nightclub was planned. As men congregated in the hotel foyer, an equal number of prostitutes suddenly exited a nearby room then paraded in line to join them. Each woman wore a black mini-skirt, a tight yellow blouse, and black stiletto heeled shoes, broadcasting Golkar colors. The beaming *Bapaks* fell into pairs with the woman and the excited, two-toned crowd rode off in busloads.[20] At the time, this episode could have epitomized political power and sexual license in Indonesia.

Getting to Gender Equilibrium

Dharma Wanita and nationalist policies provided solidly defined forces for women to contest.[21] Many sought ways around nationally imposed "norms" and even as wives and mothers became active and vocal about their marriages, families, subservience, and opportunities. As Indonesian women overwhelmingly control the social quality of everyday home life, their husbands felt less certain in their roles as masters of their abodes as their wives grew more assertive. Indonesian men dread the laughter and ridicule of women, whether from wives, mothers, sisters, co-workers, or friends. While a man may strut and swagger about the office, he will less freely behave so at home, fearing female derision and loss of face.

Increasingly, as alternatives to the confines of married life and its compliant image of *ibu*ism, Indonesian women sought educations—becoming doctors, lawyers, artists, journalists, intellectuals, and teachers. Many enjoyed newfound opportunities and freedoms to the degree that a new syndrome arose whereby elite and educated women decided to remain single. While initially revolutionary in Indonesia, today female singularity is no longer the bizarre rarity of times past. Still, these women often are termed *nyentric,* ("eccentric"), notwithstanding their achievements. Obviously, opportunities for women exist in large urban regions that remain nonexistent in remote villages. As noted by Daniel Lev in *Fantasizing the Feminine in Indonesia,* "[t]he primary assets of the women's movement (again, as elsewhere) now belong largely to educated women from well-off families in urban Indonesia."[22]

Nonetheless, numerous women of the outer islands have become less repressively *tradisi* ("traditional") and more public and business-oriented in recent years (especially on the heels of tourism and trade). Now women from Timor, Flores, Sumba, Sumatra, and other islands routinely travel to Jakarta or Bali to sell textiles and other arts in tourist and urban centers. Thus, a sort of female *rantau*—traveling to other lands—emerged in the late twentieth century and continues on. Moreover, as noted of customary societies, women find ways to sidestep or subvert male dominance in significant realms. Through the spread of tales, derision of men, and control of family and neighborhood domestic life, women manage to exercise extensive power, even if hidden or uncelebrated.

The New Order government, in an effort to curb overpopulation in Java, instituted a program of Family Planning (*Keluarga Berencana*) encouraging couples to bear only two children. Contraception, however, was predominantly applied to women. Inter-uterine devices (IUDs), banned in Europe and North America (due to their tendency to foster infections), were placed in Indonesian women. In a tropical environment where many women bathed in rivers or took on infections from men, the IUDs caused tremendous problems. Numerous women developed severe or fatal disease, and many women became sterile. This created a backlash of fear regarding birth control, particularly in village regions. While relatively effective in Java (and to a degree in Bali), people suspiciously avoided the family planning program elsewhere. Since then, however, safer means of contraception are available in Indonesia, but the miseries caused by IUDs greatly reinforced people's ideas about the dangers of curbing fertility.

On March 9, 2006, *The Jakarta Post* published a story on the Internet entitled "Women Take to the Streets to Condemn Sharia, Porn Bill."[23] Marking International Women's Day, the protestors drew attention to female persecution in regions like Banda Aceh under *sharia* (conservative Muslim) law. Religious vigilantes had bullied many women for not wearing headscarves or for walking outside at night unaccompanied by a man. Women could also suffer fines for exposing their hair, shoulders, or legs, under a "pornography" bill before the House of Representatives—which would not curtail the sexual freedom of men. Protestors called on the government to focus on pressing issues of human trafficking and domestic violence and to remove the onus of immorality from women. As Islamic Fundamentalism has grown in Indonesia, so have restrictions upon females. Women marching through Jakarta proclaimed that the pornography bill was a move back to the old days when they had little autonomy.

SEX AND THE SUPERNATURAL

Sorcery is a mystical act to be mystically combated.[24]

Metaphysical Beliefs Regarding Sex and Reproduction

Ancestors "operate" through sexuality in many regions, following marriage alliances or proscriptions. Where lineages remain critical, misfortunes might befall one who chooses to marry outside of prescribed alliances or exchange circles. Calamities have a way of happening to reinforce metaphysical beliefs, and Indonesians speak of many befalling those who defied marital rules. A man may wed on another island, then fall ill or remain childless. People will then attribute misfortunes or illness within his parental family to his defiance of rightful patterns of marriage. Assertions will follow that the wrath of violated ancestors inflicted misery upon their descendants.

Sexual dangers threaten people everywhere. *Gaib hitam* (black magic) might strike a person via betel nut, food, water, or poison hidden beneath a long thumbnail. Curses afflict people through body excretions, women's fluids, and the sexually symbolic liquid indigo dye. Small amounts of such matter can be placed in anything one ingests to harm a victim. *Gaib hijau* (green magic) lends a practitioner irresistibility to anyone desired. Men and women practice this, but *gaib perempuan* (woman magic) is a widely feared form of male sorcery in which women fall under a man's spell. People speak of unsavory men, who inexplicably attract women or achieve multiple marriages, as using this practice.

Myths throughout Indonesia center upon women who have died in child-birth or grief. Their ghosts take multiple forms and manifest at night. Some kill or castrate men, some seduce them and absorb their powers, and all represent the perilous side of the feminine. Balinese celebrate the dark Hindu goddess Durga yet dread local female spirits. Tales of menacing ghosts often place them near rivers. The ghost of a woman who died without children, but still seeks them through drowning the living, might pull some one crossing a river underwater.

Female spirits simultaneously take on positive and negative aspects. In eastern Indonesia, people speak of "sea wives." On the Maluku island of Aru, divers forge relationships with underwater female spirits, who in turn assist them in finding pearls. Divers repay the spirits with white plates. If a man does exceedingly well, he must return an offering in kind to his sea wife; otherwise, she will haunt his household and possibly cause death among his children. Thus, children of Aru often wear protective cords with talismans to repel their fathers' undersea wives.[25]

In eastern Sumba in the 1960s, an aging village king and his wife remained childless. Rumor had it that their arranged marriage was never consummated. According to villagers, the *raja* ("king") preferred consorting with women who lived beneath the sea. Periodically, he traveled with his entourage to a coastal area at some distance for aquatic trysts. Villagers report that he could stay underwater for days. Upon death, this king left no successor, and for some time his village fell into disarray. People suspected that he had left debts unpaid to his sea wives and that they haunted his household and disrupted the village order.[26]

Stories of seas wives and underwater liaisons may provide men with further "sexual" empowerment, if only mystical. In the case of the king above, his underwater trysts fulfilled a cultural expectation of manhood while enhancing his mystical powers, even if no children resulted. Regarding divers of Aru, a risk occurs in sea wife alliances, where consequences might outweigh benefits if not closely watched. Described as a compelling form of "deep play" for men elsewhere,[27] risk intensifies games of chance, dangerous encounters, and sex. Following this, one might lose all or gain immensely in the end, increasing the stakes and pleasures.

HISTORICAL AND PRESENT PLACES OF HOMOSEXUALITY IN INDONESIA

*Banci*s are part and parcel of Indonesian society. Although mostly concentrated in urban centers, they are also found in rural areas.[28]

Indonesian societies tend to accept alternative expressions of gender—the most long-established termed *banci*. Androgynous in dress, these men behave as women, and through history they held special places in the social order of things, such as matchmakers, artisans, performers, healers, or ritual specialists. More recently, lesbians are increasingly visible and vocal across Indonesia. People refer to them as *tom boi* or *lesbi*, borrowing from English language terms. Indonesians customarily have exercised far more tolerance of sexual diversity when compared with much of the world, and (barring recent resurgences in religious fundamentalism) this continues today.

Male homosexuals have always been visible in Indonesia. Now lesbians (*lesbi*) have entered public awareness. Many formerly remained unmarried or took on something of a "tomboy" appearance. In villages, people will tease an unmarried girl with a short haircut with remarks such as, "Her breasts are really just apples." Stories throughout the outer islands describe "marriages" between women, where one takes on the appearance of a man. These carry little indication of censure or immorality but form novel tales of eccentricity.

To many Indonesians, the *banci* represents a third gender. It seems that anywhere one travels throughout Indonesia, a *banci* appears as part of local society. In the Soe region of West Timor, a famed weaver referred to by locals as *tante* ("aunt") was actually a man dressed in traditional women's village garb, producing fine cloth on a loom. He lived alone in a home among other villagers and appeared incorporated into local life. In fact, he instructed village girls in weaving.[29] People may giggle at or tease *banci*s, but they generally enjoy acceptance within communities; in some communities, *banci*s are said to possess special skills or powers. One scholar from Indonesia noted: "As much as *banci* are denigrated, they are also tolerated."[30] This has been the case as long as anyone remembers.

*Banci*s might be popular entertainers. This has been so for centuries and appears in many contexts currently. A certain young man managed a *warung* in East Sumba in the early 1990s, regaling customers by lip-synching tunes to Diana Ross tapes. In the town's annual talent show in 1993, this *banci* took first prize in his category by crooning "Baby Love." Wrapped in a self-styled tight female gown of pseudo-gold-*lamé,* he performed in a woman's bouffant wig. The crowd cheered him wildly.[31]

In 1982, Indonesia's first gay and lesbian organization was founded, in part by scholar and activist Dédé Oetomo. He also helped publish *Gaya Nusantara* in 1987—the longest-running gay and lesbian magazine in Indonesia. Homosexuality in Indonesia initially gained global interest through the number of gay Europeans living in Bali in the early twentieth century. Many were artists, writers, or musicians. The relatively free atmosphere of Balinese culture attracted numerous gay men seeking a community devoid of repressive European mores. Consequently, the art movement that blossomed in the 1930s largely grew out of these Europeans' influences within a tolerant Balinese social environment.

Today, the gay scene manifests in urban Indonesia in similar ways to many Western cities. In Jakarta, gay nightclubs have become popular and the sight of transgendered people in public is not uncommon. Away from metropolitan or tourist centers, sexual diversity carries on as before, as people find ways to live as they are in communities that accommodate them.

NOTES

1. See Anthony Reid, *Southeast Asia in the Age of Commerce 1450–1680, Vol. One: The Lands below the Winds* (New Haven: Yale University Press, 1988), 146–172.

2. Reid, *Southeast Asia in the Age of Commerce,* 146.

3. Ward Keeler, *Javanese Shadow Plays, Javanese Selves* (Princeton: Princeton University Press, 1987), 39, paraphrased here.

4. Anna Lowenhaupt Tsing, "Alien Romance," in *Fantasizing the Feminine in Indonesia,* ed. Laurie J. Sears (Durham: Duke University Press, 1996), 299.

5. Clifford Geertz, "Deep Play: Notes on the Balinese Cockfight," in *The Interpretation of Cultures,* by the same author (New York: Basic Books, 1973), 418.

6. Cok Sawitri, "Is Sex a Secret in Bali?" *Latitudes* 5 (June, 2001): 42–45.

7. In fact, the same values applied to most of the European world until the nineteenth century. Romance and desire as the grounds for marriage is relatively recent in Western thought as well.

8. See Janet Hoskins, *Biographical Objects: How Things Tell the Stories of People's Lives* (New York: Routledge, 1998), 121–136.

9. See Janet Hoskins, "Why Do Ladies Sing the Blues? Indigo Dyeing, Cloth Production, and Gender Symbolism in Kodi." in *Cloth and Human Experience,* ed. Annette B. Weiner and Jane Schneider (Washington: Smithsonian Institution Press, 1989), 141–173.

10. Valerio Valeri, "Both Nature and Culture: Reflections on Menstrual and Parturitional Taboos in Huaulu (Seram)," in *Power & Difference: Gender in Island Southeast Asia,* ed. Jane Monnig Atkinson and Shelly Errington (Stanford: Stanford University Press, 1990), 270.

11. Valeri, Both Nature and Culture, 242–243.

12. David Mitchell, personal communication, 1993.

13. Julia Suryakusuma, "The State and Sexuality in New Order Indonesia," in *Fantasizing the Feminine in Indonesia,* ed. Laurie J. Sears (Durham: Duke University Press, 1996), 115. This is an expression among Indonesian military wives. The author goes on to write that the "goat" is a second wife.

14. Raden Adjeng Kartini, *Letters of a Javanese Princess,* trans. by Agnes Louise Symmers (Lanhem: University Press of America, 1985), 146.

15. Susan Rodgers, "The Symbolic Representation of Women in a Changing Batak Culture," in *Power & Difference: Gender in Island Southeast Asia,* ed. Jane Monnig Atkinson and Shelly Errington (Stanford: Stanford University Press, 1990), 312.

16. See Suryakusuma, "The State and Sexuality," 92–93. I am indebted to this article for much of the historical information regarding the Dharma Wanita organization in Indonesian political contexts and its effects upon marriage, family life, and women's freedom.

17. See Suryakusuma, "The State and Sexuality," 99–100, paraphrased here.

18. Suryakusama, "The State and Sexuality," 103, paraphrased.

19. Raden Kartini, the author discussed in Chapter 3, served as a model for Javanese woman.

20. Jill Forshee, based on fieldwork in 1999.
21. See Daniel Lev, "On the Other Hand?" in *Fantasizing the Feminine in Indonesia,* ed. Laurie J. Sears (Durham: Duke University Press, 1996), 191–203.
22. Lev, "On the Other Hand?" 201.
23. "Women Take to the Streets to Condemn Sharia, Porn Bill." *The Jakarta Post,* March 9, 2006, http://www.thejakartapost.com/headlines.asp.
24. Clifford Geertz, *The Religion of Java* (Chicago: University of Chicago Press, 1976), 110.
25. See Patricia Spyer, *The Memory of Trade: Modernity's Entanglements on an Eastern Indonesian Island* (Durham: Duke University Press, 2000), 147–150.
26. Jill Forshee, based on fieldwork in 1993 and 2004.
27. See Geertz, "Deep Play, 412–453.
28. Dede Oetomo, "Gender and Sexual Orientation in Indonesia," in *Fantasizing the Feminine in Indonesia,* ed. Laurie J. Sears (Durham: Duke University Press, 1996), 260.
29. Jill Forshee, based on fieldwork in 1999.
30. Oetomo, "Gender and Sexual Orientation," 262.
31. Jill Forshee, based on fieldwork in 1993.

SUGGESTED READING

Atkinson, Jane Monnig, and Shelley Errington. *Power & Difference: Gender in Island Southeast Asia.* Stanford: Stanford University Press, 1990.
Blackwood, Evelyn. *Webs of Power: Women, Kin, and Community in a Sumatran Village.* New York: Rowman and Littlefield Publishers, 1999.
Forshee, Jill. *Between the Folds: Stories of Cloth, Lives, and Travels from Sumba.* Honolulu: University of Hawaii Press, 2000.
Geertz, Hildred. "Indonesian Cultures and Communities." In Ruth T. McVey, ed., *Indonesia* (5–84). New Haven: Yale Southeast Asian Studies, 1963.
Hoskins, Janet. *Biographical Objects: How Things Tell the Stories of People's Lives.* New York: Routledge, 1998.
Hoskins, Janet. "Why Do Ladies Sing the Blues? Indigo Dyeing, Cloth Production, and Gender Symbolism in Kodi." In Annette B. Weiner and Jane Schneider, eds., *Cloth and Human Experience,* 141–173. Washington: Smithsonian Institution Press, 1989.
Ong, Aiwa, and Michael G. Peletz, eds. *Bewitching Women, Pious Men: Gender and Body Politics in Southeast Asia.* Berkeley: University of California Press, 1995.
Sears, Laurie J., ed. *Fantasizing the Feminine in Indonesia.* Durham: Duke University Press, 1996.
Tsing, Anna Lowenhaupt. *In the Realm of the Diamond Queen: Marginality in an Out-of-the-Way Place.* Princeton: Princeton University Press, 1993.
Wolf, Diane Lauren. *Factory Daughters: Gender, Household Dynamics, and Rural Industrialization in Java.* Berkeley: University of California Press, 1992.

7

Festivals and Leisure Activities

Indonesians tend to savor festivals and leisure activities above all other pastimes. Festivals often carry religious significance. They also mark times of year and punctuate life. Whether grand pageants or humbler family celebrations, people put their best efforts into decorations and gaiety. Leisure pursuits include festivals but also extend to competitions and games, informal socializing, cockfights, going to markets, riding motorbikes, creating functional crafts like baskets, and gambling. As sociality is fundamental to being Indonesian, enjoying activities with others characterizes life. People revel in a "more the merrier" spirit at galas amid large crowds. Radio, television, films, home videos and DVDs have infiltrated people's spare time; yet sociability persists as groups of Indonesians enjoy these together. The frequency of festive events and socializing prevent most Indonesians from ever becoming "coach potatoes."

LEISURE ACTIVITIES

Socializing

Chatting, or *omong,* happens anywhere people meet—on porches, buses, streets, or at markets. Riding public transport, strangers discuss prices of food or news. People rarely remain silent while traveling if someone sits nearby. Indonesians invariably prefer venturing out with a *kawan* ("companion"). Sharing experiences with another is more *enak* ("pleasant").

Inquisitiveness and initiating conversation extend to most anyone who appears normal. As a stranger passes a home, residents freely call out,

"Mau ke mana?" ("Where are you going?")—an altogether reasonable question eliciting answers like, "I'm going home," or "I'm out for a walk." Unacquainted Indonesians passing on streets will acknowledge each other out of mutual respect. Greeting others is both leisure activity and norm of polite social behavior and can lead to conversation. Further, sharing betel nut (or for many men, smoking) enhances leisure time and accompanies the *omong* (chatting) of Indonesians. As consummate "porch-sitters," many islanders relax on mats and chewing betel suits this social mode.

Going to market is the most common day-to-day activity for many. Here people converge in the most ubiquitous public institution of Indonesian social life. Public markets spotlight local realities through a dynamic range of social vignettes. People discuss recent scandals, news spreads of special events, women brag or commiserate on children or marriages, well-dressed singles flirt, and young men sometimes fight. Indonesian markets are carnival-like stages for leisure and life as people buy necessities. Bargaining (*tawar menawar,* or "bidding back and forth") is an animated market "sport," often relentlessly pursued. While most Indonesians use money at markets, some still barter in rural areas.

Sports (Olahraga)

Pencak silat (system of self-defense) or *silat* is an ancient martial art form likely originating in western Sumatra in the seventh century. Historically boys had to master *silat* before permitted to venture to other lands on the *rantau.* Public schools in the Minangkabau region of Sumatra teach the sport to students. In its movements, *silat* appears as both dance and athleticism, employing a wide range of specific motions and attack techniques. Variations of *silat* have developed and people across Indonesia, Southeast Asia, and around the world now practice it. Proponents of *pencak silat* are trying to achieve the status of an Olympic sport.

The Manggarai people of western Flores hold ceremonial whip fights called *caci.* Players wield three-meter long whips of sharp rattan or bound cane and wear protective headgear with water buffalo motifs. Wearing Manggarai *sarungs* and decorative belled anklets, men carry protective shields of rawhide, yet their upper bodies remain naked. This is one of Indonesia's most "macho" battles. Contestants taunt and insult each other into action and whips inflict deep, bloody cuts, leaving scars largely on arms and shoulders. Attackers, however, fiercely aim whips at faces, necks, or hands of opponents. Some say that scars (if not indicating many losses) attract local women. Gongs, drums, and singing enliven the matches.

Cockfighting evolved with other tournaments of fighting tigers, elephants, and buffaloes held by royal courts. Spilling of blood entertained the masses and likely fulfilled ritual sacrifices essential for fertility, purification, and conquests of war.[1] Cockfights have been part of Indonesian life as long as anyone knows. Today millions of men keep fighting cocks under large, airy baskets, feeding, grooming, and exercising them as beloved pets. As remarked of centuries past, "Of all such opportunities for gambling, cockfighting was by far the most popular for reasons which probably have to do with the close identification of the rooster with the male ego."[2] All religions (except animism) and the national government ban the sport, yet its popularity never wanes.

Formats vary, but fights are always frenzies of violence. Balinese attach razor sharp spurs to their roosters' legs, and the winning bird often slices the other open. Bouts are short and explosive, as cocks fly at each other with heads thrust forward and wings beating wildly. Cockfights are spectacles of pure fury and betting is fast and frantic. Contests embody men's struggles for masculinity, status, attacking enemies, and aiming for grand achievement while risking utter loss. An entwinement of male passions and risk-taking has perpetuated cockfighting in Indonesia.

World-famed for its annual *Pasola* pageant, West Sumba attracts thousands to watch hundreds of horsemen "jousting" and flinging (now blunted) spears. Festooned in colorful headgear, pom-poms, cloth, and bells, men and horses enact a battle evoking medieval European pageantry. Skill on horseback astounds audiences as men shift swiftly, riding sideways to avoid a spear, and then spring upright while battling at full speed. Formerly *Pasola* necessitated deaths, as spilled blood fulfilled the ritual. With spears now blunted (by law), riders aim at vulnerable areas, sending fierce blows to the temple. Most years at least one man dies. *Pasola* celebrates sea worms arriving at coasts annually. An abundance of worms bodes bountiful rice harvests. In recent times, many foreigners have attended this festival, including Dutch royalty—heightening the prestige of the event.

Horseracing has spread to most of Indonesia. Sumbanese breed horses for export and racing is a passionate sport on the island. The neighboring island of Sumbawa produces small pony-like horses for racing. A major annual event called *Maen Jaran* (horseracing) celebrates the end of harvest. Young boys ride as jockeys in madly competitive races. Now horseracing marks all major festivals in Sumbawa, including national holidays. Horses wear colorful bridles and pom-poms and owners of winners enjoy acclaim. The races incite heavy gambling, in which people pool their money to bet greater sums.

Bull racing, called *Kerapan Sapi,* occurs from July to October as a unique pageant of the island of Madura. Begun long ago with competitions between plowing teams, these have evolved into a major sport and, as horse racing, a prime wagering event. The ultimate 130-meter race includes 100 bulls adorned with gold. All must be Madurese stock and conform to specific physical traits. Before races begin, a procession of bulls bedecked in colorful ribbons, flowers, yokes, and jeweled headpieces marches in a festive parade through town streets. Brightly decorated parasols shade the bulls and drums and flutes accompany the promenade. When races start, *gamelan* orchestras and gongs begin to play, exciting bulls and adding festive atmosphere.

Most Indonesians cannot swim and fear the water. Yet, a surfing craze has engrossed Bali youth for decades—through contact with surfing tourists on their southern coast. Now Balinese have gone on to world championships. Boats have raced through the Maluku waters for centuries. Seafaring peoples such as Bugis and Makasar still join races in displays of superior boatbuilding and navigational skill. Traditional fishermen of Sulawesi now sail in an annual race between roughly 100 outriggers traveling more than 300 nautical miles. Boat races in long, narrow craft occur yearly on the Musi River in South Sumatra and traditional boats race upon the rivers of Kalimantan. Indonesians competed in the Traditional Boat Race at the 2005 Southeast Asian Games, with a man and a woman each winning a silver medal.

Western sports like volleyball, soccer, tennis, and badminton are common in Indonesia today, played vigorously and drawing crowds. Volleyball games appear almost anywhere. Soccer players draw immense enthusiasm, publicity, and fans. In Sumatra, Java, and Sulawesi, an older contest similar to badminton entailed wooden bats hitting back and forth small bamboo tubes with extending feathers. The imported game of badminton thus really took on through the islands. Many fashion their own shuttlecocks or "birdies" and nets. Indonesian Rudy Hartono won the "All England Informal World Championship" in badminton for seven consecutive years.

The ancient game *Sepak takraw* or *sepak raga* ("kick basket") evolved into a modern sport played at the annual Southeast Asia Games. Now internationally known by the Thai term *takraw,* this historically noncompetitive game compares to "hackey sack" popular in the West. The Dutch found men playing *takraw* on the Banda Islands in the early seventeenth century.[3] As casually played in Indonesia, *takraw* has not changed greatly. Men deftly keep aloft a hollow ball of woven rattan (about 8 inches in diameter) with their feet. While some show off skill by repeatedly kicking the ball upward, they eventually pass it to another. The rattan ball thus soars around a circle in a cooperative game—creating a kind of airborne consensus.

Games of Adults

Congklak (cowrie shell) traces back to ancient Egypt as among the world's oldest known games. Likely introduced to Indonesia centuries back by Indian or Arab traders, this game is as popular today as it was in the past. *Congklak* consists of a long (roughly 18 inches) carved wooden board with seven cup-like indentations on each side and one at each end. Initially, 98 cowrie shells, stones, or beads sit evenly divided in the recessions. The object of this game is to move as many pieces into one's "home" cup—the indented space at the end of the board to the left. *Congklak* looks simple but requires skill, strategy, and much practice. Wooden boards may be crudely carved or elegantly crafted.

Board games like chess and checkers, likely introduced from India, engage many Indonesians. Europeans chronicled these games in Java and Sumatra in the early sixteenth century. Bataks of northern Sumatra consistently exhibit the greatest prowess at chess in recent times.[4] Chess imaginably appealed to aristocrats early on by the character of its pieces (kings, queens, pawns, etc.) and by the strategic battlefield basis of the competition.

Probably introduced by the Chinese and later popularized by Europeans, card games break out everywhere. Indonesians play many versions, including poker, canasta, euchre, card renditions of Chinese *mah jong,* and local inventions. As do cockfights, high betting offers exalted gain or crippling loss, adding a perilous thrill for players. Islam and Christianity forbid gambling, which seems to increase its enticement.

Dice may have come from India to Southeast Asia in ancient times.[5] People of the Malukus used dice by the mid-sixteenth century. A Javanese version of the epic *Mahabharata* features the loss of the heroic, warring Pandawa kingdom through a king gambling with the enemy using dice.[6] As with cards, Indonesians bet on dice games, which are especially popular at markets.

Divination and fortune telling are not only ritual practices, but also leisure pursuits among friends. Indonesians seek answers to problems or auspicious personal information through reading cards, throwing dice, drawing and interpreting pictures, analyzing dreams, and mimicking shamanistic techniques. Sharing future predictions intrigues many and those who show skill enjoy popularity.

Games of Youth

Boys often own handcrafted wooden tops and hold contests for the longest spin or for knocking another's top over. An ancient toy in Indonesia, tops often emit humming or whistling sounds and feature whirling attachments.

Their antiquity and wide variation suggest that tops may once have functioned at divinations or life rituals. They persist in popularity and cleverness of design.

Some Indonesians hold a peculiar passion for kite flying. In Bali, kites shaped as dragons, gods, animals, and symbols fill the skies in the dry season. Masterly crafted of colorful waxed paper and bamboo supports, they take innumerable shapes with extravagant long tails. Some kites make sounds believed to echo celestial voices. Boys and fathers share in a love and construction of kites. Some contests involve attempts to bring other kites down, creating games of war. These "fighting kites" have no tails and their strings contain small bits of glass to sever strings of opponents. Boys develop strong emotional attachments to their special kites, as do men with their favorite fighting cocks. While pleasing their owners, kites provide imaginative, colorful, air-borne displays for all to enjoy watching.

Marble matches absorb boys as a favorite pastime with friends. A popular game involves a small circle drawn on the ground. Players try to knock marbles within the circle outward by using one marble from the outside. Each tries to knock all marbles out of the enclosed space, including his own. If a player succeeds in striking other marbles beyond the circle, but his own remains within it, he forfeits his marble. The object is to strike out marbles along with one's own, then keep the other marbles. Boys enjoy collecting marbles of all kinds.

Across the islands children play with hand-made, painted cars and trucks of wood, plastic bottles, or even dried pomelo (like a grapefruit) skin. Usually made by male relatives, these toy vehicles often include details such as windows and seats. Children pull them along by strings. Some suggest "folk art" in their ingenuity, craft, charm, and color. As simple as they appear compared to manufactured counterparts, Indonesian children delight in them. In fact, many children happily walk with a small wheel on the end of a stick, a most basic toy. Ordinary Indonesians can rarely afford to buy many factory-made toys like dolls, trucks, or computerized games, yet their children's lives seem none the worse for it.

Young girls play a version of jump rope using parallel "ropes" actually woven with rubber bands. In turns, each tries to leap over the incrementally elevating ropes until they reach neck height. Some talented jumpers are able to leap over these. As the ropes are soft rubber, girls are not apt to be scraped if missing a jump. They also play games similar to jacks, using shells, bones, or ceramic pieces. Most often, girls enjoy contests like hopscotch. They etch game patterns onto the ground, then hop on one leg using stone markers for their finish points.

Often children inherit festival decorations or crafted animal forms from rituals as toys. Javanese children love to receive the hobbyhorse-like props ridden by men in ceremonies. These woven and painted make-believe creatures add much to their imaginative play.

Favored Leisure Pursuits

Indonesians like to feel happy (*senang*), which overwhelmingly applies to their free time. Activities can be simple or elaborate, as long as people *senang*. Thus, leisure hours are less often spent on personal work projects than they are on enjoying life. In their approach toward leisure as a means to happiness, Indonesians may have the right idea.

Strolling (*jalan-jalan*) is a simple way to relax and nearly everywhere people take lingering walks in the cool of late day. Along the way, they encounter others, view neighborhood changes, or simply talk while walking slowly. The habit of strolling compels Indonesians in cities and villages, as a completion of the day. As they promenade, people ask where they are going, to which they reply *jalan-jalan*—a perfectly logical answer.

Snacking is a favorite Indonesian national pastime. People frequent shops, kiosks, carts, and *warungs* to buy cookies, potato chips, candy, peanuts, fried bananas, *tahu* and *tempe,* sweet ice dishes, and other treats. They then sit to enjoy their snacks or return home to share food together. Snacking is fun, inexpensive, and social—made more pleasant by talk and joking.

Indonesian village women often do not sit completely idle when relaxing with friends. They weave, sew, make basketry, spin cotton into yarn, or embroidery, while talking with companions. Women frequently carry out daily endeavors in groups, thus work time coincides with social time. Sharing and voicing ethical opinions concerning tales or problems of their villages, families, neighbors, and enemies; such talk spreads and becomes embedded in local ideas and lore.

Most artisans continue polishing a carving, painting a mask, or twining end threads on a textile as they visit with others. Some whittle, crochet, or even husk corn while conversing. Aside from late at night or periods of hard work requiring concentration, any time might be appropriate for socializing. This affords a pleasant, relaxed feeling to those finishing off their arts and allows for other to give praise or suggestions.

Karaoke has been a craze across Indonesia for some time now. The humblest of outer island huts might contain a *karaoke* set, drawing neighbors in the evenings to show their talents and imagine stardom. Songs range among pop hits from both hemispheres. All lounges and even restaurants seem to feature *karaoke* for Indonesian customers. In the 1999 presidential race, the ambitious candidate who opened the short-lived *Warung Wiranto* chain across the islands (Chapter 5) also campaigned on television as a dashing *karaoke* star. Whether this heralded his defeat remains speculative.

Films have long fascinated Indonesians. As with television, the Suharto government strictly censored and determined content of movies.[7] Now radio, television, home videos, and DVDs are part of leisure life across the islands. Indonesian films sometimes adapt elements of other cultures. Still, the plots, values, comic and tragic sensibilities, and emotionality are "profoundly Indonesian."[8] One notes how Indonesian films overwhelmingly center upon order and disorder and do not feature absolute "bad guys."[9] This reflects ancient, core outlooks—including ambiguity of thought and interpretations not based in absolutisms. As in many other Indonesian arts and tales, there is more than one right approach or analysis in most situations.

A demand for Western and pan-Asian films increased since the loosening of censorship following the New Order era. People especially relish action films, romances, and musicals. India's Bollywood cinematic extravaganzas became a craze in Indonesia, viewed in theaters and on televisions. Not surprisingly, Indonesians delight in the rhythmic music, colorful costumes, good-looking actors, and lavish musical sequences of these films.

Controlled and censored by the Suharto family during the New Order era,[10] television programming grew far more liberal following the president's downfall. In fact, after his demise, television stations were flooded with talk shows and satires denouncing his leadership, family, and the corruption he fostered. An explosiveness of media expression occurred in Indonesia after the New Order, following years of suppression of free speech.

Indonesians owning televisions usually watch the evening news and take interest in world events. Soap operas are popular with many women. Those imported from Mexico and dubbed in Indonesian hold special appeal, as they appear more glamorous and racy than Indonesian productions. Men like American boxing matches. Musical variety shows (including the recent *Indonesian Idol* inspired by the production, *American Idol*), comedies, dramas, dubbed Indian epics, "ethnic" performances from various island groups, and game shows entertain Indonesian viewers. Television advertisements can be quite influential, as they introduce modern products, play upon vanity, and champion popular culture.

Pornographic material from around the world now appears via magazines, videos, and DVDs in even remote Indonesia. Wildly enticing and popular with men, these frequently have fed misconceptions or ill-placed bravado regarding sex. They also portray foreigners as lascivious and immoral. Banned by religious leaders, pornography becomes all the more intriguing. Computers in public offices sometimes "crash" by an overload of surreptitiously downloaded porn sites.

FESTIVALS

Festivals as Processions

Power served pomp, not pomp power.[11]

Historically, rulers staged grand festivals to display their authority through impressing the masses. These featured competitions, performances, dances, music, and majestic parades. Spectacles of grandeur constituted the substance of power of Balinese kingdoms. Ceremonies and magnificent celebrations publicly dramatized the "ruling obsessions of the Balinese culture: social inequality and status pride. It was thus a theatre state in which kings and princes were the impresarios, the priests the directors, and the peasants the supporting cast, stage, crew, and audience."[12] Pageantry continuously legitimized rulers and elites in Southeast Asia.

This carries on through processions like Balinese cremation ceremonies. These may draw thousands and tremendous effort goes into massive decorations and construction of the requisite tower. Moreover, those attending enjoy food and entertainment by *gamelan* orchestras. As predominant status symbols for Balinese, cremations festivals perpetuate their ongoing value.

Processions shape a basic scheme for numerous festivals, elevating their grandeur through dazzling pomp, color, music, and performances—paraded before as many onlookers as possible. The cover of this book illustrates a priestess in Bali carried aloft in a colorful procession. Sumatran Minangkabau women stage lavish parades wearing distinctive head cloths of matrilineages. Javanese family pageants follow weddings, displaying adorned brides borne on palanquins and grooms following on horseback. Ritual processions between villages mark marriages on many islands. These announce relations between clan groups while flaunting wealth and standing by the numbers of people involved and their splendid costumes.

In central Java, grandiose parades honor the Prophet Mohammed's birthday, called *Maulud*. Groups of men bear large platforms with decorated mountains of rice. Marching from palaces to mosques, accompanying multitudes pray for community well being. People then take bits of the "mountain" as blessings. Similar processions honor God with "floats" displaying rice molded into male and female forms. At some stage of the parades, *gamelan* orchestras resound, drawing yet larger crowds and creating greater spectacles.

In South Sulawesi, Muslims celebrate *Maulud* by honoring their Islamic ancestors' initial arrival to the island. Symbolic ships with sails of many colors float in procession on water. Later, cloth of the sails goes to the poor. Most Islamic rituals emphasize giving alms to those in need, as this fulfills one of the five pillars of Islam, called *zakah*.

Some Indonesians perform celebratory dances on boats as they sail to events on other islands. Such colorful, sea-born processions animate waterways between the Tanimbar Islands of the Maluku archipelago in eastern Indonesia. As distances are not far between some islands, the seas become a staging ground for ritual parades of boats and people, sailing ceremoniously from one place to the next.

The *Reog Ponorogo* (Masked Dance of Ponogoro) procession of East Java follows a cavalry of men on large, flat hobbyhorses of woven, painted bamboo. The central marcher wears a gigantic mask of a tiger's face under a heavy, bed-sized platform of peacock feathers. Masked dancers and musicians follow. This boisterous parade celebrates local myths of the tiger and peacock and the territory of Ponorogo and appears at all illustrious events.

People of East Sumba organize an enormous procession each year near the end of the long dry season (often in November)—as restless heat weighs upon villages awaiting the monsoon rains. Known as the "hungry season," (*musim lapar*), the past year's food stores are growing depleted and rains must arrive for gardens to grow. The necessary "Rain Prayers" require massive processions and rituals to call down the rains. Early in the morning, men congregate at the most ancient gravesite of the region. Thousands then march more than 3 miles to the sea—a human stream in *ikat* fabric—following *Marapu* priests on horseback. None may eat or drink until nightfall. Finally, where a river meets the sea, priests seek signs of mythical red crocodiles. People believe that these amphibians swim up Sumba's rivers, metaphorically symbolizing sexual intercourse and fertilization. If sighted, the vast crowd grows wild with excitement. Men then slaughter and cook water buffalos and drink palm wine. By evening, the mood is raucously festive through the abundance of rice, meat and wine. People say that rain usually falls within a week.[13]

Festivals of Faith and Happiness

"[W]e come upon the visible of other periods and it offers us company."[14]

The most spectacular festive ritual held in Bali occurs to purify the world. Called *Ekadasa Rudra* (roughly translated as "Eleven Directions of Evil"), this transpires once every century at Bali's most sacred temple, Besakih (the last in 1979). The destructive side of the Hindu God Siwa (Shiva) is the "evil," which Balinese also honor. Thus, the dualism of good and evil becomes ritually acknowledged as Balinese cosmology. Extraordinary shrines and towering altars embellish *Ekadasa Rudra,* as do sumptuous throngs of people and dancers.

Wayang performances (celebrating many occasions) electrify the darkness of night (even using oil lamps!) as they captivate audiences under

"Rain Prayers," a procession of thousands of men in East Sumba calling down the rains in the late dry season. 1994. Courtesy of Jill Forshee.

community pavilions or in private homes. Mystical and intimate in atmosphere, these productions create close communal feeling and excited anticipation. As people have known the *wayang* stories and characters for so long, they become engrossed by any given performance. Divine personalities of the ancient Indian *Ramayana* and *Mahabharata,* now long localized by Indonesians to their liking, perform to a *gamelan* orchestra. A quintessentially Indonesian musical grouping—a *gamelan* set includes gongs of different sizes and tones, drums, flutes, xylophones, stringed instruments, and often male and female singers—altogether producing a richly ethereal, otherworldly ambience.

Indeed, the enchanting effect of the music, voices, and characters of the puppet play mesmerizes viewers, who often respond emotionally to particular heroes or sequences. During battle scenes, the orchestra becomes explosively loud and dramatic, enhancing each clash of weaponry and victory of performing puppets through percussion. Performances typically go on until dawn. As mentioned, "according to tradition, everyone at a *wayang* performance is safe from the evil influences that normally plague people."[15] Thus an aesthetic, performative space becomes a sort of supernatural safety zone, while entertaining all. The quality and extensiveness of the performance and the number of people it attracts bestow honor upon its sponsors.

The Islamic holy day of *Idul Adha* (Sacrificial Feast) commemorates the biblical story of God giving Abraham a ram to sacrifice in place of his son. *Idul Adha* coincides with a day of sacrifice of goats and sheep by those on the *haj* (pilgrimage) to Mecca. Indonesian Muslims ritually slaughter goats on this day and then distribute meat to the poor, fulfilling a duty to give alms.

Idul Fitri (Purifying Feast) follows the Islamic month of fasting, *Ramadan,* called *Puasa* in Indonesian. During this time, nothing may pass through a Muslim's lips between dawn and dusk, including food, drinks (even water), betel nut, or cigarette smoke. People then might partake of all in the evenings. Many arise before dawn so as to eat and drink sufficiently to sustain them through the day. Some Indonesians practice "partial *Puasa*s," by giving up smoking or consuming little by day. Usually, Muslims of higher classes are strictest regarding rules and practices of *Puasa*.

Idul Fitri provides a festive climax including extensive visiting and well wishing. Many buy new clothes or hold special feasts on this day to rejoice in the end of fasting. The most crucial ritual act of *Idul Fitri,* however, is an individual plea for forgiveness following status differences. Young and lower status people beg their superiors to pardon them for any offenses (however inadvertent) they may have caused over the past year. This serves as a community reprieve of ill feeling, honors elders and elites, and lightens any sense of guilt for those asking forgiveness.

Nonetheless, much of the visiting carries a festive mood as all wear new clothing and hosts provide sumptuous food for guests. Thus, humility, mercy, and social status intermix during *Idul Fitri* gatherings. Christians often also partake in the pleasant socializing of this time. *Idul Fitri* suggests something of Christmas in its festive manifestations. Colored lights and gold tinsel embellish Indonesian cities, much like holiday decorations in the West. Jakarta never appears as festive or attractive as during *Idul Fitri.*

Indonesian Christians hold more rituals at Easter than at Christmas. This likely reflects the historically local importance of rituals for the dead and ceremonies honoring ancestors. Catholics of Larantuka in eastern Flores have incorporated their own life cycle rituals with the birth and death of Christ since their conversion in the sixteenth century. Easter inspires a devout vigil for many Christians, beginning on Saturday night until the time of Christ's resurrection on Sunday morning.

Catholics of the Toba Batak mix traditional ritual dances with Christian rituals. Asmats of West Papua receive Catholic communion in traditional headdresses and face paint.[16] Sumba's Christians drape *ikat* textiles with cross motifs over coffins of their dead. A large cement Sumbanese rendition of Christ clad in a traditionally worn *ikat* costume stands before a Catholic

Church in the town of Waingapu. As always, newer world faiths overlay old ways in ceremonies and imagery.

Christmas across Indonesia typically revolves around church events rather than major festivities at home. People dress up and sing seasonal hymns but rarely decorate their homes or buy and exchange gifts as in the West. Christmas is a time of socializing and people will take sweets to friends, sometimes visiting several homes in succession. While a holy day, Christmas does not carry the religious power of Easter.

The Non-Leisured Indonesians

Lest it seem that all Indonesians enjoy abundant leisure time, the opposite condition is more often true. The poor cannot often afford the luxuries of relaxation or recreation and spend their time seeking ways to survive, often at minimal levels. Some parents work two to three jobs to support their families. Many employed by industries—both Indonesian and multi-national—receive almost no time off; some even sleeping at their work sites. Men and women working at stores, hotels, or as housekeepers might work 12-hour days or longer, seven days a week.

Foreign companies such as Nike have exploited cheap labor markets and a general paucity of workers' rights in Indonesia, while providing minimum pay, long hours, unhealthy work environments, and none of the benefits Americans expect. In Irian Jaya (West Papua), the American-owned Freeport Mine's contribution to the economic welfare of surrounding peoples has been more than negated by its policy of irrevocably displacing them from their lands and rendering regions toxic from industrial wastes. Multinational companies have been protected by the Indonesian military, taking lives of those protesting their presence and policies. Such abuses have continuously fueled West Papua's decades long independence movement.

A permanent yet resilient underclass has survived in Indonesia for many centuries. These were the poor who built grand monuments to kings, struggled for shelter through Suharto's ill-conceived urban renewal projects, and made their homes in shantytowns and garbage dumps. This continues, as described in Chapter 4. In examining life across Indonesia, an honest general description of festivals and leisure activities must take into account the millions who seldom partake of them. Poverty represents the less-than-festive side of Indonesian society. For years, Indonesian thinkers and commentators persistently have expressed concern regarding problems of poverty and international exploitation. The coming years will reveal whether equitable or "democratic" social improvements take place or whether Indonesia will carry on—notwithstanding its beauty and cultural richness—following a latter-day commercial feudalism. If so, the ruling lords will no longer be regional sultans, kings, or even Indonesian leaders, but rather, expanding corporate powers that currently seem to be inheriting the earth.

NOTES

1. See Anthony Reid, *Southeast Asia in the Age of Commerce 1450–1680, Volume One: The Lands below the Winds* (New Haven: Yale University Press, 1988), 189–190.

2. Reid, *Southeast Asia in the Age of Commerce,* 199.

3. Reid, *Southeast Asia in the Age of Commerce,* 199–200, paraphrased here.

4. See Reid, *Southeast Asia in the Age of Commerce,* 198.

5. See Reid, *Southeast Asia in the Age of Commerce,* 196.

6. See Reid, *Southeast Asia in the Age of Commerce,* 196–197.

7. See Sen, Krishna and David T. Hill, *Media, Culture, and Politics in Indonesia* (South Melbourne, Australia: Oxford University Press, 2000), 137–163. See also Karl Heider, *Indonesian Cinema: National Culture on Screen* (Honolulu: University of Hawaii Press, 1991).

8. See Heider, *Indonesian Cinema,* 7.

9. Heider, *Indonesian Cinema,* 35, paraphrased here.

10. See Sen and Hill, *Media, Culture, and Politics in Indonesia,* 108–136.

11. Clifford Geertz, *Negara: The Theatre State in Nineteenth-Century Bali* (Princeton: Princeton University Press, 1980), 13.

12. Geertz, *Negara,* 13.

13. See Jill Forshee, *Between the Folds: Stories of Cloth, Lives, and Travels from Sumba* (Honolulu: University of Hawaii Press, 2001), 181, 191, 192.

14. John Berger, *The Shape of a Pocket* (New York: Vintage Books, 2003), 21.

15. Alit Djajasoebrata, *Shadow Theatre in Java: The Puppets, Performance, and Repertoire* (Amsterdam: The Pepin Press, 1999), 11.

16. See James J. Fox, ed., *Religion and Ritual: Indonesian Heritage Series* (Singapore: Archipelago Press, 1998), 128–129.

SUGGESTED READING

Craig, Timothy J., and Richard King, eds. *Global Goes Local: Popular Culture in Asia.* Honolulu: University of Hawaii Press, 2002.

Fox, James J. *Religion and Ritual—Indonesian Heritage Series.* Singapore: Archipelago Press, 1999.

Geertz, Clifford. "Deep Play/Notes on the Balinese Cockfight." In *The Interpretation of Cultures: Selected Essays by Clifford Geertz* (pp. 412–453). New York: Basic Books, 1973.

Geertz, Clifford. *Negara: The Theatre State in Nineteenth Century Bali.* Princeton: Princeton University Press, 1980.

Harnish, David D. *Bridges to the Ancestors: Music, Myth, and Cultural Politics at an Indonesian Festival.* Honolulu: University of Hawaii Press, 2005.

Heider, Karl G. *Indonesian Cinema: National Culture on Screen.* Honolulu: University of Hawaii Press, 1980.

Reid, Anthony. "Festivals and Amusements." In *Southeast Asia in the Age of Commerce 1450–1680, Volume One: The Lands below the Winds* (chap. 5). New Haven: Yale University Press, 1988.

Sedyawati, Edi. *Performing Arts—Indonesian Heritage Series.* Singapore: Archipelago Press, 1999.

Sen, Krishna, and David T. Hill. *Media, Culture, and Politics in Indonesia.* South Melbourne, Australia: Oxford University Press, 2000.

8

Music, Dance, and Traditional Theater

Music, dance, and traditional theater provide vitality, expression, and fulfill ceremonial events. Indonesian performance arts emerge from deep roots in ancient cultures and a pervasive practice of intricate group cooperation. These arts demand mastery, attunement to subtlety, balance, and formal elegance. They also lend themselves to innovation, multiple interpretations, and reflect an Indonesian genius for adaptability and creating hybrid forms. This chapter briefly touches upon the richness of music, dance, and traditional theater of the Indonesian islands.[1]

MUSIC

Gamelan

Gamelan (meaning orchestra) ensembles epitomize Indonesian music to much of the world. This distinctive composite of instruments probably took form through an ancient merging of male drums and gongs sets with string and wind instruments of female ensembles. At some point, men evidently took over the playing of most instruments. Bali and Java—the centers of *gamelan*—produce divergent styles of music. *Gamelan* elaborated through court cultures in Bali and Java—where instruments took on lavish forms. There are multiple styles of *gamelan* throughout these islands and discussion of each is impossible here.

Javanese music tends to be soft and sustained in subtle compositions, likened to a breeze across the senses by some. While relaxing and pleasurable, *gamelan* is exceedingly complex and abstract in its performance and for those trying to understand it. Elusiveness characterizes *gamelan* of Java, reflecting

Gamelan orchestra of the court of the Sultan of Yogyakarta, Java. 1990. Courtesy of Jill Forshee.

other aspects of its culture—such as social interaction, stories, and arts. The astounding reality of most *gamelan* performances is that musicians play solely by ear—without a score or conductor. These complex musical movements can include up to 17 beats to a bar and some pieces accompanying dances may contain 15 different harmonizing layers.

Gamelan instruments in Java carry definite pitches, corresponding to two tuning systems. A complete *gamelan* set is actually two orchestras—never played simultaneously, but sometimes alternately, within a performance.[2] While often capable of seven tones, most ensembles use five tones following a pentatonic scale. Javanese orchestras contain large gongs, xylophones, also called metallophones (*gender* is a leading type) of diverse sizes and shapes with large to small keys, and kettle gongs graduating in size along rows—all cast in bronze. Large, elongated two-ended drums (*kendhang*), a two-stringed bowed lute (*rebab*), a bamboo flute (*suling*), and often male or female singers complete the ensemble.

The *rebab* (lute) and *gender* (main xylophone) lead the melodies in ensembles, especially in softer sections of a performance. The *gender* also elaborates on melody while other metallophones complement, play in parallel octaves, or enrich the music through low, abstract tones. Bronze kettle gongs mediate the music of other instruments and signal a change in the tempo. Large, hanging gongs sound at the beginning and end of a piece and at specific intervals within the arrangement. So subtle is the timing of these intervals that some regard the sounding of the gong at the right moment as the most difficult skill in *gamelan*. Instruments fall into two sound groups: loud and soft. Melodic instruments are usually soft, like the *rebab, gender,* and *suling.* *Gamelan* ensembles usually include between 10 to 40 musicians.

Specific sections of an ensemble perform three functions: Singers and instruments carrying the central melody, instruments controlling timing of the music, and instruments underscoring the musical composition. As concisely described, "*Gamelan* integrates a great variety of musical lines in shifting degrees of aural clarity."[3]

While exquisitely crafted and carved elegance distinguishes Java's *gamelan* instruments, Balinese prefer more baroquely carved designs. Gilded and often painted red, *gamelan* ensembles in Bali play faster music with a more vibrant tone. Balinese enjoy loud, rousing *gamelan* music, reflecting their exuberance in ceremonial forms. Clashing cymbals characterize Bali style and men strike metallophones with relatively large wooden mallets to increase their sound level. The *gender* metallophone often sits over bamboo resonators to create a more shimmering, vibrating sound.[4] One unique type of Balinese *gamelan* centers on long bamboo flutes.

Tuning instruments in Bali follows two scale systems, but only one scale for each ensemble. Villages, not individuals, own *gamelan* instruments. Each village tunes its ensemble slightly differently so that instruments cannot be traded or stolen and used elsewhere. Thus, each village maintains an exclusive sound. Turning down a lane, one might encounter a group of young men "jamming" together on *gamelan* instruments in a driveway. While in Java *gamelan* typically appears at special occasions, the Balinese practice it constantly. Music drifts through the air in much of Bali, like part of the natural environment.

Musical Bamboo

Easily available to Indonesians, bamboo is an excellent material for music. Even standing in natural groves, bamboo responds to the wind with its own peculiar sounds. Bamboo xylophones make up *gamelan gambang* (traditional xylophone) of Bali, and musicians also use slit bamboo drums. In Sumatra, Tapanuli music can involve grouped bamboo or wood xylophones playing together. The sound differs greatly from metallophones, producing light, pleasantly resonant melodies. In Kalimantan, people fashion elaborately shaped mouth organs of several bamboo pieces bound together (called *kledi*), played through a carved perpendicular mouthpiece. Bamboo zithers make music on a number of islands. Logical instruments for bamboo, flutes take their shapes from the material. Diverse sorts of bamboo flutes produce melodies across the islands—from Sumatra to West Papua, where Asmat people use wide bamboo sections as wind instruments. Well-crafted bamboo flutes from Makasar, South Sulawesi feature flared ends made of a tight spiral of lontar leaf, adding resonance to the instruments. The ubiquitous bamboo flute sounds across the archipelago.

An *angklung* consists of three or four bamboo tubes held together within a bamboo frame. A player holds the instrument by the left hand and shakes it with the right. Each loosely set piece of bamboo produces a different note. *Angklung* ensembles contain at least 10 instruments suspended from one large frame, a wooden xylophone, a large kettle gong and a larger hanging gong. This type of ensemble is traditional in western Java.

Folk music of the Banyumas area bordering Central and West Java employs diverse bamboo instruments, including flutes and *angklung*. *Calung* is the newest of such music, using a wooden xylophone with bamboo instruments with those of imported styles. Now becoming an eclectic, popular music, *calung* blends styles from Java with Portuguese, Western, and Indian influences. Some *calung* groups use a bamboo zither and flute along with *maracas*, cymbals, and tambourines. Yet these all mix into a five-toned octave of *gamelan* music, forming the basis of the compositions.[5]

Percussive Music

While some central Indonesian *gamelan* ensembles might be predominantly percussive, other islands and peoples deserve attention. In some regions, music is more percussive than melodic, which is not to say that melody is absent. Yet ensembles in regions of outer island Indonesia are simpler than those of courtly central cultures, play to local rituals and dances, and tend to produce predominantly percussive music.

In eastern Indonesia iron gongs usually substitute for those of bronze. Produced in a port town of Sumba from recast 50-gallon oil drums, these relatively cheap gongs sell well locally and on neighboring islands. With a sufficiently resonant sound, they often form the percussive base for music of the Lesser Sunda Islands and beyond.

Drumming often predominates the music of these islands. In Timor, Tetum women dance while beating small drums held under one arm. The drums provide the rhythm of their dancing and cause a curved posture to their bodies as they gracefully move. In Sumba, variably tuned drums play for days during funeral events and other ceremonies. Sumbanese also carry out contests with different types of drums, including those imported from other islands. A peculiar two-toned drum is found only in Sumba, made of stretched deer hide on either end. Between the tympanic sides the base of the drum contains about 100 wooden wedges, driven inward to lock together and held in place by leather cords. To change the tone of a drum, the wedges are either loosened or made tighter, altering the tension of the drumheads and thus the sound. These porcupine-like instruments hang from trees or stands and receive full forced beats, sometimes by women.

Sasak people of Lombok employ a basically percussive *gamelan*. This ancient, traditional ensemble includes drums, cymbals, large gongs, and gong chimes. Male dancers perform to the music, also playing heavy, long drums strapped to their shoulders. They compete in drumming while showing physical strength and agility. Still, their music interlocks cooperatively as they dance and strike dramatic postures. The dancing and drumming builds in intensity until a gong sounds. This vibrant musical dance competition is one of the few remaining traditional forms of the Sasak people.

Northern Sumatra contains numerous, rich drumming traditions. The Toba Batak perform drum ensembles in which one man plays five long drums melodically while another plays a sixth drum for accents and patterns of rhythm. This type of tuned drum set is called *taganing* and is extremely rare in the world.[6] Yet the drumming is now seldom performed, as Batak say that the sounds call down ancestral spirits, which many now fear (most Toba Bataks are Protestant and have been dissuaded from animistic practices). This is but one type of drum music that involves peoples of coastal Sumatra, Kalimantan, and the Riau Islands, echoing a strong percussive tradition of Malay groups.

Distinctive drums of West Papua (Irian Jaya) are hourglass shaped, carved in wood with a cassowary skin drumhead. Sacred drums of this shape from the region of Lake Sentani play only at hidden ceremonies within exclusive men's houses. All drums of this region bear a carved, central band. This is called a waist belt in local language and represents a similar belt worn by headmen that bestows protective powers. As indigenous West Papuan peoples have disputed their incorporation into Indonesia since the beginning, headmen and special powers hold profound importance to the present as people feel little sense of belonging to a nation state—and powerless within it. In their own societies, Papuan men are secretive of rituals in men's houses. Thus, while anthropologists have recorded certain ceremonies, much remains hidden of the special music and beliefs of peoples of Irian Jaya. Such drums beat away from outsiders, defying typically Indonesian notions of ceremony.

Singing

A style of folk singing called *tangis* ("to cry") is popular in Sumba. This may have evolved from the "keening" dirges women traditionally sing for the dead. Keening sounds like combined crying and singing—a sort of rising and falling wailing with an underlying tune. Two-stringed lutes (*jungga*) accompany sad ballads of loss, parables, or the lovelorn.

Yet some have compared this droned singing, in Sumba and Roti, to songs of eastern Arnhemland in Northern Australia. Peoples of these regions sing in a descending vocal pattern. Songs of lamentation in Sumba might compare to those of the Yirrkala people of Arnhemland, as remarked by a Sumbanese man.[7] While people of Sumba have never been seafaring to any extent, fishermen of Roti long have traveled far in their boats. *Trepang* (sea cucumbers), an Asian delicacy, were abundant in northern Australian waters and drew many Indonesians to Arhemland's shores in ancient times. As Sumba and Roti sit relatively close to Australia, and Rotinese have long ventured to sea, such influences were possible.

In Flores women perform a type of choral singing remarkably similar to that of the Balkans. Indeed, some theorize that migrations of Balkan peoples in prehistoric times culminated in parts of eastern Indonesia. While this cannot be proved, Europeans possibly migrated to the Lesser Sunda Islands (Nusa Tenggara Timur) bringing artifacts, types of song, and musical instruments (such as the lute). That such ancient links insinuate through music makes it all the more compelling to study.

Popular Music

Playing instruments and singing melodies together is universal among the young. Batak play a two-stringed lute (*hasapi*) in a quickly plucked, mandolin style. Their songs follow the tempo as lively folk music. This is typical in many parts of Indonesia, where people often play guitars or lutes and sing. Among the Bugis in rural villages or small towns in South Sulawesi, group singing with two-stringed plucked lutes has become a common pastime. Some groups practice and develop their music and singing to the point that they play at special events. In Sumba people play lutes and mouth harps while others sing. Like the young who play *gamelan* in back lane Bali, youth across Indonesia get together to make music, from relatively traditional styles to pop and rock hits. The city of Ambon (in the Maluku archipelago) developed a special type of folk singing incorporating ukuleles, creating a unique "islander" sound. Ambon music has become a unique style on international recordings, featured in the American production, "Steeling around the World Hawaiian Style."

Keroncong and *dangdut* are relatively contemporary popular music types in Indonesia. Some Indonesians consider that *keroncong* began through Portuguese influence in a specific part of Jakarta, developing through the twentieth century. Modern ensembles include a guitar, flute, violin, ukulele, banjo, cello, two small lutes, and string bass. The flute, violin, or lead singer carries the melody. *Keroncong* instruments are all plucked, so that a cello produces rhythm, as does a drum. Syncopated rhythms of differing lengths characterize this music. *Keroncong* appeals largely to an older generation from the times of national independence. Nostalgic and slow in tempo, it sings of nationalistic pride, nature, and times past. *Keroncong* likely sounds "corny" to the younger generation, who thrive on international pop music, Indonesian rock stars, or the enticing dance rhythms of *dangdut*.

Dangdut wafts on buses, streets, and markets throughout the archipelago, although its appeal is ostensibly to relatively poor Muslim youth. It carries rhythms inspired by Indian, Malaysian, and Arabic influences, yet adapted to a Western scale. Beginning in the 1950s, (as did all Indonesian pop music) *dangdut* has continuously absorbed new influences to the point of becoming a form of rock. Rhythms of *dangdut* are sensual and syncopated, often accompanying a popular dance from Malaysia called *joget*. This undulating dance moves with graceful restraint to the rhythms, using arm and hand motions evocative of classical dances. *Joget* dancers often shift their heads from side to side in time to the music. Young men especially like to show off their talents at dancing, and *joget* permits dancing alone, with someone else, or in a line. While the tempo is vibrant, *dangdut* lyrics are melancholic and yearning and often sing of broken hearts. (In fact, another pop genre is called *cengeng lagu*—"whining songs" of broken hearts!) Rhoma Irama is a famous contemporary *dangdut* star, whose lyrics carry critiques of modern social problems, while bringing the musical form into the rock genre.

Iwan Falls and his band *Kantata Samsara* have been beloved rock stars for years in Indonesia. His many hits successfully combined Indonesian and Western rhythms and scales, producing resonant and even elegant hybrids enjoyed by many Westerners. Currently, new faces dominate the pop music scene. One vivacious young woman, Ully Sigar, composes and sings songs completely focused upon environmental awareness. Colorful, eccentrically dressed, and animated, she has become a new pop icon in Indonesia.

Ingenious Indonesian composers have created scintillating fusions of *gamelan* with Western classical, jazz, or pop elements. These make use of electronic media and computers and some fusion music especially highlights the adaptability of *gamelan* with other musical forms.

DANCE

Mask Dancing

Masks (*topeng*) defined characters at the courtly dance dramas of Javanese kings. In fact, these masks largely were about glorifying kings past and present and their heroic deeds. To this day, many masked dramas of Java tell of Panji, an adventurous prince of long ago embodying all Javanese ideals of noble refinement. Against all odds, Panji triumphs in the end. As with puppet characters, the precise physical features of a Panji mask make him readily identifiable to the audience. These performances include arrays of masked characters, many paralleling those of the shadow play.

In Bali, masks invigorate most festivals and sacred rituals. Balinese invariably strive toward drama and elaboration in their arts and the island's extraordinary masks reflect this. The most dramatic and world-famous masked characters are the *Barong*, a fabulous and morally good creature from the underworld, and its counterpart *Rangda*, a powerfully evil witch who plagues villages. The *Barong* inevitably wins in the end after much music, dance drama, and audience excitement.

Such elaborate masks include human or horsehair, shredded leaves of plants, carved teeth, colorful fabric, real or simulated gold, and many layers of paint. The *Barong* incorporates a full body costume of gold-painted leather and leaf strips. Worn by two people, the fantastic creature resembles a hybrid lion, a caterpillar, and a fabulous Chinese festival dragon. *Rangda* wears a raging mane of hair and a ferocious face, with bulging eyes, long fangs, and a hanging tongue—features symbolic of wildness and devilry in Bali. While these masked beings clearly define good and evil, the stories they enact are not simple. Rather, "[t]he *barong* performance is the expression, through theater, entrancement, and celebration, of the whole complex of the Balinese mythic and religious world—the choreography involves not just a troupe of dancers and musicians, but a whole village."[8]

Other masked dance dramas in Bali tell *babad* (meaning "history" or "chronicle") tales—ancient stories based upon genealogies. These provide cores around which performers weave improvisations demonstrating the relevance of the tale to more recent events.[9] According to one scholar, masks are the only visual forms that represent the *babad* tales in Bali dramas.[10] Yet, their stories often contain new renditions or invented episodes and thus continue to reflect both historical and modern concerns and shifts.

The *Hudoq* ritual mask dance of East Kalimantan Dayaks begins riceplanting season and celebrates the harvest. Of a style and elaboration seen nowhere else, the masks represent crop pests or fearsome beasts to scare off evil spirits. Consisting of numerous parts in wildly diverse shapes, these masks

The *Barong* exits a temple compound in Bali to take part in a dance drama. 1992. Courtesy of Jill Forshee.

are masterpieces of imagination and craft. Some bear delicately carved swirls extending beyond the body, some feature intricate beadwork combined with other materials, and others have upright feather crowns. Some masks extend to a full body costume of banana leaves or grass. Usually 11 dancers perform the *Hudoq* ceremony to the sounds of gongs and a small drum. Hand and feet movements create the dance, as arms fly upward then slap down and feet stamp upon the ground. One foot crosses the other with each stamp, causing bodies to sway. Dancers thus proceed in a circle until they have covered the arena. Finally, they sit in the center waiting for spirits to possess them. A twitch of bodies signals possession and they stand to dance once more. When finished, they sit and all present regard the spirits as departed. The entire ceremony takes lead from a ritual specialist.

The Asmat of West Papua wear masks evoking the costume of the Balinese *Barong*. The *jipai* covers the head and body to the legs. Head sections are of wood, but the body mask might be woven, with extending grasses at the bottom. These are secret creations in men's houses as part of months-long preparations. Eventually, a *jipai* covers a man who wants to make contact with his ancestors,

Hudoq dance performed by Bahau men of the Middle Mahakam, East Kalimantan, 1992. The dance is performed by men wearing *Hudoq* masks and banana or areca nut leaves as part of a ritual to ensure *padi* (rice plant) spirits return to the rice seed about to be planted. Hudoq photo 1992. © Elizabeth Oley. Used by permission.

during a special event commemorating the departed. The masked figures perform dances before the men's house at various times during the special day.

Dances of Bali

Many regard the *legong* as Bali's most elegant dance form, accompanied by *gamelan.* This secular dance graces temple anniversaries while increasingly performed for tourists. Three pubescent girls become tightly bound at the torsos by wrapped fabric, then embellished with gorgeous costumes of exquisite gold neckpieces and cloth panels over colorful silk *sarungs.* Crowned with golden headgear bearing frangipani blossoms, the girls perform a graceful dance of largely arm and hand movements, while shifting their heads and moving their eyes expressively. The central dancer provides the most animation while the others follow her dance in perfect synchrony. The tight binding adds grace to the dancers' motions, causing their bodies to arch and sway as they move their feet. Near the end of the dance, the music grows loud and frenzied and the girls dance more vigorously to its doubled tempo.

The *baris gede* is a sacred dance involving a number of dancers depicting great warriors and performed at temple anniversaries and cremation ceremonies. The *baris tunggal* is a secular dance by one man presented for entertainment. Males of all ages perform these dances. All wear a conical headdress of glittering leaves, metallic inlays, or shells and opulently embellished silver,

Legong dancers in Bali. Courtesy of M. J. Adams.

gold, and white costumes. Movements involve rapidly darting, intense eye movements (implying vigilance); elegantly lifted, bent legs (often sustained in pose); and upturned toes. Men dancing the *baris* master exquisite grace in their finger movements, which flicker and curve upward.

Bali's most internationally famed dance is the *kecak* (monkey dance). Walter Spies, an influential European artist, choreographed it in 1931. The indigenous Balinese, nonetheless, made the *kecak* dance their own. The *kecak* resembles a human *mandala*. About 100 men sit in a circle surrounding one or two women, who dance in fetching postures. Often the only accompaniment is the loud, frog-like sounds the men emit in syncopated harmony, with interludes of individual singers. The men never rise, but sway back and forth and lean back to lying positions while continuing their rhythmic chants. The dance is a spectacle unlike any other.

Javanese Dances

The *bedhaya* and *serimpi* dances exemplify refined courtly performances of Central Java and enjoy royal patronage today. Dancers wear fine *batik sarungs* with trailing fabrics. The also make use of gossamer sashes to create or enhance motions. In gold headdresses they demonstrate ideals of perfection through almost imperceptibly subtle movements of a finger or foot. The *bedhaya* only recently was performed outside of palaces of Central Java. As a sacred heirloom of Central Javanese courts, women danced the *bedhaya* in palaces on special occasions. Indonesians believe that Sultan Agung of Mataram created this dance form in the early seventeenth century. Young boys in women's garb originally performed the dance. This ancient dance carries on through a selection of nine dancers deemed most refined and beautiful in the region. Filled with subtle symbolism, the *bedhaya* epitomizes refinement in Central Java. Through slow movements, dancers create a tranquil atmosphere of solemnity and wellbeing.[11] Long silken sashes enhance graceful gestures as dancers deftly hold or shift the fabrics with delicacy.

The *serimpi* dance also developed centuries back in Central Java courts. Usually four female dancers perform this dance, in various renditions composed and choreographed during reigns of different rulers. The oldest known form of *serimpi* dates to the late eighteenth century.

Serimpi dances also make use of flowing sashes and enact set postures such as sitting, standing while rearranging positions of sashes with gracefully bent knees, and an upright stance with an extended arm holding a Javanese *kris* (a curving, slender dagger symbolizing power of rulers). This dance and its ideal postures and movements are still used in Javanese courts to train princesses in grace and balance.

Randai of West Sumatra

The traditional narrative dance drama of *randai* of the Minangkabau region of western Sumatra is embedded in complex cultural systems. Long following the custom of *rantau*, young *Minangkabau* men have left their villages to gain wealth and experience, and prestige upon return. This tradition "is thematically woven through the practice and content of *randai*."[12] *Randai* was preparation for the *rantau*, allowing elders to educate young men in proper conduct, expectations, and what to avoid on their 6- to 12-month journeys. *Randai* is both dance and theatrical performance. As noted by Craig Latrell in his *Asian Theatre Journal* article, "Widening the Circle": "Since almost every *randai* story includes an episode in which the hero vanquishes comic villains using *pencak silat*, performances even today provide an opportunity to show off and perfect moves through hand-to-hand combat and dagger (*keris*) fighting."[13]

A *randai* performance takes the shape of people sitting or moving around a circle. A musical ensemble accompanies the event, consisting of a flute, lute, small gongs, and drums. Before each scene, dancers perform in a ring, clapping hands and slapping legs. A song becomes the narration and actors sitting in the center of the ring engage in dialogues. All others remain squatting around the circle defining the perimeter of the performance. Costumes are black or white trousers, loose, and low-crotched. Mandarin collared shirts, beaded headcloths, and large sashes around waists complete *randai* apparel.

A form of folk entertainment, *randai* occurs after harvests or at special events. *Randai* works in complement to the *rantau* and the matrilineal system of the Minangkabau. The circle is eminently important to Minankabau culture, in that "it may symbolize unity, inclusiveness, or the union of seen and unseen halves of the cosmos."[14] Circles or enclosed sacred spaces mark dances and rituals throughout Indonesia. Inclusion within a bounded social world is a prime Indonesian value. It then follows that "*randai*'s *lingkaran* [circle] expresses in performance terms something essential to the Minangkabau, which is repeated over and over in different ways in other areas of the culture."[15] This repetition of meaningful motifs binds many Indonesian societies to their pasts and their presents, empowering them to adapt to their futures.

The *Padoa* Dancers of Savu

Another circular dance takes place on the small eastern Indonesian island of Savu, beginning in the dry season and lasting through the harvests. The *padoa* dancers creatively generate their own vivid percussion. They dance with rhythmic footwork wearing small palm leaf boxes attached to their feet, filled with grains or beans. These make rattling sounds and add liveliness and tempo to the dance. These ancient dances feature young men and women circling in their finest *ikat* fabrics, denoting clans. A man sings a song in the center of the circle, then dancers repeat it as they link arms and continue their rhythmic circling. The *padoa* furnishes the ideal opportunity for flirting and courtship among the young dancers, which energizes everyone. Circles might include 30 men and women, circling to generate community feeling and good will of ancestors toward their harvests, in the driest region of Indonesia.

Circles dances take place among the Toraja of Sulawesi, people in East Sumba, the Tetum and other groups of Timor, on Solor, and beyond. Whether for harvest or in celebration, these events seem quintessentially Indonesian in symbolizing the significance of community and the ongoing cyclic nature of life.

Padoa dancers of Savu provide their own rhythm with palm leaf boxes attached to their feet, filled with dried beans or gains. 1993. Courtesy of Jill Forshee.

THEATER

Wayang Puppet Theater

Wayang performances originated, by many accounts, in Java, where people blended Indian legends with local ones. A stone inscription from central Java dating from 907 A.D. mentions a "wayang performance held in honor of the gods."[16] Many of the colors and motifs of *wayang* puppets derive from the *pasisir* (coastal trading) culture of northern Java, influenced more than other Indonesian regions by Chinese trade and aesthetics. Rich in artistic influences and vibrant innovations, *pasisir* culture produced amalgamated, elegant, and distinctive art forms that spread to the court cultures of central Java.

The *wayang* became based in what are called *purwa* stories; ancient tales depicting celestial occurrences, the divine, and a course of events considered predestined as a part of cosmic law. *Wayang purwa* originally appeared only in Java and Bali, and other places where Javanese people settled, such as southern Sumatra, south Borneo (Kalimantan), and Surinam[17] (South America via Dutch colonialism).

Skilled and ingenious puppet masters, called *dalang,* bring the puppets to life through complex movements and speaking and singing in an astounding range of voices—from an evil old witch to a refined young woman to a noble warrior-hero. The puppeteer also manipulates a number of *wayang* at once, quickly shifting his voice to represent his range of characters. All of the puppets in a performance stand lined up, impaled (by their supporting sticks) into a soft banana plant trunk. The *dalang* selects them as needed for their parts in the drama and then returns them to the trunk.

Like other Indonesian arts, *wayang* characters and performances involve a moral dimension and function to remind people of the right and wrong ways to behave in this world. Thus, evil and good define the plots and characters of *wayang* plays. Some people believe that these performances emit a protective power, with certain plays chasing off evil spirits.[18] An ongoing belief in spirits permeates these events, persisting from ancient animist ideas of the world, yet making full sense in modern times.

All puppets and props conform to categories—nobles, servants, villains, animals, heroes, sacred trees, and mountains that follow, in varying degrees, the concepts of refined (*halus*) or coarse (*kasar*) in their aesthetic features. Specific characters might appear within a performance as several different puppets, depicting changing moods and circumstances. Audiences, however, will still recognize each character by hairstyle, size, body type, stance, and facial features, not to mention the specific voices of the *dalang*. The nobler the character, the more elongated and slanted the eyes become, with the nose correspondingly long and slender, and nearly closed mouths with thin lips. Opposite types of features distinguish less elite puppets, progressing from unpolished commoners to hideous ogres. Positions of heads also indicate qualities of character. A bowed head signifies a calm, patient, dedicated personality—high virtues in Java. A head held high evokes the opposite traits—impatience, aggression, and irritability—negative personal attitudes in Java.[19]

Wayang puppets evoke ancient ideals of perfection for men and women.[20] The heroic characters Arjuna (from the *Mahabarata*) and Rama (from the *Ramayana*) represent the noblest of male attributes, while their feminine counterparts, such as Sita (*Ramayana*) and Rara Ireng (*Mahabarata*) embody culturally ideal qualities for women. Many Indonesians love and even emulate these heroes and heroines, who have never become irrelevant and carry roles in current films and television shows.

Over the centuries, new ideas and characters have entered the *wayang* repertoire. Special styles developed in places like Yogyakarta and Solo (Surakarta) in Java, following tastes and desires of rulers. As have other arts, the puppets and stories have always changed with the times. Balinese puppets are more realistic than those from Java, which distort their depictions of humans and animals. Indeed, the heads of many Javanese shadow puppets resemble side views of hands as they attempt shadowed faces on walls (similar to how many Westerners entertain children). This peculiar misshaping of human heads may result from Islamic prohibitions on representations of people or animals, creatures that only God may create. Unlimited by such rules, Bali Hindus are more innovative as well as realistic with their puppet designs.

Significantly, the *wayang* cast also includes clowns. Serious performances contain interruptions as clowns enter the shadow screen stage and provide comic relief, enacting an opposite mood and reestablishing balance for an emotional audience after tragic or dramatic scenes. This repeatedly demonstrates the importance of equilibrium in Indonesian arts and life. One notes that "the Javanese word for clown (*badut*) is derived from *badot,* meaning 'healer.' Both groups are thought to be inspired by higher powers."[21] Clowns thus "heal" some of life's sorrows.

Semar is the major *wayang* clown and the eldest of his family and cohort. Originally a God himself, he was sent to earth to guide the hero in a story through various hardships. Paradoxically, Semar personifies the physical opposites of Javanese or Balinese ideals of refinement. Fat and misshapen, with ever-running eyes and nose and an immense backside,

The bulbous clown Semar (right) and his son Petruk. American Society for Eastern Arts, Courtesy of David Weitzman.

he uncontrollably breaks wind. His flatulence incites hilarity throughout the audience. At times, another puppet repeatedly whacks his behind with a stick, a standard source of laughter. Although at first Semar might appear as a foolish "slob," he is perhaps the most loved character among the entire *wayang* cast. Semar is gross, magical, mysterious, powerful, loyal, wise, and always morally good. He counterbalances the elegant characters of righteousness by his distinctive appearance and idiosyncrasies. As remarked of ironies surrounding Semar:

Semar, for all his great potency, not only must play servant to high-status figures, but he must put up with the constant insults, teasing, and tricks to which his sons subject him ... to their own father they are rude and hostile in a manner both scandalous and, to spectators, vastly entertaining ... [they] treat Semar with a kind of jocular scorn out of kilter with all the notions of respect for one's elders Javanese normally espouse.[22]

In this way, some *wayang* characters defy certain cultural ideals to better distinguish them. Semar also presents ambiguity in his highly atypical manner of being good. Again, Indonesians strive to achieve a balance of forces between opposites such as good and evil (or elegant and crude), which emerges in their artistic creations and characters, whether carved, painted, sung, danced, or performed.

NOTES

1. Due to constraints on space, I have limited the "Traditional Theater" section of this chapter to a discussion of the shadow play. However, several forms (such as Sumatran *randai* and Balinese and Javanese mask dances) also function as theatrical performances.

2. Edi Sedyawati, ed., *Performing Arts: Indonesian Heritage Series* (Archipelago Press, 1999), 31.

3. Ward Keeler, *Javanese Shadow Plays, Javanese Selves* (Princeton: Princeton University Press, 1987), 225.

4. Sedyawati, *Performing Arts,* 32.

5. See Sedyawati, *Performing Arts,* 34–35.

6. Sedyawati, *Performing Arts,* 36.

7. See Douglas Myers, "Outside Influences on the Music of Nusa Tenggara Timur," Part Two, http://www.archipelago.emag.com/acad/NTT.html, 1996. During fieldwork in 1999, people in Sumba also spoke to Jill Forshee about connections to northern Australia in ancient times.

8. Fred B. Eiseman, Jr., *Bali—Sekala & Niskala: Volume I: Essays on Religion, Ritual and Art* (Hong Kong: Periplus Editions, 1990), 293.

9. Paraphrased from Margaret J. Wiener, *Visible and Invisible Realms: Power Magic, and Colonial Conquest in Bali* (Chicago: 1995), 86.

10. Wiener, *Visible and Invisible Realms,* 385 n.12.

11. Sedyawati, *Performing Arts,* 76, paraphrased.

12. Craig Latrell, "Widening the Circle: The Refiguring of West Sumatran *Randai,*" *Asian Theatre Journal* 16, no. 2 (1999): 248–259.

13. Latrell, "Widening the Circle," 2.
14. Latrell, "Widening the Circle," 3.
15. Latrell, "Widening the Circle," 4.
16. Alit Djajasoebrata, *Shadow Theatre in Java: The Puppets, Performances, and Repertoire* (Amsterdam: The Pepin Press, 1999), 17.
17. Djajasoebrata, *Shadow Theatre in Java,* 16.
18. Djajasoebrata, *Shadow Theatre in Java,* paraphrased here, 9.
19. Djajasoebrata, *Shadow Theatre in Java,* 42.
20. For descriptions of the specific attributes of the classical *wayang kulit* cast of puppets, see Djajasoebrata's *Shadow Theatre in Java.* This book provides many excellent color photographs and much information on the puppets, their creation, their characters, and their importance in Javanese life.
21. Djajasoebrata, *Shadow Theatre in Java,* 69.
22. Keeler, *Javanese Shadow Plays,* 212.

SUGGESTED READING

Becker, Judith. *Traditional Music in Modern Java: Gamelan in a Changing Society.* Honolulu: University of Hawaii Press, 1980.
Djajasoebrata, Alit. *Shadow Theater in Java: The Puppets, Performance, and Repertoire.* Amsterdam: The Pepin Press, 1999.
Eiseman, Fred B. *Bali, Sekala & Niskala, Volume 1: Essays on Religion, Ritual, and Art.* Bali, Indonesia: Periplus, 2004.
Heppel, Michael. "Wither Dayak Art?" in *Fragile Traditions: Indonesian Art in Jeopardy,* ed. Paul Michael Taylor (Honolulu: University of Hawaii Press, 1994), 123–138.
Keeler, Ward. *Javanese Shadow Plays, Javanese Selves.* Princeton: Princeton University Press, 1987.
Latrell, Craig. "Widening the Circle: The Refiguring of West Sumatran Randai." *Asian Theatre Journal* 16, no. 2 (1999): 248–259.
McPhee, Colin. *Music in Bali.* New Haven: Yale University Press, 1966.
Sedyawati, Edi. *Performing Arts—Indonesian Heritage Series.* Singapore: Archipelago Press, 1999.

9

Social Customs and Lifestyle: An Epilogue

We are not so deep by nature that it will break anyone's head to understand our wisdom. There is no word for selfishness in our language. Happy language where that word has never penetrated.[1]

SOCIAL CUSTOMS IN PRESENT TENSES

In 1993, an American anthropologist and her husband traveled by ferry to one of Indonesia's remote islands, Savu. A small craft took them near the shore. Several yards from the beach, local men chest deep in water surrounded the boat. Passengers began to climb upon their shoulders, luggage and all. The Americans followed, dismounting on the sand feeling both guilt and amusement. The island was quiet at the time, without electricity. There were no flights to Savu, few tourists, and overnight ships from larger islands provided the sole passage. Late in the day, they took a walk along a white beach.

As is customary in rural Indonesia, a band of children trailed behind them. When the couple sat, the group stood before them, staring and stifling giggles. The anthropologist greeted the children in Indonesian, asking their ages. All fell into hushed confusion. A sprightly seven-year-old girl stepped forward, delivering standard questions Indonesian children ask foreigners who know their language: "Where do you come from?" "How many children do you have?" "What is your profession?" "Are your parents still living?" "Do you like Indonesia?" On this day, however, a new query supplemented the interrogation: "Is Mike Tyson still in prison?"

Early that evening at their modest hotel (owned by Yemenite descendants), a generator fired up. Machines followed in sputters around the small town of fisher folk and traders and Seba became illuminated and lively. Sounds of cassettes and televisions wafted down the lanes. People strolled along the main sandy avenue, enjoying the cool air and greeting others. Across from the hotel, under a festively decorated pavilion, a singing contest between young Muslim boys commenced. An audience of well-dressed parents sat on folding chairs under fluorescent lights, proudly watching their sons. In turn, each boy covered his ears with his hands and wailed renditions of the Muslim call to prayer. An enclave of Bugis residents was holding this special event in the town center of a largely Protestant island. The affair continued into the night, while others watched with interest or went on with their own activities.

On this small island, a range of diverse social customs became evident. Customary questions asked of foreigners, the time of day the generators routinely started, a contest based in Islamic practice doubled as an enjoyable social get-together—the most pervasive social custom in Indonesia. The Protestants of the community demonstrated customary Indonesian religious tolerance, indeed many showed polite interest, toward an Islamic event. Only the part about the men carrying people to shore from the boat remains obscure, yet undoubtedly reflected relative social status, which always influences Indonesian customs.

The real surprise was how far-flung the issues of American popular culture and media had become. What did these children know of the boxer Mike Tyson and had they opinions about his imprisonment for rape? Evidently the boxer's fate concerned some people in Savu. In fact, Tyson had become a local hero through the media. As in other parts of Indonesia, following American boxing matches was now a contemporary custom for some on this island.

"LIFESTYLE" IN INDONESIAN CONTEXTS

Social customs across Indonesia are as countless as "lifestyle" is indefinable in a concise sense. The (necessarily limited) range of cultures and customs described in this book precludes a unified definition of Indonesia. In fact, such a definition is impossible. Lifestyle, however, implies a more arbitrary choice than does custom. Lifestyle is self-constructed, drawing from the options and styles available. In a modern Indonesia, lifestyles have developed emphasizing choice, style, and technology—and building upon ancient attitudes permitting flux and new expressions.

In Indonesian urban environments, lifestyle might suggest golfing, going out to restaurants and nightclubs, and owning nice cars or motorcycles.

These are eminently modern ways of spending time and money in Indonesia, largely limited to an elite class. Although elites of times past enjoyed the best of everything, their choices still involved largely materials and entertainment options of traditional culture (however many foreign influences it included). Tommy Suharto, the former president's wayward son, flaunted a notorious lifestyle of fast cars, clubbing, and cocaine. This also led to arranging the murder of a judge and eventually put him in prison. To most Indonesians, the junior Suharto's lifestyle bared the vulgar underbelly of Western-style modernity in perverse blend with entrenched New Order corruption.

Yet, lifestyle options offer positive opportunities to the creative and non-conventional. The modern visual art, literary, and musical movements of Indonesia evolved from people who carried out something besides typical ways of life. All involved breaking with social customs and creating images, prose, or music of something "other" in the face of conservative societies or repressive regimes. All required audacity.

Certainly, Pramoedya Toer did not relish his lifestyle as a novelist and political critic during his long years of imprisonment in Buru Island's penal colony. Yet he wrote his famous *Buru Quartet* under such conditions. After his release, Toer expressed from his Jakarta home long-pondered views on lifestyle and simple ways to happiness:

I came to know well the mind, heart, and even the hypocritical face of the New Order regime. I learned many ways of maintaining my health at almost no cost; that life is actually very simple but has been made complex by a small group of authoritarian people for a glittering lifestyle; that the slaughter Indonesia experienced is a demonstration of cannibalism, of an animal devouring its foe just to make itself feel stronger. Then, too, I also learned that a smile, even a false smile, is an antidote for stress and feelings of hopelessness, that even as it relaxes one's muscles, it serves to sooth one's nerves.[2]

Senang-Senang

Senang-senang (being content, relaxed, and happy) can be an ideal of living, if not a sustained lifestyle. On many islands, people congregate on porches or *balé*, sitting on woven *tikar* mats. Often no other furniture elevates the high-ranking, so people of lower status or the young sit at the edges in social deference. People invite others to their homes by asking them to come to their porch or floor. By evening, groups congregate—playing cards, eating, talking, and laughing by kerosene or fluorescent lamplight. Floors of homes serve the living: vibrant, visceral, and stained by the stuff of life—food, betel spit, and the occasional accident. A minimum of furniture leaves floors sharply defined as social foundations, while accenting the superiority of sacred, upper regions of households.

Much gaiety and outright hilarity animates these spaces, especially when hosting guests. Social customs throughout Indonesia require hosts to immediately offer guests coffee or tea. To refuse creates insult. The same applies to betel nut, which often arrives before drinks. People love to tell and hear stories; the more bizarre or ludicrous the better. Immensely rich with themes ancient and recent, the persistence of Indonesian folklore "tells" custom—especially through tales of breeching it—thus reinforcing its value. People also enjoy sparring and poking fun at one another. Laughter is a favorite Indonesian pastime and can become uproarious. As a great social leveler, laughter draws all ages and ranks into shared enjoyment. Like Southeast Asians in general, Indonesians display a broad tolerance (and even enjoyment) of eccentricity. If anything, eccentric people stimulate good stories.

In cities, people also sit on porches or walkways at night, similarly greeting others and getting together for games or chats. Within (ever-threatened) urban *kampung*s, modest ways of life reflect those in provincial regions. People offer drinks and snacks, chew betel nut or smoke, and enjoy neighborhood amiability. Socializing is Indonesia's most widespread and spontaneous social custom, readily available and relatively free of cost.

Parties (*pestas*) or grandiose spectacles (*perayaans*) are ongoing customs, regardless of holidays. Elaborate ornamentation, abundance of good food, and entertaining music create successful celebrations. Indonesians prefer public places with a lively (*ramai*), festive ambience. If too quiet, guests dismiss a place as *kurang ramai* (not lively) and leave in pursuit of more spirited places. As do houses and people, everything should exude spirit (*semangat*) no matter how modern or urban.

LASTING SOCIAL CUSTOMS

Among some groups, modern times have all the more accentuated the priority of older cultural forms, rather than rendering them obsolete. This precedence emphasizes the inviolable value people place upon local identity and social belonging and their crucial positions in the cosmological order. A resurgent expression of local pride and prestige symbols has stimulated a big comeback of old-style, hand chiseled, and human dragged stone megaliths in Sumba. Balinese cremation ceremonies have never been grander and children diligently study traditional dances. *Gamelan* is an increasingly popular musical form spreading around the world, yet fundamental to cultures and customs in Java and Bali, where it retains tremendous value. Further, the ancient supremacy of fine boatbuilding and seafaring from South Sulawesi sails on through current grand races in Indonesian waters. To maintain indispensable aspects of their humanity, Indonesians pick and choose from what modernization offers them. In this way, important elements of older, local cultures remain stubbornly resilient.

Through troubled political and economic times, Indonesians returned to time-honored ways of doing things. The terrorist bombings in Bali prompted a groundswell in prayers, offerings, and ceremonies across the island, as people reflected on their neglect of the sacred during years of commercial prosperity through tourism. Today it seems that more processions than ever fill Bali's lanes, as people carry offerings to temples. While tourism has waned, people's needs, beliefs, and arts go on—drawing from deeper roots and recreating culture and life.

DYNAMIC CUSTOMARY FORMS

Social status and rank remain critical in Indonesia, despite many years of alleged democracy. True rank carries sumptuary privileges that still rely upon traditional forms of regalia, most evidently in clothing. Customary dress also identifies where people "belong" across the islands. Clothing of contemporary global style places those who wear it with as much definition as do *adat* garments. Like technology, it mediates a shift to the modern in appearance and partially in thought.[3] Technology (through computer games, iPods, television, etc.) also induces distraction—an insular "buzz" away from life's tangible perils and joys.

Indonesian technocrats were the handmaidens of the New Order, whose mechanisms induced ongoing distraction from the somber realities of the nation's people. While they created much of great benefit across the islands, they also squandered millions on ill-conceived technological monstrosities benefiting only investors, many left unfinished and in decay. Still, Indonesians were not naïve regarding this wastefulness and many ridiculed or opposed government projects, even when Suharto's political position was solid. Many did not aspire to all things modern, technological, or "advanced," especially the poor. The corruption, pollution, deforestation, homelessness, drugs, street violence, crime, and other plagues of the industrialized world have weighed heavily upon Indonesia. After years of tumult and economic woes, many value their cultures and customs all the more. This feeds a resurgence of customary forms, including those that people make by hand or perform for an audience.

Cloth is what numerous women best make and has always brought them pride. Just as women affect the balance of social life, the weaver producing smoothly woven cloth is an exemplary model of female posture in much of Indonesia. As a consistent focal point of their vision, dexterity, and imagination, cloth has long been a "canvas" for expression, devotion, and even passion for many. Yet women also defy the exemplary and assert other powers in life. As customary managers of household finances, many became cleverly entrepreneurial during the economic crisis of the late 1990s. Now the traditional position of staying at home has become passé for some, as they travel for trade and business and enjoy wider connections.

In Sumba in 1993, however, cloth enhanced an alternative "exemplary model" of the feminine while enhancing eccentricity and passion. A certain *banci* (transvestite) named Willem worked at a small family *warung* in the eastern town of Melolo. From behind a lace curtain, he played vintage tapes of Diana Ross and the Supremes as he cooked for customers. The curtain suddenly sweeping aside, Willem would make a dramatic entrance, then carry food to a table. Dressed in a floral *sarung,* a woman's silk blouse, and a makeshift hat of plastic tropical fruit, he moved sinuously to the music. He eventually became recorded into an anthropologist's notebook as "Willem, Vamp of Melolo."[4] At the annual regional talent show, Willem stood on stage clad in a self-styled gown of locally woven, simulated "gold *lamé*" commissioned from a village woman. Wearing a bouffant wig, he lip-synched "Baby Love" with emotional flourish to a rapt audience and won his category of the event. Part of a society that included *banci*s, making use of traditional weaving skill, and finally producing a transgendered rendition of a global pop icon and coming out a winner, Willem had managed to follow social customs and proclaim a lifestyle.

A NEW ORDER AND BEYOND

Taman Mini Indonesia (Beautiful Indonesia) represented a nationalistic park to inspire visitors to imagine Indonesia as a nation. It rendered the New Order slogan, "Unity in Diversity" into theme park form and enabled the Suhartos to survey their domain—if only in simulation. However, that was the point. Here social and environmental realities could not enter into a mythical Indonesian "Disneyland" (which had inspired its creation). Beautiful Indonesia recreated the archipelago and bestowed a monumental "gift" upon Indonesians, demonstrating government largesse. The park contained well-produced replicas of traditional houses of ethnic groups representing each province of the archipelago. They sat frozen in a reconstructed context that "erased the difference between past, present, and future, and thus flattened time—and, with it, histories, including the extraordinary violence of the New Order's own origins—into a continuously presented present."[5]

Taman Mini Indonesia installed a permanent appearance of order, by displaying a community of customary dwellings of cultures across the archipelago and rendering it idyllic. Fundamentally, the park made a statement about how rulers in Jakarta regarded their islands' peoples, by arbitrarily reconstructing Indonesia as it never was and never would be—as a single place bounded by Javanese authority and design. Often even educated Javanese were notoriously ignorant of their country's geography and indifferent to its diverse cultures. Notions of cultural superiority blinded many Javanese in power to the validity of others in their nation. In current times, the center of national power (ideally) will need to acknowledge respectfully its multiple societies, while demonstrating competence and true potency of leadership. Yet Indonesia has fallen into a dangerous disunity, no longer even artificially depictive by a theme park. In the vacuum of Megawati's free-for-all presidency, in response to the corruption and excesses of crony-capitalism (including multi-national interests), and following the slow pace of reforms:

There is growing concern that commercial interests are dominating the media, and that they are no longer voicing "the conscience of the people" as their banners often proclaim. Conspicuous consumption is displayed in all urban centers, while the poor multitudes are still standing in line for rice rations. Elaborate billion-rupiah cemeteries are being built, while millions of the living have no proper shelter.[6]

Such realities have fueled Islamic Fundamentalism in Indonesia, and incited violence from organized terrorist groups and street gangs. This has created and exacerbated animosities between religious groups, resulting in incidents like the murder of young schoolgirls walking home in Sulawesi. Amid such horrors, social customs and lifestyle close their doors in fear.

Still, a new generation in Indonesia enjoys access to information and freedom to express ideas as never before. The Internet opened a far-reaching dialogue with others (including between terrorist groups), though computers are not the privilege of poor. Young Indonesians everywhere now imagine themselves as different from their former leaders and seek new directions for their country. These may not be the ways of Western democracy, but following other values and goals. Further, Indonesia's many islands and great ethnic diversity will complicate its direction through differing cultures and priorities. The nation's future remains unpredictable.

Currently the first directly elected president, Susilo Bambang Yudhoyono, still holds power and some slow changes have begun to take root, beginning government reforms supported by many Indonesians. Yet, the nation's international debts weigh heavily and self-interested Indonesian and international bureaucrats burden institutions. Further, the recent series of volcanic eruptions, earthquakes, and tsunamis have devastated communities and left people newly disenchanted with their government. The country badly needs a strong reformist policy drawing together many factions in Indonesia, in the interest of better living conditions, good governance, social balance, and order. This will require that foreign and national elites transcend their own narrow interests and permit ordinary Indonesians to thrive in their cultures, customs, and futures.

On August 15, 1902, Raden Kartini wrote from Java in a letter to a Dutch friend:

I can tell you much of our gentle people; you must learn to know and love them as I do. There are so many poets and artists among them, and where a people has a feeling for poetry, the most beautiful thing in life, they cannot be lacking in the instincts of civilization.[7]

NOTES

1. Raden Adjeng Kartini, *Letters of a Javanese Princess* (Lanhem: University Press of America, 1985 [1920]), 179.

2. Pramoedya Ananta Toer, *The Mute's Soliloquay: A Memoir,* Trans. by Willem Samuels (New York: Hyperion East, 1999), 315–316.

3. See Rudolph Mrázek, *Engineers of a Happy Land: Technology and Nationalism in a Colony* (Princeton: Princeton University Press, 2002).

4. Jill Forshee, "Sumba Performed: Twenty Years of Stylin' Animism" (Paper presented at the Association of Asian Performance Fifth Annual Conference, University of San Francisco Campus, July 27–28, 2005).

5. John Pemberton, *On the Subject of "Java"* (Ithaca: Cornell University Press, 1994), 155.

6. H. S. Dillon, "Development and Governance: Where Is Indonesia Heading?" *The Jakarta Post On-line,* http://www.thejakartapost.com/headlines.asp, April 13, 2006.

7. Kartini, *Letters of a Javanese Princess,* 179.

SUGGESTED READING

Anderson, Benedict R. O'G. *Mythology and Tolerance of the Javanese.* Ithaca: Cornell University Press, 1997.

Morrell, Elizabeth. *Securing a Place: Small-Scale Artisans in Modern Indonesia.* Ithaca: Cornell University Southeast Asian Publications, 2006.

Mrázek, Rudolph. *Engineers of a Happy Land: Technology and Nationalism in a Colony.* Princeton: Princeton University Press, 2002.

Pemberton, John. *On the Subject of Java.* Ithaca: Cornell University Press, 1994.

Rigg, Jonathan, ed. *The Human Environment: Indonesian Heritage Series.* Singapore: Editions Didier Miller, 1996.

Toer, Pramoedya Ananta. *Tales from Jakarta: Caricatures of Circumstances and Their Human Beings.* Ithaca: Cornell University Press, 1999.

Glossary

Aceh. Northernmost region of Sumatra devastated by the tsunami of December 2004. Likely an original landing point for Indian and Arabic Muslim traders. Marco Polo traveled to Aceh in 1292, recording the first Islamic sultanate in Southeast Asia.

Adat. Customary laws and practices throughout Indonesia. The ancient, correct way of doing things.

Agama. Religion.

Amuk. To rage wildly. To run berserk and violently lash out in all directions. Often follows a personal problem or insult. Usually an affliction of men.

Asli. Indigenous, with local precedence.

Asmat. Indigenous Papuan people of southern coastal Irian Jaya, or West Papua. Makers of fantastic ceremonial costumes. Traditionally animist hunter-gatherers.

Austronesians. A group migrating from southern China through islands of Indonesia (around 3000 B.C.), west to the island of Madagascar (Africa), and east as far as Hawaii and Easter Island. Little is known of them, except through some metal artifacts and the language they spread. The Austonesian language group is the largest in the world.

Bagus. Beautiful, good, or exemplary. Applied to objects and people.

Balé or Balai. Outdoor pavilion for guests.

Bali. Island between Java and Lombok. The only predominantly Hindu island in Indonesia.

Banci. Transvestite or homosexual male.

Bapak. Polite term of address for married or older man. It means both Mr. and father, depending on context. Often shortened to "Pak."

Barong. Fabulous Balinese mythical creature in costumed performances. The barong resembles a giant caterpillar, a lion, and Chinese festival god combined.

Batak. People of northern Sumatra (of seven sub-groups). Known for impressive, elegantly carved traditional houses, called rumah gorga (carved house) as well as traditionally fine carved pieces.

Batik. Wax-resist dye process in which wax is applied to fabric in patterns. When dyed, the waxed sections cannot absorb color. An ancient, refined art of Java still thriving today.

Bedhaya. Sacred heirloom female dance performed in courts in Central Java, using elegant sashes to accentuate slow, graceful, precise movements.

Borobudur. Largest Buddhist monument in Indonesia and the world. An immensely complex, mandala-like open-air temple built between about 760–833 A.D. under the Central Java Sailendra dynasty.

Bride price. Goods given to a bride's family by a groom's family to secure a marriage. Customary practice involving livestock and gold items.

Bugis. Islamic ethnic group of southern central Sulawesi. Boatbuilding, seafaring, and often settling on coasts of other islands.

Candi. Temple in Bali or Java.

Dalang. Wayang kulit puppet master enacting all the voices for up to 100 characters and skillfully manipulating the shadow puppets.

Dangdut. A popular musical fusion incorporating Indian, Malaysian, and Arabic rhythms. Song lyrics are melancholic but rhythms are lively, syncopated, and invite dancing. Popular among Islamic youth and others.

Dapur. Kitchen area of a household, often a separate structure behind a main house.

Dayak. Indigenous, non-Islamic, inland people of Kalimantan.

Dewi Sri. The rice goddess in Bali and Java. A high-ranking deity to which many make offerings.

Dharma. Religious duty following Hinduism and Buddhism.

Dharma Wanita. On obligatory association for wives of civil servants under Suharto's New Order, encouraging women to remain subservient housewives and supporters of the nation.

Dukun. Indigenous healer or shaman.

Ekadasa Rudra. Spectacular ritual held every hundred years at Bali's most sacred temple, Besakih, in order to purify the world and balance evil forces.

Enak. Pleasurable. Describes good food, pleasant sensations, and enjoyable times.

Gaib. Magic, of which gaib hitam (black magic) is most feared. Gaib hijau (green magic) is love magic to seduce another. Some men practice gaib perempuan (woman magic) to make them irresistible to women.

Gamelan. Javanese or Balinese orchestra of mainly gongs and xylophone-like instruments.

Gotong-royong. Community mutual cooperation common to Indonesian societies.

Gunung. Mountain.

Haj. Muslim pilgrimage to Mecca.

Halus. Refined, sensitive, and graceful. Halus is an Indonesian ideal applied to speech, behavior, dance, arts, and so on. It opposes kasar, meaning crude or rude.

Hikayat. A chronicle in Malay language written in Arabic script.

Hudoq. Dramatic mask dance to contact spirits by certain Dayak groups in Kalimantan.

Ibu. Polite term of address for older or married women. It means both "mother" and "Mrs." Sometimes shortened to Bu.

Idul Fitri. A time of celebration and feasting after the end of the Muslim fasting month of Ramadan.

Ikat. The word means "to bind." Like batik, a resist dye technique, except that bundles of yarns to form a cloth are wrapped in tight palm leaf strips and immersed through successive submersions in dye before a textile is actually woven. Ikat typifies eastern Indonesian fabrics.

Irian Jaya or West Papua. The western half of the island of Papua (New Guinea), ceded to Indonesia by Dutch in 1963. An area of ongoing independence movements. Indonesia's easternmost region.

Jago. Rooster, playboy, a man successful with women. Also an independent male entrepreneur.

Jamu. Indigenous herbal tonic for many ailments. Men drink jamu to increase their virility.

Java. Fourth largest island in Indonesia and most densely populated, containing almost half of Indonesia's population of roughly 240 million people.

Jelek. Ugly or evil.

Jilbab. A Muslim head cloth for women that exposes the face but covers the hair, ears, and neck.

Joget. Undulating, graceful, rhythmic dancing often performed to dangdut music. Popular contemporary dance form of the young in Indonesia.

Kain. A generic word for cloth, but in Bali and Java signifying a long stretch of cloth wrapped around the body to form an ankle length skirt fastened at the waist. Often such kain is made of batik cotton or silk.

Kaki lima. A wheeled pushcart selling diverse foods along the lanes of towns and cities. Kaki lima means "five legs," referring to wheels, vendor legs and stick. Kaki lima vendors typically sound bells, gongs, metal wires, stick beats, or vocally chant to indicate what they sell.

Kalimantan. Indonesia's largest island, formerly called Borneo. Northern sections of the island belong to Malaysia. Home of the Dayak and the Iban people.

Karma. Hindu and Buddhist belief that one's deeds ultimately determine one's fate.

Kecap manis. Important Indonesian seasoning, like molasses. The English word "ketchup" came from this Indonesian term.

Keris or Kris. A graceful dagger with a wavy double blade. Said to contain the power of a ruler.

Korupsi. Corruption, especially on the part of the government and wealthy cronies, reaching great heights during the New Order.

Kurang ajar. Ignorant, without learning. The ultimate insult in Indonesia.

Ladang. Dry rice agriculture still practiced in upland or dry regions of Indonesia, such as Sumba and Timor. Fields rely upon rain and not irrigation.

Latah. A nervous condition that affects women after a sudden shock. They then become irrational and behave or speak in sexually explicit and inappropriate ways. Often a local healer or shaman (dukun) will help relieve the condition.

Lesbi or Tom Boi. Lesbian. Probably relatively accepted in much of Indonesia in times past, but recently part of public consciousness as lesbians became more visible, especially in urban cultural communities.

Lontar Palm. An adaptable species of palm (Borassus sundaicus) producing paper, sugar, syrup, building materials, and sustenance. Lontar leaves provided paper for ancient Indonesian texts.

Mahabarata (Mahabharata in India). A long Hindu epic of a war between the Pandawa brothers and their cousins, the Korawas. Indonesians adapted this Indian story into their own. Enacted in dances, plays, and puppet performances. Also popular as soap opera and film themes.

Majapahit. A great kingdom of East Java from about 1294 to 1478, sending envoys to eastern Indonesia and claiming sovereignty over much of what is today the nation. Eventually taken over by the Islamic empire of Mataram (from Central and North Java), many say that the courts of Majapahit fled to Bali, greatly influencing its culture.

Makasar. Islamic ethic group of southwestern Sulawesi. Rivals of the Bugis in seafaring.

Maluku (formerly Moluccas). Eastern province of Indonesia including the islands of Ambon, Seram, Halmahera, Ternate, Tanimbar, Banda, and others. Region of the "Spice Islands."

Marapu. Persistent belief system of people of Sumba, making the island an animist holdout compared to neighboring Christianized islands of Flores, Savu, and Timor and the largely Muslim island of Sumbawa.

Maulud. The Prophet Muhammad's birthday, celebrated in Java by parades carrying immense mountains of decorated rice.

Megalith. Large, chiseled stone monument, often a grave marker.

Meru. Pagoda-like roof (often tiered) on Balinese altars or temples. Symbol of Mt. Meru, the sacred center of Hindu cosmology.

Mesjid. Mosque.

Mie. Noodles, often stir-fried in a wok as mie goreng (fried noodles) or used in soups.

Minangkabau. A Muslim yet steadfast matrilineal descent group of western Sumatra. Their traditional clan homes (rumah gadang) are among the most impressive and elegant in Indonesia, with arching rooflines suggesting water buffalo horns.

Musim lapar. The hungry season. This especially applies to the southeastern islands, where rain might not fall for half the year.

Musyawarah. Community meeting where people try to reach consensus on an issue.

Nasi. Cooked rice, the staple of Indonesia.

Nyentrik. Eccentric person; Orang nyentrik.

Odalan. Festival celebrating the anniversary of a Balinese temple.

Omong. Casual conversation, chatting.

Orang. Person. Indonesian language often makes no distinction denoting gender, including pronouns. The term for man is "laki-laki" and for women "perempuan," used to differentiate sexes.

Orang laut. Sea people, often Bugis originating in Sulawesi or Bajau from the Sulu Archipelago, but including other island peoples.

Orang tuna rumah. Homeless person, street person.

Orde Baru. New Order Indonesia, under President Suharto after the downfall of Sukarno.

Pacar. Either a boyfriend or a girlfriend.

Pancasila. Five basic principles of the Republic of Indonesia: Belief in one God; just and civilized social order; unity of Indonesia; guided democracy through the wisdom of representative resolutions; and social justice for all.

Pasar. Public market containing many vendors.

Pasola. Spectacular annual horse jousting and spearing contest in West Sumba, celebrating the arrival of sea worms (nyale) boding success of the rice harvest.

Perahu. A general term for boat, which might be of many types.

Pinisi. Cargo boat of the Bugis seafaring people of South Sulawesi. Extremely well crafted of teak or ironwood and up to 70 feet in length.

Priyayi. The historically elite class of Java.

Puasa. The Indonesian term for the Muslim fasting month of Ramadan.

Pura. Balinese temple.

Qur'an (Koran). Book containing the word of God as told to the prophet Muhammad. The ultimate divine authority for Muslims.

Raja. King.

Ramai. Lively, bustling, spirited, crowded. Indonesians enjoy events and places that are ramai. The opposite is kurang ramai, meaning dull, lifeless, or lacking spirit.

Ramayana. The Indian epic of King Rama and the abduction of his wife Sita by the evil Rawana. The subject of many dances, plays, shadow puppet performances and television dramas.

Randai. Traditional narrative circular dance performance of Minangkabau men, incorporating martial arts called pencak silat, acting, storytelling, and a musical ensemble.

Rangda. A hideous witch in Balinese masked dance drama always defeated by the barong.

Rantau. A journey by men away from their homelands to gain knowledge, experience, and wealth. A long custom in western Sumatra and carried out in other parts of Indonesia.

Rapi. Neatly dressed, also implying a modern sleekness.

Rasa. Can mean feeling, taste of food, sensation, or expressing one's thoughts about a matter.

Rumah. Basic term for house applied to other structures, such as rumah makan ("eating house") for a restaurant.

Rumah adat. Traditional clan house where ritual events take place. These display the most impressive architecture of a regional group.

Run. Small island among the Banda Islands in eastern Indonesia traded by the English to the Dutch in exchange for Manhattan Island in the mid-seventeenth century. One of the "Spice Islands" where nutmeg flourished.

Rupiah. Indonesia's currency.

Sambal. Indonesian hot sauce, made in many ways.

Sarung. A basic garment for men and women across Indonesia. A cloth sewn together at each end forming a tube people step into and pull up to the waist, then fasten in a variety of styles.

Sastra. Literature in a fine sense.

Saté. Meat coated with spicy peanut sauce and cooked on skewers over open grills. A popular street food.

Sawah. Wet rice agriculture.

Semangat. Spiritual force within many things. People and houses should contain semangat.

Senang. To enjoy or like. To feel happy. If especially relaxed and enjoying oneself with others, this may be expressed as senang-senang.

Seni rupa. Visual arts: painting, drawing, carving, sculpture and so on.

Sepak takraw. An ancient game of kicking a hollow woven rattan ball to keep it in the air, still popular in Indonesia. Something like "hacky sack" played in the United States.

Sharia. Conservative Islamic law.

Sholat or Solat. Muslim prayers performed five times daily.

Sirih-pinang. Betel nut (pinang) from the areca palm and a catkin (sirih) from the piper plant, chewed in combination with powdered lime (kapur). Sometimes a piper leaf wraps all ingredients. A mild narcotic of central social importance in Indonesia.

Slametan or Selamatan. Ritual held in Java on occasions such as marriage, birth, death, appeasing village spirits, illness, or the seventh month of pregnancy. This includes relatives and often neighbors in a communal feast.

Spice Islands. Eastern islands of the Maluku archipelago originally drawing Europeans to Indonesia in the early sixteenth century in search of spices: especially nutmeg and cloves that many believed prevented the plague. These islands included Ternate, Tidore, Makian, Halmahera, Seram, Ambon, and the Banda Islands.

Srivijaya. A great trading Buddhist empire of Sumatra between the eighth and fourteenth centuries, controlling maritime commerce through the Straits of Melaka.

Subak. An organization of rice farmers in Bali who work the land and maintain the irrigation system.

Suharto. President of Indonesia from 1965 to 1998, a period called New Order Indonesia.

Sukarno. The first president of Indonesia (after the end of World War II) and long a part of the struggle for independence from Holland.

Sulawesi. Third largest island of Indonesia. Home of the Muslim Bugis and Makasar, and the Toraja people, among others.

Sultan. Muslim king.

Sumatra. Indonesia's westernmost and second largest island. Home to the Minangkabau and Batak, among others.

Susilo Bambang Yudhoyono. Current President of Indonesia—the first elected by direct vote in September, 2004. Usually called "S.B.Y." by Indonesians.

Tahu. Tofu. Basic protein food made from fermented soybeans.

Taman Mini Indonesia. "Beautiful Indonesia in Miniature." A nationalistic theme park in Jakarta commissioned by Mrs. Suharto after a trip to Disneyland.

Tempeh. A fermented, compressed soybean food from Java. Referred to as "poor people's meat," tempeh is actually much higher in protein.

Tikar. A plaited mat of grass or palm leaves used in much of Indonesia to sit upon, for meals, and entertaining guests.

Topeng. Carved masks, usually of wood. Topeng dance dramas are numerous on Bali and Java representing hundreds of characters.

Toraja. A group in the mountains of central South Sulawesi, practicing the indigenous belief system, Aluk to dolo, "ways of the ancestors" combined with Christianity. Toraja build spectacular, carved, arched-roofed clan homes called tongkonan.

Transmigrasi. A policy deployed by President Suharto's government to transmigrate people away from densely populated Java onto other less populated islands, where they would continue to carry on wet rice agriculture.

Uma. Term for house in many eastern Indonesian areas.

V.O.C. Vereenigde Oost Indische Compagnie or Dutch East Indies Company.

Wallace Line. Imaginary geographical boundary running north and south between Bali and Lombok separating two distinct climate zones of Indonesia, with differing types of flora and fauna.

Warung. Indonesia's predominant public eating establishment, serving a range of fast or ready-made dishes. Stir-fries and curries are popular. Warungs range from a simple table with a communal bench to places with separate tables, music, and more varied fare.

Wayang kulit. Flat, leather shadow puppets used in performances especially popular in Java and Bali.

Selected Bibliography

Adams, Kathleen M. *Art as Politics: Re-Crafting Identities, Tourism, and Power in Tana Toraja, Indonesia.* Honolulu: University of Hawaii Press, 2006.

Adams, Marie Jeanne. *System and Meaning in East Sumba Textile Design: A Study in Traditional Indonesian Art.* New Haven: Yale University, Southeast Asia Studies, 1969.

Adams, Marie Jeanne, Jill Forshee, Alit Djajasoebrata, and Linda Hansen. *Decorative Arts of Sumba.* Amsterdam: The Pepin Press, 1999.

Ammayao, Aurora and Roy W. Hamilton. *The Art of Rice: Spirit and Sustenance in Asia.* Los Angeles: The Fowler Museum of Cultural History, University of California, 2004.

Anderson, Benedict R. O'G. *Mythology and Tolerance of the Javanese.* Ithaca: Cornell Modern Indonesia Project, 1994.

Aragon, Lorraine V. *Fields of the Lord: Animism, Christian Minorities, and State Development in Indonesia.* Honolulu: University of Hawaii Press, 2000.

Atkinson, Jane Monnig, and Shelley Errington, eds. *Power & Difference: Gender in Island Southeast Asia.* Stanford: Stanford University Press, 1990.

Barbier, Jean Paul, ed. *Messages in Stone: Statues and Sculptures from Tribal Indonesia in the Collections of the Barbier-Mueller Museum.* Milan: Skira, 1999.

Barnes, Ruth. *The Ikat Textiles of Lamalera: A Study of an Eastern Indonesian Weaving Tradition.* Leiden: E. J. Brill, 1989.

Becker, Judith. *Traditional Music in Modern Java: Gamelan in a Changing Society.* Honolulu: University of Hawaii Press, 1980.

Bellwood, Peter. *Prehistory of the Indo-Malaysian Archipelago.* Honolulu: University of Hawaii Press, 1997.

Blackwood, Evelyn. *Webs of Power: Women, Kin, and Community in a Sumatran Village.* New York: Rowman and Littlefield, 1999.

Causey, Andrew. *Hard Bargaining in Sumatra: Western Travelers and Toba Bataks in the Marketplace of Souvenirs.* Honolulu: University of Hawaii Press, 2003.

Chambert-Loir, Henri, and Anthony Reid, eds. *The Potent Dead: Ancestors, Saints, and Heroes in Contemporary Indonesia.* Honolulu: University of Hawaii Press, 2002.

Covarrubias, Miguel. *Island of Bali.* New York: Alfred A. Knopf, 1956 [Reprint from 1937].

Cribb, Robert. *Historical Atlas of Indonesia.* Honolulu: University of Hawaii Press, 2000.

Djajasoebrata, Alit. *Shadow Theater in Java: The Puppets, Performance, and Repertoire.* Amsterdam: The Pepin Press, 1999.

Dumarcay, Jacques. *The House in Southeast Asia.* Michael Smithies, trans. and ed. Singapore: Oxford University Press, 1987.

Echols, John M., and Hassan Shadily. *Kamus Indonesia-Inggis: An Indonesian-English Dictionary.* Jakarta: Gramedia, 1989.

———. *Kamus Inggris-Indonesia: An English-Indonesian Dictionary.* Ithaca: Cornell University Press, 1975.

Eiseman, Fred B. *Bali, Sekala & Niskala, Volume 1: Essays on Religion, Ritual, and Art.* Hong Kong: Periplus Editions, 1990.

Ellen, Roy. *On the Edge of the Banda Zone: Past and Present in the Social Organization of a Moluccan Trading Network.* Honolulu: University of Hawaii Press, 2003.

Elliot, Inger McCabe. *Batik: Fabled Cloth of Java.* rev. ed. Hong Kong: Periplus, 2004.

Elmslie, Jim. *Irian Jaya under the Gun: Indonesian Economic Development versus West Papuan Nationalism.* Honolulu: University of Hawaii Press, 2002.

Feldman, Jerome. *The Eloquent Dead: Ancestral Sculpture of Indonesia and Southeast Asia.* Los Angeles: UCLA Museum of Cultural History, 1985.

Fischer, Joseph, ed. *Modern Indonesian Art: Three Generations of Tradition and Change, 1945–1990.* Singapore: Singapore National Printers, Ltd., 1990.

———, ed. *Threads of Tradition: Textiles of Indonesia and Sarawak.* Berkeley: Lowie Museum of Anthropology, University of California, 1979.

Forshee, Jill. *Between the Folds: Stories of Cloth, Lives, and Travels from Sumba.* Honolulu: University of Hawaii Press, 2000.

Forshee, Jill, ed., with Christina Fink and Sandra Cate. *Traders, Travelers, and Tourists in Southeast Asia.* Berkeley: Center for Southeast Asia Studies, Monograph No. 36, University of California at Berkeley.

Forth, Gregory. *Beneath the Volcano: Religion, Cosmology and Spirit Classification among the Nage of Eastern Indonesia.* Leiden: KITLV Press, 1998.

Fox, James J. *Harvest of the Palm: Ecological Change in Eastern Indonesia.* Cambridge, MA: Harvard University Press, 1977.

———, ed. *Religion and Ritual: Indonesian Heritage Series.* Singapore: Archipelago Press, 1999.

Fraser-Lu, Sylvia. *Indonesian Batik: Processes, Patterns and Places.* Singapore: Oxford University Press, 1988.

Geertz, Clifford. *Agricultural Involution: The Process of Ecological Change in Indonesia.* Berkeley: University of California Press, 1963.

———. "Deep Play/Notes on the Balinese Cockfight." In *The Interpretation of Cultures: Selected Essays by Clifford Geertz* (pp. 412–453). New York: Basic Books, 1973.

———. *Negara: The Theatre State in Nineteenth Century Bali.* Princeton: Princeton University Press, 1980.

———. *The Religion of Java.* Chicago: University of Chicago Press, 1976.

Geertz, Hildred. *Images of Power: Balinese Paintings Made for Gregory Bateson and Margaret Mead.* Honolulu: University of Hawaii Press, 1994.

———. *The Life of a Balinese Temple: Artistry, Imagination, and History in a Peasant Village.* Honolulu: University of Hawaii Press, 2004.

Geertz, Hildred, and Ida Bagus Madé Togog. *Tales from a Charmed Life: A Balinese Painter Reminisces.* Honolulu: University of Hawaii Press, 2005.

George, Kenneth. *Showing Signs of Violence: The Cultural Politics of a Twentieth-Century Headhunting Ritual.* Berkeley: The University of California Press, 1996.

Gittinger, Mattiebelle, ed. *To Speak with Cloth: Studies in Indonesian Textiles.* Los Angeles: Museum of Cultural History, University of California, 1998.

Hamilton, Roy W. and Ruth Barnes, eds. *Gift of the Cotton Maiden: Textiles of Flores and the Solor Islands.* Los Angeles: University of California, Museum of Cultural History, 1994.

Harnish, David D. *Bridges to the Ancestors: Music, Myth, and Cultural Politics at an Indonesian Festival.* Honolulu: University of Hawaii Press, 2005.

Heider, Karl G. *Indonesian Cinema: National Culture on Screen.* Honolulu: University of Hawaii Press. 1980.

Herbert, Mimi. *Voices of the Puppet Masters: The Wayang Golek Theater in Indonesia.* Honolulu: University of Hawaii Press, 2002.

Hitchcock, Michael. *Indonesian Textiles.* New York: HarperCollins, 1991.

Holt, Claire. *Art in Indonesia: Continuities and Change.* Ithaca: Cornell University Press, 1967.

Hooker, M. Barry. *Indonesian Islam: Social Change through Contemporary Fatawa.* Honolulu: University of Hawaii Press, 2003.

Hoskins, Janet. *Biographical Objects: How Things Tell the Stories of People's Lives.* New York: Routledge, 1998.

————. "Why Do Ladies Sing the Blues? Indigo Dyeing, Cloth Production, and Gender Symbolism in Kodi." In *Cloth and Human Experience,* ed. Annette B. Weiner and Jane Schneider (pp. 141–173). Washington: Smithsonian Institution Press, 1989.

Kartini, Raden Adjeng. *Letters of a Javanese Princess.* Lanham: University Press of America, 1985.

Keeler, Ward. *Javanese Shadow Plays, Javanese Selves.* Princeton: Princeton University Press, 1987.

Kipp, Rita Smith. *Disassociated Identities: Ethnicity, Religion, and Class in an Indonesian Society.* Ann Arbor: University of Michigan Press, 1993.

Kipp, Rita Smith, and Susan Rodgers, eds. *Indonesian Religions in Transition.* Tucson: University of Arizona Press, 1987.

Lansing, J. Stephen. *Perfect Order: Recognizing Complexity in Bali.* Princeton: Princeton University Press, 2006.

Latrell, Craig. "Widening the Circle: The Refiguring of West Sumatran *Randai.*" *Asian Theatre Journal* 16, no. 2 (1999): 248–259.

Lev, Daniel S., and Ruth McVey. *Making Indonesia.* Ithaca: Cornell University Southeast Asian Studies Publications, 1999.

Lubis, Mochtar. *Indonesia: Land under the Rainbow.* Singapore: Oxford University Press, 1990.

Mangunwijaya, Y. B. *The Weaverbirds.* trans. Thomas M. Hunter. Jakarta: The Lontar Foundation, 1991.

McGlynn, John, ed. *Language and Literature: Indonesian Heritage Series.* Singapore: Archipelago Press, 1999.

McKinnon, Susan. *From a Shattered Sun: Hierarchy, Gender, and Alliance in the Tanimbar Islands.* Madison: University of Wisconsin Press, 1991.

McPhee, Colin. *Music in Bali.* New Haven: Yale University Press, 1966.

Miller, Keith Ruskin. *Indonesian Street Food Secrets: A Culinary Travel Odyssey.* Portland, OR: Hawkibinkler Press, 2003.

Milton, Giles. *Nathaniel's Nutmeg: How One Man's Courage Changed the Course of History.* London: Hodder and Stroughton, 1999.

Morrell, Elizabeth. *Securing a Place: Small-Scale Artisans in Modern Indonesia.* Ithaca: Cornell University Southeast Asian Publications, 2006.

Mrázek, Rudolph. *Engineers of a Happy Land: Technology and Nationalism in a Colony.* Princeton: Princeton University Press, 2002.

Niessen, Sandra. *Batak Cloth and Clothing: A Dynamic Indonesian Tradition* (The Asia Collection). Oxford: Oxford University Press, 1994.

Owen, Norman G. *The Emergence of Modern Indonesia.* Ithaca: Cornell University Southeast Asian Studies Publications, 2005.

Pemberton, John. *On the Subject of "Java."* Ithaca: Cornell University Press, 1994.

Pospos, P. "Me and Toba." In *Telling Lives, Telling History: Autobiography and Historical Imagination in Modern Indonesia*, trans. and ed. Susan Rodgers (pp. 81–148). Berkeley: University of California Press, 1995.

Prijotomo, Josef. *Ideas and Forms of Javanese Architecture.* Yogyakarta, Indonesia: Gadjah Mada University Press, 1988.

Radjab, Muhamad. "Village Childhood (The Autobiography of a Minangkabau Child)" In *Telling Lives, Telling History: Autobiography and Historical Imagination in Modern Indonesia*, trans. and ed. Susan Rodgers (pp. 149–320), 1995.

Rawson, Philip. *The Art of Southeast Asia.* London: Thames and Hudson, 1967.

Reid, Anthony. *Southeast Asia in the Age of Commerce 1450–1680, Volume One: The Lands below the Winds.* New Haven: Yale University Press, 1988.

Richter, Anne. *Arts and Crafts of Indonesia.* San Francisco: Chronicle Books, 1994.

Ricklefs, M. C. *A History of Modern Indonesia Since c.1300.* 2nd ed. Stanford: Stanford University Press, 1993.

Rigg, Jonathan, ed. *The Human Environment: Indonesian Heritage Series.* Singapore: Editions Didier Miller, 1996.

Sears, Laurie J., ed. *Fantasizing the Feminine in Indonesia.* Durham: Duke University Press, 1996.

Sedyawati, Edi, ed. *Performing Arts: Indonesian Heritage Series.* Singapore: Archipelago Press, 1999.

Sen, Krishna, and David T. Hill. *Media, Culture, and Politics in Indonesia.* South Melbourne, Australia: Oxford University Press, 2000.

Shulte Nordholdt, Henk, ed. *Outward Appearances: Dress, State, and Society in Indonesia.* Leiden: KITLV Press, 1997.

Soemantri, Hildred, ed. *Visual Art: Indonesian Heritage Series.* Singapore: Archipelago Press, 1999.

Spyer, Patricia. *The Memory of Trade: Modernity's Entanglements on an Eastern Indonesian Island.* Durham: Duke University Press, 2000.

Sunindyo, Saraswati. "City Garbage from the Nongo River." In *Fantasizing the Feminine in Indonesia*, ed. Laurie J. Sears (pp. xii–xvi). Durham: Duke University Press, 1996.

———. "Murder, Gender, and the Media: Sexualizing Politics and Violence." In *Fantasizing the Feminine in Indonesia*, ed. Laurie J. Sears (pp. 120–139). Durham: Duke University Press, 1996.

Taylor, Jean Gelman. *Indonesia: Peoples and Histories.* New Haven: Yale University Press, 2004.

Taylor, Paul Michael and Lorraine V. Aragon. *Beyond the Java Sea: Art of Indonesia's Outer Islands.* Washington, D.C.: Smithsonian Institution, 1991.

Tjahjono, Gunawan, ed. *Architecture: Indonesian Heritage Series*. Singapore: Archipelago Press, 2001.

Toer, Ananta Pramoedya. *The Buru Quartet* (4 Volume Series), trans. Max Lane. New York: Penguin Books, 1997.

———. *The Mute's Soliloquy*, trans. Willem Samuels. New York: Hyperion East, 1999.

———. *Tales from Jakarta: Caricatures of Circumstances and Their Human Beings*. Ithaca: Cornell University Press, 1999.

Tsing, Anna Lowenhaupt. *In the Realm of the Diamond Queen: Marginality in an Out-of-the Way Place*. Princeton: Princeton University Press, 1993.

Vickers, Adrian. *Bali: A Paradise Created*. Berkeley: Periplus Editions, 1989.

———, ed. *Being Modern in Bali: Image and Change*. New Haven: Yale University Southeast Asian Studies, 1996.

———. *A History of Modern Indonesia*. Cambridge: Cambridge University Press, 2006.

Wallace, Alfred Russel. *The Malay Archipelago*. New York: Dover, 1962 [1869].

Waterson, Roxana. *The Living House: An Anthropology of Architecture in South-East Asia*. London: Thames and Hudson, 1997.

Watson, C. W., and Roy Ellen, eds. *Understanding Witchcraft and Sorcery in Southeast Asia*. Honolulu: University of Hawaii Press, 1993.

Weitzman, David. *Rama and Sita: A Tale from Ancient Java*. Illustrated by the author. Boston: David R. Godine, 2002.

Wiener, Margaret J. *Visible and Invisible Realms: Power, Magic, and Colonial Conquest in Bali*. Chicago: The University of Chicago Press, 1995.

Wijaya, Made. *Architecture of Bali: A Source Book of Traditional and Modern Forms*. Honolulu: University of Hawaii Press, 2003.

Winchester, Simon. *Krakatoa, The Day the World Exploded: August 27, 1883*. New York: Perennial (HarperCollins), 2004.

Wolf, Diane Lauren. *Factory Daughters: Gender, Household Dynamics, and Rural Industrialization in Java*. Berkeley: University of California Press, 1992.

Wright, Astri. "Painting the People," In *Modern Indonesian Art*. ed. Joseph Fischer, pp. 106–157. Singapore: Singapore National Printers, 1990.

———. *Soul, Spirit, and Mountain: Preoccupations of Contemporary Indonesian Painters*. New York: Oxford University Press, 1994.

Yeager, Ruth Marie, and Mark Ivan Jacobson. *Textiles of Western Timor: Regional Variations in Historical Perspective*. Bangkok: White Lotus Press, 2002.

Index

Aboriginal people, 6, 13

Aceh, 1; female persecution in, 168; independence, battle for, 21; tsunami, December 26, 2004, 1, 2, 47, 111, 112; war against Portuguese, 12–13

Adat (customary law), 31, 37–43, 83, 97, 211

Adipurnomo, Nindityo, 61

Affandi, 60, 61

Africa, 1, 6, 128

Agriculture, 2; slash-and-burn, 3–4; volcanic ash and, 3; wet-rice, 3, 4, 8, 10, 129, 137

Agung, Sultan, 200

"All England Informal World Championship," 176

Alleys *(gangs),* 43

Alomang, Yosepha, 77

Alor, 3, 52

Alphabet, *ka-ga-nga,* 67

Ambon, 6, 14, 20, 194

American Allies, 17

Ancestors and powers of the dead, 38–43

Angola, 7

Animism, 4, 29–32

Arabia, 1, 8, 35, 52

Arabs, 6, 133

Archaeological findings, 6

Archipelago *(nusantara),* 11; before European arrival, 8–10; volcanic, 1–3

Architecture, 83–84, 111–21; churches, 115–17; graves and tombs, 119–21; headstones *(penjis),* 121; megaliths, 6, 41, 119, 120, 121, 210; monuments, public, 3, 18, 117–18; mosques, 111–12; phallus-vagina *(lingga-yoni),* 89; public buildings, 117; temples *(Candi* or *Pura),* 10, 11, 57–58, 112–15. *See also* Housing

Arnhemland, 194

Art, 51–67; dyes, 63–64; masks *(topeng),* 56–57; modern, 58–62; story cloths, 65; temple painting, 57–58; textiles, 62–67; visual, premodern, 52–53. *See also* Puppets *(wayang* performances)

Asian monetary crisis, 21

Asmats, 184, 192, 197

ASRI (The Yogyakarta Academy of Art), 61

Asterix (comic book), 76

Australia, 3, 6, 13, 23, 91, 138, 194

Australo-Melanesians, 6

Austronesians, 6, 67, 68, 128

Badminton, 176

Bahasa Indonesia, 7, 13, 32

Balai Pustaka (Bureau of Literature), 71, 72

Bali Aga, 115

Balinese, 2; art, 59–60; caste system of, 34, 89; churches, 116; cockfighting, 43, 175; cremation ceremonies, 39–41,

ABOUT THE AUTHOR

JILL FORSHEE is a cultural anthropologist and Visiting Scholar at the Center for Southeast Asia Studies, University of California, Berkeley. Author of *Between the Folds: Stories of Cloth, Lives, and Travels from Sumba* (2000), she has written numerous articles about Indonesia.

Recent Titles in
Culture and Customs of Asia

Culture and Customs of Taiwan
Gary Marvin Davison and Barbara E. Reed

Culture and Customs of Japan
Norika Kamachi

Culture and Customs of Korea
Donald N. Clark

Culture and Customs of Vietnam
Mark W. McLeod and Nguyen Thi Dieu

Culture and Customs of the Philippines
Paul Rodell

Culture and Customs of China
Richard Gunde

Culture and Customs of India
Carol E. Henderson

Culture and Customs of Thailand
Arne Kislenko

Culture and Customs of Afghanistan
Hafizullah Emadi

Culture and Customs of Pakistan
Iftikhar H. Malik